On the cover:

Top:
Solidarity with sanitation strikers, Nantes, France.

Lower Left:
Wally and daughter Anita, 2 1/2,
on hospital strike picket line, 1959
Photo by June Linder

Lower right:
Chicago PLP May Day marchers invade
Nazis' turf. (I'm in center, near front.)

A Life
of
Labor and Love

A Red Memoir

Wally Linder

Dedication

This memoir is dedicated to Anita, Andrew, Doyle, Andrea, Jerry, Eli, Pascal, Peter, Kevin, Crystal, Isa, Anton and Gavan, to the memories of Esther, Toni and Vera, and to my comrades in the Progressive Labor Party, all of whom enriched my life beyond measure.

Introduction

The origin of this memoir has many layers. The first time it might have even entered my consciousness was maybe forty years ago when a comrade, Grover Furr, suggested that I write my life story because he thought it contained many lessons that others could learn from. I dismissed the idea and forgot about it for decades. Then about twenty years ago, my children said I should start writing down an account of my life, if only so my grandchildren could learn about their roots. With this in mind, in the early 2000s I signed up for two Elder Hostel courses entitled, "Turning Memories into Memoirs."

In each course, we were assigned to write stories on particular topics. (It was at the second one, led by Denis Ledoux, that I first met Vera DuMont, who later became my partner for seventeen years, and was the person who, to a great degree, kept on my back to write a memoir.) Even though I read many instructions from Denis on "how to get started," I never made an effort to begin. However, once I became partially disabled and had to hire two home health aides to take on the various chores that were increasingly beyond my capabilities, "suddenly" blocks of time opened up. I no longer had excuses. I knew I had the opportunity to start writing.

I realized I had already written many stories which gave me a head start: a six-part series printed in PLP's newspaper *Challenge* on my decade-long experiences working on the railroad and in the rail workers' union; a number of eulogies I had been asked to prepare for family members and close friends (I seemed to be the person who was always asked to address these memorial services); and scores of pictures I had put up on my apartment walls, all of which brought back a flood of memories and became my "material." Finally there were the interviews with me about my life conducted by "Radio Rookie" Kady Bulnes for the New York public radio station WNYC which refreshed my memories of about half the stories that have appeared in this memoir.

Of course, when one begins writing, it triggers other memories of events and experiences long forgotten. Once started, I couldn't stop. In the early days, I would send out copies to family members and friends for comments. They were all positive, which further encouraged me to continue non-stop.

At this juncture, I think I have recorded a fairly complete memoir (is it ever complete?), comprising 73 stories, hopefully in a comprehensible order. Some of them refer to the same events and experiences because stories overlap from event to event, from individual to individual. I have tried to limit such repetition where possible.

In reality, this memoir has been a collective undertaking. It has encompassed all those who were part of my life, who urged me on, who made invaluable suggestions and who themselves were the subjects of my writing. What can I say about having a father who, on the one hand, had a personal encounter with Socialist presidential candidate Eugene V. Debs, and at the other end of the spectrum scared the hell out of billionaire John D. Rockefeller? Now that's "material"!

Finally, I think it has been important to put down on these pages many of the lessons and mistakes drawn from my life, which I hope will help readers to improve not only their own lives, but also to create a more equitable world for all those whose labors produce everything of value for everyone to enjoy.

Acknowledgements

I would be remiss if I did not acknowledge the vital roles played by my expert editor Maura Murphy, for her patience, excellent copy editing and invaluable suggestions and advice; to ace proofreader Alexis Mulman; to Denis Ledoux in overseeing the creation and production of the actual memoir; to Sally Lunt for the complicated task of correlating the pictures and captions with the stories and inserting changes; to my home health aides, Rema and Sondra, for their tending to all the tasks that freed me from the problems engendered by my myositis disability, which allowed me the time to write this memoir; to Rick Foard for searching his archives to supply some of the pictures I needed to accompany the stories; to Paul Heymont for agreeing to supervise the handling and shipping of those copies that may be ordered through the advertisement in *Challenge*; to nephew Alec for various references in the "railroad" stories and for escorting me to National Parks; and last, but certainly not least, to my grandchildren: to Peter for teaching his computer-illiterate grandfather the systems and operations of my new computer and helping to select and put together all the photos, as well as arranging for their electronic transmission to Sally; to Kevin for setting up the new computer; to Eli for solving some of the problems with the new computer; and to Eli's boyfriend Pascal for setting up and linking the new printer to the new computer.

Truly, my memoir has had many "authors."

—Wally Linder, March 21, 2019

Contents

Chapter One
Early Years

Who is this Short Kid "Bunny"?

When I was eight years old living in Monticello, New York, I was quite short for my age. It must have been in my genes. My father was 5 feet 4 inches "tall" and my mother was barely 4 feet 10. The bangs cutting across my forehead made me appear even shorter.

In my early years, when my classmates were lined up in size order on the stairs in school, preparing for a fire drill or waiting to march to the playground, I was always the first in line. "You're the leader, Walter," the teacher would always say. So one day, when I stood on one side of the stairs, everyone else, as a prank, lined up on the other side.

"Walter, you're out of line," the teacher scolded.

"No," I said, "I'm the leader, Mrs. Birdsall. *They're* all out of line." The children snickered, and Mrs. Birdsall couldn't help but laugh.

My family was always scraping by financially so I wore a lot of hand-me-down clothes, inherited from a wealthy, slightly older and taller cousin living in Brooklyn. Although his clothes were always of the finest quality, one could not fail to notice they never fit quite right on little "Bunny." That was a nickname that had originated in infancy. My parents hadn't yet selected a name for me at birth, so when my Pop saw me lying in my crib, he said I looked like "a little bunny rabbit." The name stuck.

When I was 12 we moved to Brooklyn and as a budding teenager, I was determined not to be introduced to my new city friends as "Bunny," so "Wally" was born. However, my mother continued to call me Bun until she died in 1982 at 84, when little Bun was 52, and my 70-year-old nephew Alec still uses the name to this day.

Although I was short, I was pretty well-proportioned, extremely fast and athletic, often winning races against boys several years older. The very name Bunny connotated quickness, elusiveness, small but lithe. My agility helped me excel in baseball where I played centerfield. It won me respect from my playmates and warded off attacks from the bigger boys. I had an overall healthy appearance. So it was that my contracting double pneumonia in the winter of 1938-39 surprised my family and friends. My complexion paled and I lost quite a few pounds. Now I looked even slighter than ever.

The pneumonia reached its climax one night when my temperature soared above 105°. I slept continuously for 36 hours, in a near coma, with my mother at my bedside the entire time, sponging me periodically with alcohol. When I awoke, the fever had broken. The crisis was over.

I was home from school for two whole months, then returned to the classroom for a week but immediately caught a cold, and was home for another week. When I went back to school, I contracted the chicken pox so it was back to my bed for another two weeks.

Throughout this succession of illnesses, my third-grade teacher, Mrs. Birdsall, brought me my school work twice a week, enabling me to keep up with the rest of my class. But, of course, there were hours on end during which I had to find other things with which to occupy myself. The sports pages were one option. But my mother felt that wasn't enough for her son. She fed me many books, two of which I particularly remember: A *Child's History of the World* and *A Child's Geography of the World*, which filled me with knowledge that I have remembered throughout my entire life.

In addition, my mother — a classical music enthusiast — fed me books on that subject. One was *The Great Composers* by Walter Damrosch. While learning little about music itself, to this day I recall that Beethoven was born in 1770 and died in 1827. She always had the classical music station WQXR on all day, so those sounds permeated my brain and contributed to my fondness of classical music throughout my life.

After the pneumonia, my oversized clothes were now even looser; I could never quite grow into them. But during these illnesses my parents had promised that upon my recovery they would take me to Hammond & Cooke, the local "exclusive" department store, and outfit me in a brand new wardrobe. And so they did. My battle had had some reward.

Life Lessons My Parents Taught Me

When I was growing up, dinners in my house did not exactly reflect a varied fare. My mother generally cooked the meals. My father did the shopping, following my mother's list.

Dinner nearly always consisted of an inexpensive cut of red meat (until my mother took a nutrition course during the food rationing in World War II), or chicken, but never fish — "too expensive" she said — a baked potato, one or two green vegetables and a salad. Now and then spaghetti, but no casseroles, no bread with dinner, rarely anything "fancy." Certainly not salami or hot dogs. But I must admit, my mother baked a great lemon-filled chocolate cake and delicious nut-filled cookies.

When she served something I didn't like (green peas), while she wasn't looking I would dump it on my father's plate, which he sympathetically accepted. If she served two vegetables, I would switch with my father — my green peas traded for his string beans. Salad always included iceberg lettuce. I'd never heard of romaine or green leaf or Boston lettuce until after I left home. If I didn't leave a clean plate she'd become very upset.

19

Later, when my father began working nights, things changed — no more "trading." Then I would try to steer dinner discussion with my mother (my sister, ten years older than I, was long gone from the house) to something she loved, like classical music or the theater. If I succeeded in distracting her, I seized the moment to clear my plate of stuff I didn't like or couldn't finish, dumping it into the garbage. It worked quite often.

One advantage I drew from much of the above occurred when my mother went to work in 1942 in a pocketbook factory. With my father working nights after having done the food shopping during the day, it was left to me to cook dinners for my mother and me. So, after doing my homework and going outside to play ball, I would return to put a meal on the table to eat when she came home from work. Generally I followed the menus I was used to, with a few changes to suit my preferences. I knew how to prepare the meals from having watched my mother cook while growing up.

My mother had what I would call a neurotic temperament. She would become as overwrought over the most minor problem — the head of lettuce turned out to be brown inside — as she would over something really serious, like a broken leg. My mother constantly worried about me: about whether I would know the right foods, make the right choices, go to college, become a professional, and so on.

However, I remember my father taking the long view. If I didn't eat the peas, I'd still grow up — I wouldn't waste away. I'd be healthy enough. This mirrored my father's overall temperament, especially towards me. I think he believed that if he and my mother raised me reasonably well, I'd make it. But to make the "right" choices, I would have to learn through trial and error.

I think these contrasting attitudes of my parents — reflected during meals, among other times — somewhat influenced my adult life. I know my mother was using whatever income that was available to shop and serve meals as judiciously as possible. (Some have labeled me as being frugal — a Great Depression left-over?) From her I learned the importance of eating well, what foods to shop for (which was my responsibility throughout my married life), what was necessary to maintain good health. I think this must have had an important influence on my physical condition. While I did contract the usual childhood diseases, as an adult I've been pretty healthy, getting a cold maybe once every few years and never having spent a day in a hospital until I was 71 (and then only two nights). My mother's influence certainly played a role here.

But emotionally and somewhat intellectually, I think I learned from my father in trying to figure out the long view as best as I could and in varying degrees, from helping to raise my own children to handling periodic crises — the death of an infant daughter, my sister's suicide, to the sudden death of my first wife Esther (hit by an automobile driven illegally) and the death from cancer of my second wife Toni, as well as the death of my late third partner, Vera. I think whatever ability I possessed to face up to these crises is a tribute to my father's influence. (The development of my political understanding and my world view, is the subject of another story.)

Tom Mooney — An 8-Year-Old's Hero

Starting in my early years, my parents had impressed upon me the importance of the history of militant labor struggles led by workers and communists that had occurred in their lifetimes. (My mother started early: when I was three years old she taught me the alphabet from the headlines in the Communist Party's newspaper, the *Daily Worker.*)

One story was the frame-up of Tom Mooney, a working-class leader who had been imprisoned for 22 years. Along with co-defendant Warren Billings, Mooney had been charged with setting off a dynamite explosion that had killed ten people on July 22, 1916, during a World War I preparedness parade, amid anti-war protesters marching down San Francisco's Market Street.

Both workers were sentenced to be hanged, but soon it was revealed that perjured testimony had been used in the trial and several witnesses had been coached by the prosecutors. Within two years a worldwide campaign to "Free Tom Mooney!" — which Mooney himself helped organize from inside prison walls — forced the reduction of the death sentence to life imprisonment. The campaign continued until finally the global protests bore fruit. On January 7, 1939, Mooney was pardoned and freed.

I was eight years old at the time. My parents, having told me this story, then turned on our old Stromberg-Carlson floor-model radio (there was no television at that time) to listen to the broadcast of Mooney's release as he walked out of prison. The cheers of thousands greeting him were deafening. As I sat on the floor of our living room, I remember that the cheers coming from the radio speaker sounded like static, and drowned out the voice of the announcer describing the event. The static went on and on, minute after minute after minute. Tears of joy streamed down my face. The announcer's voice finally broke through to describe Mooney leading a victory parade of thousands up San Francisco's Market Street, the very same spot where the frame-up had begun back in 1916.

That seemingly endless static has been burned into my consciousness for more than three-quarters of a century. My parents impressed upon me the value of a working class united in protest against the ravages of what I later came to learn was a system based on profits extorted from workers' labor. It was the first of many such experiences which helped launch me on a lifetime of struggle to end that system. And it all began with that static in 1939.

It's Not How Tall or Shy You Are But Who You Marry

As a child I was greatly concerned about my height. I was usually among the shortest in my classes in school. As it happened, my mother, who had taught me how to read when I was three to four years old, held me out of kindergarten. Thus I started school in the first grade, reading far better than my classmates.

I guess this ability pushed me to the head of the class. (Was this the reason I was elected class president in the second, third and fourth grades?) By that time my teacher, Mrs. Choate, started giving me fifth-grade work. So it was that I skipped the fifth year entirely to enter the sixth grade, where I was somewhat younger (and shorter) than my classmates.

But school work didn't satisfy me. I developed athletically. I was fast, which helped to compensate for my shortness. In basketball, I developed an outside hook shot, thwarting the taller boys from blocking it. In football, I played end (now called wide receiver), catching forward passes and running like the wind.

In one incident when I was 15, I was playing on our neighborhood club football team, the "Spades" Social Athletic Club (S.A.C.) of which I was president. I never wore regular football equipment (it encumbered me) — only an old green sweater and corduroy pants. At the start of the game, our wily coach, Eddie Shumsky, told me to stand on the sidelines, sort of mixed in with the crowd of spectators on the edge of the Wingate Stadium field. (This field, as it turned out, was across the street from what became Murrow High School, where my grandchildren attended classes years later).

When my team received the kickoff, Eddie told them to run the ball to the opposite side of the field from where I was standing, thereby inducing the ref to position the ball for the first play from scrimmage a good distance from me. Of course, no one on the opposing team noticed me in my "unfootball"-like garb. We called this the "sleeper play." On the first down, I emerged from the crowd, alone, unguarded; the quarterback threw me a forward pass and I ran like hell, partly out of fear of being tackled. By the time the opposing defenders realized what was happening, I had crossed the goal line and scored a touchdown. (Why they never protested I'll never know.) After that, no one thought of me as "short."

Such athletic ability, alongside my progress in school — plus a knack for organization — enabled me to fit in, despite the fact that as a teenager I didn't smoke, all the rage among my friends in the 1940s.

As I finished Midwood High School and moved on to City College, my participation in athletics waned, my worry about my height receded but my shyness remained. This was accentuated by the paucity of my relationships with the opposite sex. When I was 19, in my second year at City, I didn't hang out with my friends from my Spades days. Neither athletics nor school work helped me any longer. Shyness, not my height, was the big hurdle.

Every so often I screwed up enough courage to ask a girl for a date, but it never went beyond one or two outings. (At 24, a girlfriend materialized but I ended it after a year — see my "Esther" story.) I'd had this great fear that I'd never get married. When I did meet the woman who became my first wife, she was my exact opposite: very outgoing, uninhibited and definitely more mature than I. She was to change my personality, and my life.

In my naïveté, I thought this had just "happened". I learned the truth later thanks to a conversation with my daughter Anita, who at the time was just coming out of a messy divorce. We were comparing the maturity of our respective spouses at the ages when we had married, she at 20 and I at 25. She then related a conversation she had had with her mother, my wife Esther. Esther told her she had recognized my shyness at the very same time that she had fallen in love with whatever qualities I had. She had said to herself, "This guy is worth a lot of work." She told my daughter I became her "project." And in many ways her "work" succeeded.

A Baseball Life 1 — "Take Me Out To the Ball Game…"

In 1936, when I was six years old, baseball became my life. My family — father Abe, mother Ann and sister June — was living in a four-family house at 60 St. John Street in Monticello, New York. We had moved there from Brooklyn in 1931, during the Great Depression. My father, an immigrant from Russia, had been unemployed for two years. A friend had promised him a job as a cashier in the Miss Monticello Diner. So for the next eleven years I spent my childhood in that small town of some 3,000 souls, 90 miles north of "the big city." There were lots of transplanted New Yorkers living in what was known as the "Borscht Belt," where swarms of New Yorkers spent summer vacations, swelling the local population then to more than 100,000.

My mother, a fairly accomplished pianist, gave the landlady's daughter lessons in exchange for the rent. My parents had no interest in sports but I got my first introduction to baseball from the landlady's 11-year-old son, Philly. He was a rabid fan and active ball player. He made it his personal crusade to "train" me and two playmates (who lived in the building).

In the spring of '36, Philly asked me which New York team I rooted for. When I looked perplexed, he laid it out for me. "You're lucky," he said. "You've got three choices — the Giants, the Yankees or the Dodgers — so pick one." Knowing very little about these New York teams, I began poring over the sports pages in the New York papers. It was spring training time in major league baseball and there was a lot of publicity about a highly-touted 21-year-old rookie named Joe DiMaggio. The Yanks had just called him up from the San Francisco Seals, a Yankee farm team in the Pacific Coast League. DiMaggio had set a minor league record by hitting safely in 61 consecutive games, a phenomenal feat. It was reported that the Yankees were "taking a chance" on this son of Italian immigrants because he had a bum knee. Still, they paid $25,000 to acquire him, a huge sum during the Depression.

"Joltin' Joe" — as he later became known — caught my fancy. I told Philly I had "picked one" and so began a 16-year love affair with "Joe D" and the Yankees.

It turned out to be a "good pick" since the Yanks won the next four World Series. Their other two stars, Babe Ruth and Lou Gehrig, had faded from the scene. The Babe had been traded two years before and Gehrig's career was winding down, when he was forced to retire after having played in a record 2,130 consecutive games. The "Iron Horse" played his last game on my ninth birthday, May 2, 1939, felled by an illness that was later to become known as "Lou Gehrig's disease." So now my hero, "Joe D.," became the leader of the Bronx Bombers.

It was pretty easy to be a Yankees fan since in those sixteen years, from '36 to '51 when DiMag was to retire, the Yanks were in eleven World Series; they won it ten times, more than the other 15 major league teams combined!

Philly, my friends Daniel and Marshall and I played baseball every chance we got. During summer vacations I listened to the Yankee radio broadcasts virtually every day. (There was no night baseball then.) In 1938 something called television appeared so we would go to our friend Roy Fleischer's house — his father owned the RCA dealership and the only TV set in town — to watch a cloudy picture on a four-foot-high set with a 4-inch by 8-inch screen. For the first time I actually "saw" DiMag lead the Yanks to a four-game World Series sweep of the Cincinnati Reds.

MY FIRST GAME — LIVE!

Usually once a year my family rode the Short Line bus to New York City to visit my Aunt Thelma who lived in the borough of Staten Island. Three months after my 11th birthday, my aunt's son Larry, 15 — knowing my devotion to DiMaggio — offered to take me to a Yankee game. I was beside myself with excitement. I would actually see my hero in person! The big day came when on July 31, 1941, we made the hour-and-a-half trip via a bus and ferry ride to Manhattan and then took the subway all the way north to the Bronx.

Luckily for me, the Yanks had a scheduled doubleheader against the Detroit Tigers that day — two games for 55¢ sitting in the right-field bleachers. DiMag got one hit in the first game, and was walked twice intentionally. The Tigers had tied the game in the ninth inning, so we remained glued to our seats until the 13th. With Red Rolfe on second, the Tigers decided not to pitch to DiMag so again they walked him intentionally. It proved their undoing. The next batter, Charley "King Kong" Keller, hit a three-run homer to give the Yanks the victory in the first game. I was ecstatic. Suddenly cousin Larry announced we were leaving. "What about the second game?" I cried. "We've already seen 1½ games," he replied. "That's enough for me. Besides, we've got a long trip home." I later read that Joe D. hit his 25th homer in the second game, a three-run blast, part of a 5-0 Yankee win. Somewhat disappointed at being unable to witness that one, I was still thankful to have seen my first Yankee game "in the flesh."

Actually this was the 14th consecutive game in which DiMag had gotten at least one hit. He would go on to get at least one hit in the next 42 games, setting an all-time record of 56, a feat unequalled to this day and one that many believe will never be broken. So I was present for part of Joltin' Joe's amazing streak!

THE BIG MOVE

The following summer my mother surprised me. She said she felt she had made a mistake with my sister, allowing her to spend her high school years in such a small town (although my sister did graduate as salutatorian, second in her class). "Too provincial," she remarked. My mother said she wanted me to have a "broader cultural outlook" as a teenager, which "could only be gained by moving to New York City."

I was dumbstruck. What I had looked forward to just once a year — a trip to "the big city" — would now become my whole life! Silently I thought it *would* give me a broader outlook — in Yankee Stadium.

In early September, 1942, we arrived in Brooklyn, moving into our usual three-room apartment. It was in the heart of the Flatbush neighborhood, on Clarkson Avenue between Flatbush and Bedford Avenues. When I strode to the corner of Bedford and looked left I could see Ebbetts Field, home of the Brooklyn Dodgers, a ten-minute walk away. Here I was, a Yankee fan in the heart of Dodger territory (who the Yankees had beaten in the World Series the previous year).

Little did I know at the time that, after paying the first month's rent ($30), my family's coffers amounted to $10 and neither of my parents had a job. The Second World War was on and employers were searching for workers too old to be drafted. My father, at 57, knew this and felt confident he'd land something pretty quickly.

Intrepid soul that he was, he began walking down Flatbush Avenue, stopping in store after store asking if they needed anyone. After about eight blocks he struck pay dirt, a cashier-bookkeeper's job in a men's haberdashery for about $30 a week. A few months later my mother was hired in a pocketbook factory in Manhattan for $17 a week. I felt we were riding high.

Soon after I had learned we were moving to New York, I realized that come October my Yankees would probably be playing in the World Series. Now, living in Brooklyn, with my parents gainfully employed, and with the Series a mere three weeks off, I summoned enough nerve to announce to my mother that I was going to the Yankees' World Series opener.

"How? she asked. "By subway," I replied. "Are you crazy?" she fairly shouted. "Do you think I'll let you trek an hour and a half from Brooklyn, through Manhattan to the Bronx in a strange city *by yourself* on a subway you know nothing about? Get that idea out of your head!"

I was crushed. I pleaded my case. I said I had consulted a fellow Yankee fan living a block away who had taken the subway to the Stadium many times. He explained just what train to take. Our BMT stop was just two blocks away, and that train took me to 42nd Street in Manhattan where I could switch to the IRT, directly to Yankee Stadium in the Bronx.

My mother, who knew absolutely nothing about baseball, was aware of how wedded I was to the Yankees and DiMaggio. Still reluctant to allow me take that trip alone, she decided she would accompany me to the game. I could hardly believe it. I felt obligated to explain the logistics. "Mom," I said, "you must realize that we can only sit in the bleachers — benches with no backs — and the line for the unreserved seats opens at seven A.M. so we will have to leave at five-thirty in the morning to get on line for tickets. And then," I continued hesitantly, "after finding seats, we'll have to sit for six hours because the game doesn't start until two o'clock."

I held my breath until she said, "I know how much this means to you, so I'll do it." On game day we arose at 4:30, packed a lunch and took off an hour later. For me it was a dream come true.

As we sat in the bleachers and heard the fans debating all the ins and outs of the Series, my mother would ask me what it all meant. I explained as best I could and she seemed satisfied. Then at around ten o'clock, Al Shacht, the "clown prince of baseball," dressed in a formal tuxedo, came out to entertain us. Facing the bleachers, he did his comic interpretations of various players, the umpires and plays that we might see in the game.

My mother took that in somewhat until the players appeared at noon for pre-game batting practice. Then, of all things, amid all the noise and hoopla, she proceeded to take out a book and start reading! I was absolutely amazed. I'm sure that among the over 80,000 fans in the Stadium, she was the only one reading a book.

Unfortunately, the St. Louis Cardinals, the National League pennant winners, won. They had marvelous outfielders and five balls that Yankee batters had hit to the first row in the stands for apparent home runs were caught as the outfielders fell over the low three-foot fence. I went home saddened, especially since the Cardinals went on to win the Series. World War II was on and DiMaggio was drafted, so I had to wait another five years before seeing the Yankee Clipper help win a Series, in 1947.

Four years later, I received the shock of my young baseball

life. DiMag decided to retire. Without Joltin' Joe to root for, I, too, "retired." I stopped following the Yanks and baseball altogether, not even reading the sports pages. Life without DiMaggio, I concluded, was meaningless.

Eighteen years later, my nine-year-old son Andrew asked me to take him to Shea Stadium. I asked him what that was. "It's where the Mets play," he replied. Not ready to reveal my ignorance about this new team that was replacing the Dodgers (who had taken off for Los Angeles), I agreed.

Lo and behold, the Mets won the World Series that year, 1969, only seven years after they had joined the National League. So my young son was somewhat following in the footsteps of my own early years. Stuck with the Mets, my baseball life was resurrected.

An 'Ordinary' Man

One might consider my father an ordinary man, but in the course of his ordinary life he crossed paths with the Socialist leader Eugene V. Debs, the oil tycoon John D. Rockefeller and the I.W.W. (International Workers of the World), among others. Born in Russia in 1885 as Abram Linder — known mostly as "Lin" and later as "Abe" — he was among the two million Jews who fled the virulent anti-Semitism of Tsarist Russia at the end of the 1800s, an immigrant boy, virtually penniless.

He was 10 in 1895 when he emigrated with his mother and older sister Tilly. They endured a couple of day's journey in a third-class rail carriage to the Russian border. They then took another train to a port where they boarded a ship in steerage class to New York. They had been preceded by his father, but when they arrived he was nowhere to be found; they learned he had gone to Canada, where he had another family. Abe felt he had nothing in common with him and never pursued a relationship.

Most immigrants couldn't make it beyond New York City and were crowded into Lower East Side tenements. Abe, Tilly and their mother landed in a basement around Hester Street where it wasn't unusual for five families to be living in one 12-by 12-foot room. Abe went to Public School No. 7 at Hester and

34

Chrystie Streets, while his sister went to work in a sweatshop. Two years later their mother died of tuberculosis, leaving Abe and Tilly young, orphaned and broke in a foreign country. Abe was forced to leave school at 12 but by then he had learned English and loved to read.

The legal workday was ten hours and the minimum working age was 14, limits that were often ignored. Women were paid much less than men, and Abe's sister could hardly earn enough to support herself, much less the two of them. So at 12 my dad found a factory job. Factories were dark, drafty, dirty and dangerous. Accidents were common, so he looked for other jobs. In the 1890 census, Abe was listed as living in a flophouse at 270 Bowery, along with 178 other males. For 10 cents a night one could have a straw mattress and a blanket. One night Abe shared a bed with an old man. In the morning he found the old man dead.

Within all this, my father had an irrepressible sense of humor. On one job he operated an elevator and had to work on Sundays. His boss was a religious Scotsman, so Abe asked for an hour off on Sunday morning. Assuming the time off was for church, his boss consented. But my pop, who was an atheist, went to hear a noted atheist lecture.

Another job was as a stock boy in a store owned by Abraham Kosower. The latter had accumulated the money to emigrate and buy a store on the Lower East Side by informing on Russian Jews who had tried to leave without paying "proper" bribes — he was a thoroughly despicable character. His greed was boundless. Abe was with Kosower one time when he got his foot caught in a streetcar door. Abe said Kosower's face lit up at the thought of a personal injury suit. He later deserted his wife and children and fled to New Jersey when sued for child support. The police put out an arrest warrant and caught him for selling pornography. Kosower's wife Amelia, a kindly woman who took a liking to the orphan boy Abe, invited him to visit often.

Soon Abe landed a job at Macy's, when it was located in Manhattan on 14th Street at Union Square. He had numerous run-ins with his supervisor, known as "Eagle Eye," about whom he later wrote a number of stories for the Local 65 union paper (see excerpts below), at the time the union was organizing that department store in the 1940s. His working-class experience led him to a life-long belief in Socialism and later Communism. It was from him, as well as from my mother, that I drew that outlook which shaped my life.

In 1912 he encountered the Socialist Party's leader Eugene V. Debs when the latter was running for president on the Socialist ticket. Debs had come to Union Square for a campaign speech, entering the area in a horse-drawn carriage. My father later told me it was one of the highlights of his life when he ran up to the carriage, opened the door, grabbed Debs' hand, escorted him out onto the street and exchanged a few words with the candidate.

Not long afterwards he had what one might call a confrontation with a representative of the opposite end of the political spectrum. Abe was working as a bus boy at Keene's Steak House in Manhattan. It was a fairly exclusive eatery frequented by John D. Rockefeller, the country's first billionaire. Abe's job was to clear the tables when people were finished with their meals. A curtain, through which Abe would transport the dirty dishes, separated the kitchen from the dining area. Abe had a huge bushy head of hair which, depending on one's point of view, could appear somewhat menacing, especially at a time when the press was featuring cartoons of bushy-haired bomb-throwing anarchists. (It was 1913 and striking workers at Rockefeller's Colorado mine had just suffered an infamous massacre.)

Spotting Rockefeller sitting at his table, Abe planted himself at the kitchen-side of the curtain, and began opening and closing it, glaring in Rockefeller's direction. After a few minutes of popping in and out, he caught the magnate's attention. The latter, nervous and somewhat fearful amid all the current publicity, then called over the maitre d' and demanded to know who that menacing character was. The boss saw Abe doing his thing and ordered him to stop or be fired. But Abe had achieved his goal, scaring the hell out of the oil baron.

Soon it was 1914 and the First World War had begun. U.S. entry into the conflict seemed imminent. Opposition was mounting, led partly by the I.W.W. In 1916, the latter organized a mass anti-war demonstration in Washington, D.C. My father was intent on participating. As it happened, Amelia — my future grandmother — had been inviting him to dinners at her apartment where he met one of her daughters, Ann (who later became my mother). She later told me that she had sat on the floor, entranced with my father's "sermon" condemning this imperialist war. Abe then invited her to accompany him to the Washington protest. She was thrilled. It turned out to be their first date. She said that by the time the day was over, she had fallen in love with him. They were married three years later.

In 1920 they moved to Northford, Connecticut, a small town, population 200. (A sign at the town's entrance warned "thickly settled.") Somehow they had scraped together enough money to buy the town's only general store. Not only did Abe run the place but he became the town's fourth-class postmaster. It was one of those classic places with a pot-bellied stove in its center around which the old folks would gather to warm themselves and shoot the breeze. It was in Northford that their first child, my sister June, was born in 1920.

My father loved Northford and the Yankee farmers who were his customers and neighbors. One time Ann's three sisters came to visit. They were city girls, attractive and well dressed. Abe said they drew so much attention in this little rural community that the girls were afraid to go out.

Being a city girl herself, my mother didn't like Northford. When the rent was raised on the store in 1923 my father gave in and the family moved to New York City. Abe had various cashier and bookkeeper jobs in the Twenties but then came the October 1929 stock market crash. The Great Depression had struck. I was born on what the birth certificate said was May 2, 1930, but my father disputed that. He said he had heard me squalling at 11:45 PM on May 1st, but the doctor had recorded it as 12:15 AM May 2. My father's reasoning? He said the doctor couldn't bring himself to put down May First — May Day, the international working-class holiday — as the birth date, so May 2 it became.

By the next year, 1931, Abe had been unemployed two years into the Depression. At one point my mother was so desperate that she stole food from a store to feed us. One time a relative told Abe of a company that was hiring workers. But when he went there he found that the workers were on strike and the company wanted only strikebreakers. Abe, of course, wouldn't cross the picket line. As desperate as he was, he wouldn't compromise his principles. And my mother, to her credit, supported his decision.

My Pop at the
Miss Monticello Diner

A family friend promised him a job in Monticello, NY — 90 miles from Brooklyn — as a cashier in the Miss Monticello Diner, so we packed up and left the big city for the small town of Monticello.

In 1938, June entered Brooklyn College. My mother's sisters, then living in New York, considered "a good marriage" most important and kept introducing

June to well-off young men, but June, being her father's daughter, rejected such ideas.

I spent those early years in that small town but my mother had felt it would be a mistake to spend my teenage years in such a narrow-minded, provincial setting, so in September of 1942 we moved back to Brooklyn's Flatbush neighborhood.

Since neither of my parents had a job, it was then that my father found one walking down Flatbush Avenue. It was later that I discovered that my parents had only $10 between them after paying the first month's rent ($30) for a three-room apartment in a four-story walk-up on Clarkson Avenue.

Following that, my father had a series of jobs, including at the Pierrepont Hotel in Brooklyn Heights and later at the old Mc-Calpin Hotel in Manhattan's Herald Square, where he joined the Hotel Workers union. Meanwhile, my mother got a job in a pocketbook factory, making $17 a week. Together we were able to make ends meet.

In 1949, when I was 19 and a sophomore at City College, my father decided it was time for me to buy my first suit. (Previously I had been wearing hand-me-downs discarded by a rich cousin.) He said, "Let's go to Brooks Brothers and see what we can find." I told him he was crazy; we couldn't afford anything there. "Never mind," he replied, so we went uptown and he had the Brooks' salesman bring out something my size to try on. After we got a look at a few, Pop thanked the salesman and, turning to me, said, "O.K. Now let's go downtown to Rogers Peet [a much cheaper place] and pick one out there." I was bewildered. "What's going on?" I asked. "Well," he said, "now that you know what a real classy suit looks like, we'll look for something similar at a price we can afford." Always thinking, my pop.

In 1950, while working at the McCalpin as a cashier in the dining room, my father had a heart attack and was rushed to Bellevue, a hospital to which mostly poor workers with few resources were taken. I'll never forget walking into this gigantic ward that contained patients in maybe 300 beds, all lined up against the walls. I saw my father encased in an oxygen tent. It scared me to see him there looking so helpless, but he smiled at me, "I'm O.K. sonny, don't worry, I'll be out of here in no time." Sure enough, he was, but could not return to work.

Throughout the 1950s, when my mother was still working, my father did all the cooking, shopping and cleaning in the house. He was an original "house-husband." I guess all of that rubbed off on me.

Once unable to work outside the home, he began drawing the princely sum of $40 a month in Social Security. Somehow he managed to collect $26 a week in unemployment insurance benefits, the maximum, for a full year. Then my mother got sick and had to quit work but was able to also collect $26 a week in sickness benefits. In the Spring of 1951 I was laid off from my job in the garment center (I had switched to night school at City College) and also began collecting $26 a week in unemployment benefits. "So," my father noted, "we're pulling in $88 a week without working. That's the greatest income this family has ever earned!" That remark was symptomatic of a sense of humor that carried my father over seven decades. From his face-off with Rockefeller to his "dispute" about my birth date to my suit-buying escapade to his skipping out of Bellevue Hospital, my father was always using his wits to make it through life.

By 1960 my father's condition was fading. He was confined to their apartment on Ocean Avenue near Newkirk and my mother had become his full-time caregiver. One day when she returned home from grocery shopping, she discovered he was missing. She immediately called me and I called my sister's husband Ralph. We couldn't figure how he could survive, wearing only pajamas, a bathrobe and slippers.

We went to the local subway station, Avenue H, on the Brighton line and spoke to the toll clerk. She knew him from years of seeing him in the station and yes, she had seen him entering the platform but did nothing to alert anyone. Ralph and I went to the terminals of the Brighton line, to Times Square and then all the way back to Coney Island, asking transit workers if they had seen him, but none had. We had called in to report him missing but for two days there was no word. Finally we received a call from Coney Island Hospital where he had been brought. He had been found sitting on a bench on the Coney Island Boardwalk. The ER medics examined him and found he was no worse for wear! How he lasted in his condition, how he ate, if at all, was a mystery to us. But we now realized he was nearing the end.

While his wits had carried my father through much of his life, unfortunately they could not stave off the coronary attack which struck him in 1962. He was hospitalized for a week before dying at the age of 77. What I learned from his life was a school from which I'm still graduating.

STORY WITHIN A STORY

(In the 1940s, my brother-in-law Ralph was editor of the Union Voice, organ of the union that was organizing Macy's. When he discovered that my father had been employed there at the turn of the 20th century, he thought it would be helpful to their efforts if my father could write up his experiences at the store. These are excerpts from that four-part series.)

I REMEMBER MACY'S
By Abram Linder

Who hasn't worked in Macy's?

This frequently heard question of the present century did not find its way into conversations during the Nineties. But the seed for it was planted during those formative years when the store was still located on West 14th Street.

And the one who should get sole credit for it is a man named William Pitt, who was general manager... It was his ruthless system of turnover of help that gave birth to the popular question, "Who *hasn't* worked in Macy's?"

Their merciless system of underselling and mass buying was on a level with the constant turnover of help.

The Macy's building, which faced Sixth Avenue and opened on both 13th and 14th Streets, consisted of a number of former residential red brick and four-story buildings.

In going through his inspection tours, Manager Pitt would descend the steps of a grand staircase very slowly, rolling his eyes in all directions. He would spot a victim before reaching the bottom, following which he would start at a fast trot like a ferocious tom cat. He had the look of a mesmerizer in the act of forcing a criminal's confession.

In those days, I was one of the two or three hundred cash boys and girls. Our job was to take the cash and merchandise from the sales person and bring it to the wrapping desk, from where the money was sent through a compressed air tube to the payment department. We would then get the change and package and rush back to the sales person. It was long before the cash register system was introduced into the store.

In terms of expendability and wages, we belonged to the lowest strata. The boys earned $2.50 a week and the girls $1.50 — for the very same work.

As for Manager Pitt, most of his time was taken up with hiring and firing help. In the afternoons he would be going through the building and handing people the "slip" with his initial P.

A witty little Irish girl who worked there once remarked, "He doesn't care when or how he does it. He fires 'em in between sales, the old eagle eye." Thereafter he was known to the help as Old Eagle Eye, and the advance warning of his appearance in any department was: "Watch out! Here comes Old Eagle Eye!"

If some half-starved sales girl suddenly laughed, she found herself confronted with the menacing form of Eagle Eye and he would shove the "slip" in front of her: "Pass Bearer's Salary."

I remember one instance where the victim, a teen-age girl, stood stock still for a moment and then dropped flat to the floor right behind her showcase; she had to be revived by the house physician and taken home in a carriage. And Old Eagle Eye rushed right on, looking for more victims, never turning back for a view of the mess he left behind.

In the selling line, the wage standard reached the "high" level. Male clerks received $10 a week for single men and $12 for married. A few young boys received as little as $4 or $5 a week.

Macy's 14th Street, 1912

Into my second year, after I had brought a two-wheeled bike to the repair shop and was desperately trying to ride it, I suddenly

43

became aware of a tall, menacing figure. Yes, it was Old Eagle Eye making out my slip. "Go get your salary, boy."

It was getting close to Christmas when I found myself walking up and down West 14th Street and finally stopping in front of the Macy's building, watching the well-dressed ladies coming out of fine carriages drawn by high-spirited horses and carrying immaculate livery men. I was watching the endless procession with a child's admiration when something inside reminded me that I was looking for a job.

I entered the store and headed straight for Eagle Eye's office, wondering if he would recognize me. As I came face to face with the executioner, Eagle Eye would order the cash girl to "take this boy to the toy department." In a few minutes, I was a cash boy in Macy's again.

When Christmas Eve arrived I was pretty well convinced the old man recognized me but pretended that he had not. I received my full week's pay plus a pink form advising me that my services were no longer required.

It was almost midnight when I came out of the building and brushed past two young girls who had just met the same fate. One of them sobbed out the words: "This is what they do with us. Take us on when they need us badly, work us long hours, then throw us out on the street to starve."

The poor thing, she had sized up the situation correctly.

A Mother of Many Dimensions

The fact that my mother had so many sides to her is reflected in the many times I've been compelled to refer to her in stories throughout this book, some of which will be repeated here in appropriate contexts. My mother Ann was short in stature (4 feet, 10 inches) but large in the influence she cast on those close to her and beyond in the outside world. She was born in New York City in 1898 into a middle-class family, to a despicable father and a tenderhearted mother. Her father Abraham made Silas Marner look like a big spender, tied as he was to his craving for money above all else in life. The extent of his disgusting nature was reflected in the fact that my mother, her three sisters and brother all testified against him when my grandmother Amelia filed for divorce in the 1920s, during a time when women found it extremely difficult to initiate a divorce.

As a teenager, my mother managed to extricate herself from her father once she met my own father Abe at a party at my grandmother's house. It was then, in 1916, that my father was expounding on his socialist politics [See story "An Ordinary

Man"], when he announced he would be participating in an I.W.W.-organized anti-war march protesting the impending U.S. entry into World War I. My father, 31 at the time, invited Ann, 18, to join him. And it was that day that she fell in love with him. Married three years later, they moved to Northfield, Connecticut to their general store.

It was when the landlord had raised the rent on the store that they were forced to move back to Brooklyn.

When the stock market crashed in 1929, my father lost his job. I was born in 1930, an "accident" no doubt. My father had been unemployed for two years when he was promised a cashier's job at a diner in Monticello, NY, 90 miles from the city. They moved there in 1931.

Times were hard, so my mother, who played the piano, offered to give the landlady's daughter lessons in exchange for the rent for our three-room apartment in a four-family house at 60 St. John Street. My parents made friends with those who had like-minded politics. Although there was no Communist Party club in Monticello, they joined the FSU — "Friends of the Soviet Union." There they met Pauline and Leon Sidler, who had a reputation as "left-wingers," so much so that a KKK cross was burned on their lawn.

In 1942, we moved back to Brooklyn to gain what my mother said was "a broader outlook" compared to the small town of Monticello. In the city, she took me to Broadway plays (back-row, $1.10 seats) as well as to demonstrations, including one as soon as we arrived in September. Two hundred thousand people jammed Manhattan's Union Square, calling on the U.S. to open up a "Second Front" in Western Europe to ease the burden on the Soviet Union carrying the battle against four million German soldiers on the Russian Front. In 1947, she took me to my first May Day celebration among 250,000 marchers. These were all the "non-provincial" influences she had hoped for me in the

people who gathered in New York's Union Square Thursday in a dem- Square at which 50,000 people gathered under the ... the British Communist... by the Communist Party and addressed by outstanding Communist, to eight Ferdinand Smith, secretary-treasurer of the ... National Maritime Union; Earl Brows ...due to the great meeting held some weeks ago in London's Trafalgar Marcantonio, Harlem Laborite. He this year and pase...for entrance from some speckers.

MOM   WALLY

Wally's First Demonstration, Sept. 27, 1942 — Union Square, New York City
"Open up the Second Front NOW!

move from Monticello.

Without a job, my father answered a newspaper ad offering employment, which turned out to be one for hiring scabs. My parents agreed he could not be a strikebreaker.

My father soon found a job as a cashier in a haberdashery, and my mother went to work in a pocketbook factory in Manhattan for the princely sum of $17 a week. World War II was raging. Food rationing had been instituted, leading my mother to take a nutrition course with the goal of using what food was available to feed us as healthily as possible. During that period, she began exercising daily, long before the fitness craze had seized the country. She continued for her entire life.

In my teenage years, my mother would quit her factory job in June and take me with her to Monticello for the summer months, renting a house from a friend who lived and worked in a Catskill Mountain hotel during that period. This enabled me to work as a caddy at the Concord Hotel, earning about $300 spending money for the rest of the year, and hanging out with my friends in the evenings. My mother was easily able to land another factory job each September, with unemployment at a low ebb during the war.

In 1950, my father suffered a heart attack and was forced to quit his job at Manhattan's McAlpin Hotel. It was then that he became a "house-husband" doing all the cleaning, shopping and preparing meals while my mother kept working. I was also working that year so, along with my father's monthly Social Security check of a grand $40, we got along. But then in 1960 my father had another setback and my mother was forced to leave her job to take care of him 24/7. Two years later, at the age of 77, my father died. Then one day my mother was mugged in the lobby of her apartment house on Ocean Avenue and decided she had to leave the city and move back to Monticello, where she had many friends and had few fears of being harmed.

My mother led an active life, even getting a part-time clerical job at the local Social Security office. When she was laid off during Reagan's first budget-cutting year, she applied for unemployment insurance. I told her she was probably the oldest person collecting such benefits. Every so often she would take the Short Line bus into New York and go to the theater, seeing the musical "Hair," among other plays. She was courted by an elderly gentleman, but nothing came of it.

In 1972, my sister took an overdose of sleeping pills and died. I felt I couldn't tell my mother the actual cause of June's death, so I drove to Monticello and made up some story (which I've forgotten) which I thought would be less jarring. Naturally, she was still very upset, but later she somehow read a copy of June's death certificate and saw the real cause. She realized why I had not told her the real truth at the time and forgave me.

My mother had inherited some money upon the death of her long-lost father, so I urged her to use it to travel, maybe take the Queen Mary to Europe, but she balked, saying she wanted to leave as much money as possible to Esther, me and her grandchildren. I told her we didn't need the money, but she held fast.

In January, 1980 at 82, my mother was diagnosed with stomach cancer — surprisingly not lung cancer, having smoked two packs a day until she quit when she was 60. I would drive to Monticello, pick her up and take her to Downstate Hospital in Brooklyn for monthly chemotherapy treatments and then bring her home. She was one of the early ones to smoke medical marijuana to relieve the discomfort (where she got it from she never told me). I asked the doctor friend of mine who had diagnosed the cancer how long she might last. He said two years. After a year still living alone in Monticello, I said she should come to live with Esther and me — Anita and Andrew were out of the house at college — and she agreed. It was tough on Esther, who wasn't used to living with someone with my mother's neuroses. She would constantly check our freezer, aghast at finding frankfurters there.

At one point it became too difficult for my mother to stay alone all day when Esther and I were at work, so we arranged for her to go to an old-age home in Brooklyn, coincidentally the same one to which we had brought Esther's father Sam. He would visit her every day and keep her company. Finally in January 1982, two years exactly to the time the doctor had predicted, her heart gave out and she died peacefully at the home, at the age of 84. I went to her Monticello apartment to gather some things she had left there, especially an album filled with pictures of her life, some of which are reproduced in this book.

There are many details related to me, to her daughter June and her husband Abe (or "Lin" as most people called him), which have not been included in the above account, since it was difficult for me to find the appropriate spots to insert them without interrupting the narrative, but I would be remiss if I didn't add them here.

My mother was always trying to shelter me from the harshness of the outside world. She yearned for me to become a professional, maybe a college professor, and was elated when I graduated from CCNY. I did not attend my graduation ceremony (I finished in January, 1948, but the ceremony took place in June). In fact, I didn't even go back to get my actual diploma until my mother insisted I do so; she wanted to hang it on her wall. She was shocked when I told her I wasn't pursuing a professional career but was going to work on the railroad. [For my reason, see "How the Rosenberg Case Changed My Life"]. She said she blamed herself for my choice, lamenting the fact that she had taken me to all those demonstrations and rallies when I was young, filling me with those communist politics. I told her, "Mom, that was the best thing you ever did for me. It gave me a real purpose in life." She reluctantly accepted that, and actually said she was very proud to hear I was elected president of my railroad local union.

My mother's inability to distinguish minor events from really important ones was disturbing. One example: when I was 15 and with my mother in that summer house of her friend in Monticello, she used to serve me a breakfast of two soft-boiled eggs every morning, seven days a week. I finally got tired of it and said I couldn't take it any more. She said she was giving them to me because "it was good for your health." One morning I finally exploded, striking my fork on the enameled kitchen table, chipping it slightly. My mother began screaming and moaning and lay down in bed crying hysterically, agonizing over what had been done to her friend's table. I got scared and told her I'd get some paint and smooth it over, but this didn't placate her. Things like this didn't happen too often, but often enough. If the lettuce she bought turned out to be brown inside, she would become abnormally agitated.

In a sense, these fits quite contradicted the very many positive things she brought to my overall outlook in life. I could never reconcile them.

Her relationship with my sister June was not so endearing. Although June did become a professional in my mother's eyes — as a photographer (some pictures appear in this book), a librarian and a designer — the two of them fought ferociously, for reasons I was never able to figure out. After June's first year in Brooklyn College, she had a nervous breakdown and came home. When I was 17 and searching for something in a cabinet drawer, I came across several pages my sister had written about her feelings towards my mother. She said it drove her to marry her first husband, Howie, to get away from her. While Howie seemed like a really nice fellow, they were married while he was in the Army during the war and never saw too much of each other. She met her future husband Ralph while Howie was away and she divorced him when he came home, after which she married Ralph. That marriage had a lot of problems, too. [See story about my sister June.] Unfortunately, she ended up taking her own life.

I had mixed feelings about my parents' relationship. For the most part, my father seemed easygoing, certainly with his children, but often husband and wife fought like cats and dogs. My father had an awful temper when he lost it. While this may very well happen in many marriages, it was very unnerving to me. My wife Esther said she was amazed at how I was able to maintain a relationship with my mother. When I was 22, out of college and chose to move into a cold-water flat in Manhattan's Little Italy, my mother went nuts. My father said. "Let him go out on his own," but my mother insisted it would ruin my life. "How could you let him do that," she said, rebuking my father.

But through all their fighting, my parents must have cared enough for each other to stay together. They had maintained their relationship from the move to Northford, back to Brooklyn, then through the unemployment of the Depression — which affected many married couples — and the move to Monticello, and then back to Brooklyn again. Their relationship taught me a lot about

how to avoid many of the pitfalls in marriages, and especially from my father's ability to keep life on an even keel.

In one sense, in many ways, my mother helped me chart my life, which turned out to be a very happy one. Yet in another sense I had to grapple with my mother's neuroses. I

Grandma Ann with grandchildren Anita and Andrew

guess it was my father's ability to take the long view in life that helped me deal with my mother's weaknesses, which were balanced to some degree by the strengths she offered me throughout our years together.

Chapter Two
The 1940s

Following the Red Army

As a teenager, I managed to create a small niche for myself, within the context of one of history's most cataclysmic events, World War II, by tracing the march of the Soviet Union's Red Army from Stalingrad to Berlin.

Hitler's legions seemed on the brink of following up the fall of France and the retreat of British soldiers from the disaster at Dunkirk with a potential invasion of England. The Nazis, surprisingly, instead turned East on June 22, 1941, to launch a massive invasion with four million troops — possibly the largest army in history — into the Soviet Union.

My family, along with millions of others, watched intently as the invasion moved inexorably towards Moscow. (My sister June stood in front of a Monticello movie theatre collecting money for Russian War Relief.) My father was convinced the Red Army would stop the Nazis, but I was reading reports from U.S. military "experts" that the war would be over in six weeks. Winter came and the invasion was stalled at the gates of Moscow. For the first time, Hitler's armies were not only stopped but turned back to the West. The world was astounded.

In the spring, the Germans launched another offensive, this time to the South, aiming to capture Stalingrad as the jumping-off point for the seizure of the indispensable oil of the Caucasus region. But Stalingrad was not to surrender. The Red Army and the partisans fought block by block, room by room, even as the workers in the arms factories, under unrelenting fire, churned out weapons 24 hours a day. As was later agreed by historians and even the U.S. generals, Stalingrad was the turning point of the Second World War. Millions of German troops, along with their generals, surrendered to the Soviet defenders.

As General Douglas MacArthur told the Associated Press (February 23, 1942): "The hopes of civilization rest upon the worthy banners of the courageous Russian Army." Their heroic "resistance to the heaviest blows of a hitherto undefeated enemy, followed by a smashing counterattack which is driving the enemy back into its own land" is "the greatest military achievement of all time."

It was then that I discovered my niche. Woolworth's 5-and-10¢ department stores were selling maps of every front involved in the war. I bought the one depicting the Eastern Front, 2,000-miles long, from the Arctic to the Crimea. It was sold with tiny flags on pins, one set with the Nazi swastika and one set with the Soviet hammer and sickle. I would listen to the radio and read the daily papers for the latest reports of the Red Army's march westward. Their tanks and infantry were moving along at about 40 miles a day, aided by the partisan forces behind German lines.

As each report came in, I would move the Red Army flags West and along with the retreating Nazi flags. From the spring of 1943 until April 1945 at the capture of Berlin, my "niche" illustrated one of the world's greatest military feats of all time.

As usual, my Pop was right.

FORE! Time to Strike

Born and bred in Brooklyn, N.Y., I spent summers in my teenage years in Monticello, New York, where my mother would rent an apartment in town for July and August. In 1944, at 14, I worked as a caddy at the nearby Concord Hotel, three miles away. Each morning I would hitchhike to the hotel carrying my lunch pail, which always seemed to induce drivers to pick me up. Little did I foresee that this job would lead to my first strike.

At the golf course, about 20 of us, ranging in age from 14 to 17, lined up to be hired by the golfers to carry their bags and help search for balls driven into the adjoining woods. We were paid 75 cents per bag per golfer (sometimes we carried two bags).

On our way to the golf course we'd pass guests on the lawn playing cards and watch some of them rake in $300 on a single hand. The caddies wondered: maybe they could afford to pay us another quarter, $1.00 per bag? One morning we decided to demand a raise, as well as also ask the caddymaster, our boss, to charge us only a nickel for a soda instead of the usual dime.

The night before our planned action, we wrote a leaflet to be handed to each golfer; it stated our demand: We'd carry their clubs only if they agreed to the 25¢-per-bag increase. In the morning we gathered near the shack where the golfers checked in. Jackie, the first caddy in line, presented the leaflet to the first golfer. Although the latter agreed to pay the increase, when the caddymaster realized what was happening, he told Jackie to go out at the going rate or be fired. One of the 17-year-olds stood in the back, holding a long metal pipe. He yelled, "Hold fast!" to the caddy, waving the pipe somewhat menacingly. Jackie held fast and was promptly ordered by the caddymaster to leave.

At that point we all walked off and set up a picket line at the entrance, carrying signs saying, "On Strike." In that era there were no golf carts, and — just as we'd calculated — none of the golfers were prepared to carry their own bags, so the course was effectively shut down. The hotel's millionaire owner appeared and told us to either work at the old rate or leave his property and not bother coming back.

We never found out if, or how, they operated the course the remainder of that summer. But the following year we all returned and were offered our jobs back at the new rate of $1.00 per bag — and five-cent sodas. We were amazed at the power of our unity. I was particularly impressed by the leadership shown by that 17-year-old pipe-holder.

Wally Distributes Hitler's Favorite Newspaper: The "Daily Noose"

During the early years of the Second World War, the New York Daily News adopted a pro-fascist stance, calling for a negotiated peace, and even an alliance with Nazi Germany in its "fight to destroy Soviet communism." The News had the largest circulation of any paper in the U.S., topping over two million in its Sunday edition, including hundreds of thousands of working-class readers.

In New York City, the communist-led Local 65, with 30,000 members — of which I later became a member [see "Pages from A Working Life"] — vowed to combat the News's pro-Nazi propaganda by publishing thousands of copies of a 4-page parody entitled "The Daily Noose." My sister's husband Ralph was assistant editor of the Local's paper, "Union Voice," and was responsible for launching the "Noose." It's front page portrayed a meeting of the News editorial board grouped around a large conference table behind which hung a banner depicting a huge Nazi swastika.

The "Noose" satirized several News features. A popular one was "The Inquiring Photographer," which contained street interviews alongside pictures of those being asked provocative questions aimed at affirming the paper's political outlook. It was pretty well-established that many of these "interviews" were written by the News staff. So the "Noose" ran a column entitled, "The Conspiring Photographer" which contained "answers" exposing the News's politics.

Ralph brought home a copy and when I read it I immediately asked him to get me several hundred copies to distribute to all my classes at Midwood High School. By the next afternoon students had jumped all over the "Noose." Soon the school administration got wind of it and I was called down to the principal's office. The principal was irate, telling me I was not allowed to distribute any "material" without permission and that I should "stop immediately." Fortunately by then I had gotten rid of virtually all my papers.

I told the principal I thought the "Noose" was educational material, teaching my classmates about fascism. This didn't go over too well with the principal (who, by the way, was Jewish). I felt pretty good about the whole episode, having introduced hundreds of students to a new course in the school curriculum, "Anti-Fascism 101."

A Baseball Life II — The Catch

In the 1947 World Series I was to witness a historic feat involving my boyhood hero Joe DiMaggio, and from a vantage point barely six feet away from the action.

The Yankees and the Brooklyn Dodgers were playing the sixth game of that matchup. Now, at 17, having mastered the subways, I took off by myself for the Bronx from Flatbush to join the throng awaiting what we hoped would be the deciding game of the teams' second Subway Series. The Yanks were leading three games to two and a win would clinch it.

After waiting on line for several hours, I finally secured a seat in the second row of the corner of the left-field bleachers just above the Dodgers' bullpen. The game see-sawed back and forth until the sixth inning when the Yanks, with two out and trailing 8 to 5, put two men on base. Who should come to bat but the great DiMag. Everyone knew what that might mean — a three-run homer could tie the game.

Ace reliever Hugh Casey was on the mound for the Dodgers. Coincidentally, at the start of that inning, the Dodgers' manager had inserted bench player Al Gionfrido into left field as a defensive replacement. The count on Joltin' Joe went to two balls and one strike when he took a mighty swing. The ball soared toward the left-field bleachers, right in my direction. Along with the rest of the fans around me, I stood up yelling, reaching skyward hoping to catch it.

Gionfrido was racing back towards the bullpen, 415 feet from home plate. As the ball started its descent, the diminutive left-fielder reached back and threw his gloved hand over the three-foot-high railing, snatching it for the third out. We all groaned. The crowd was shocked. At that time it was hailed as the greatest catch ever in a World Series. DiMaggio was approaching second base when the ball was caught. In a rare (for him) display of emotion, DiMag kicked the base in disgust and walked slowly back to his position in centerfield.

I'm waiting in the bleachers' second row.

Suddenly a Yankee fan in front of me in the first row jumped over the outfield railing and raced out to pat DiMaggio on the back to console him. Immediately, stadium security guards ran out to drag the guy off the field. But he was too quick. He circled around, eluding them and headed back for the bleachers, jumped back over the railing and crouched into his seat. We quickly covered him up with a blanket, hiding him from the guards. Although the next day sports writers covering the game reported that "some bum from Canarsie had taunted" DiMag, we knew differently.

The Dodgers ended up winning the game 8 to 6 and I returned home dejected, but the Yanks took the sting out of The

Catch, winning the decisive seventh game and the Series.

Years later, on a trip to the Baseball Hall of Fame, I asked the curator if he had a picture of The Catch. He dug one up and made a copy for me. Although my face was blocked out by the railing at the spot where I was standing, I knew just exactly where I was. To this day the photo hangs on my bedroom wall in my "DiMaggio section," commemorating my presence at this red-letter day in my baseball life.

I Become A Baseball Writer (and Announcer!)

How could my family's Communist background land me, a 19-year-old in 1949, as a reporter in the pressbox at Yankee Stadium and the Brooklyn Dodgers' Ebbetts Field?

At that time, baseball was my life. Ever since 1936 I had been a diehard Yankee fan, stemming from the arrival of my boyhood hero Joe DiMaggio. When my family moved from Monticello in upstate New York to Brooklyn in 1942, I was in baseball heaven — now I could actually see Joltin' Joe in the flesh!

From 1946 to 1951, every chance I got I made the hour-and-a-half journey from my Flatbush neighborhood — ten minutes from the Dodgers' Ebbetts Field, no less — to Yankee Stadium in the Bronx to cheer for the Bombers. Little did I realize that this would lead me to "cover" the Yanks in their stretch drive to the pennant against the hated Boston Red Sox, and to the World Series over the Dodgers.

In my teenage years, my parents subscribed to the Communist Party's newspaper, the *Daily Worker*, so every day I would turn to their sports page to read what was happening with the Yanks. As it happened, their two sports writers, Lester Rodney and Bill Mardo, were avid Dodgers fans. They both subscribed to the widespread view that the Yankees represented the corporate world while the Dodgers, the "Bums," were "the workers' team."

This annoyed me no end since — adopting what I viewed as a Communist class outlook — the players on the two teams had more in common with each other than they did with their respective bosses.

Back then the players had no union and were at the mercy of the owners. They were not allowed to move to another team and were sent a new contract every year to "sign or you don't play." In fact, DiMaggio would invariably hold out for more money than the Yanks would offer and sit out spring training unless they upped his salary. (One year, when he demanded $25,000 for the season, he was told it was more money than long-time co-star Lou Gehrig was making. DiMag retorted, "Well, you're underpaying him!" Of course, these days a superstar makes four times that for one game!)

In the spring of '49 some of the above thoughts were circulating in my brain, spurring me to write to Rodney and Mardo, telling them they didn't have a class view when it came to baseball players, which seemed to lead them to their pro-Dodger, anti-Yankee position. Soon afterwards they called to invite me to have lunch with them and discuss my stance. Initially they seemed to regard my thinking as "cute," but as we proceeded, things got more serious. Finally, they asked if I would like to attend the games with their press pass and then write up a "nonbiased" story for the paper.

I was floored but immediately accepted. They said they couldn't pay me but would arrange compensation by way of the Fur Workers Union. How? That union was led by the communist Ben Gold with whom Rodney and Mardo had some "influence." If I went to the union hall on West 26th Street at 8:00 a.m. every morning, I would be given an "on-strike" picket sign and directed to the shops they were organizing in the fur market. There I would stand with the sign to alert drivers to refuse to cross the picket line and not deliver any goods to those shops. I would do this for four hours until 12 noon, for which I would receive a dollar an hour, netting me $20 a week. I would then ride the subway to Yankee Stadium or Ebbetts Field and take notes during the game, mostly daytime affairs. (Night games were limited to 7 or 14 a season.) After the game, I would return to their office and type up the report for the next day's paper.

I was overjoyed — getting to see games free, and becoming a baseball writer to boot! When I told my friends about this arrangement, they asked if I could get an extra pass for them, which I did.

That year the Yanks and Red Sox were in a battle for first place in the American League, the winner to go directly to the World Series against the National League Dodgers. (In 1949, there were no playoffs; with only eight teams in each league, finishing first meant reaching the Series. In that era, the Yanks and Dodgers were perennial pennant winners.)

My pass and "job" enabled me to attend 17 Yankee-Red Sox games during the September stretch drive, including the last weekend when the Yanks trailed by a game but swept the series, DiMag's hit winning the key encounter. Truly baseball heaven for a teenager!

As it turns out, the CIO unions in New York City had a baseball league of their own in which teams representing each local played every Sunday in various parks around the city. As an addition to my "job," I was asked to attend those games and write them up for Monday's paper as well. When substitutions were made during the game, I was handed a mike to announce the change to the crowd. The players liked that so much they asked me to "keep on talking" so I ended up announcing the entire game. I had become an announcer!

My "summer of '49" ended that fall when I got a day-time job working in Manhattan's garment center.

My days as a baseball writer/announcer were over. But that experience has stayed with me ever since.

STRIKE! Anti-Racism Shuts City College

Five years after our caddy walkout, I was involved in another strike, this one with a more political character. In April 1949, I was a sophomore at the uptown campus of City College when an uproar arose involving the chairman of the Romance Languages department, a professor named Knickerbocker, and an economics instructor named Davis.

Knickerbocker had withheld a language award from a deserving Jewish student and held back the advancement of others who were also Jewish. Meanwhile, it was learned that Davis, who oversaw the Army Hall dormitory housing returning GIs, was segregating black and white students. This triggered an anti-racist campaign to demand that the two of them be fired, or a strike would shut down the campus. The action was led by the American Veterans Committee, composed of GIs who had fought in the Second World War against the racist filth spread by Hitler's Nazis.

The next morning, as we walked from the Broadway subway station uphill along 137th Street, we saw scrawled in chalk across the width of the street one word emblazoned in eight-foot-high capital letters: "STRIKE!" That was one of the best "leaflets" I ever saw.

We reached the center of the campus and saw two dozen students at the administration building marching in a circle carrying strike signs. Suddenly a swarm of cops drove up and began manhandling the picketers and arresting them, shoving them into police vans. Some of you may know one of those arrested, Bert Lessuck.

A mass of students was standing across the street. When we witnessed the police attack, we moved as one, surging forward

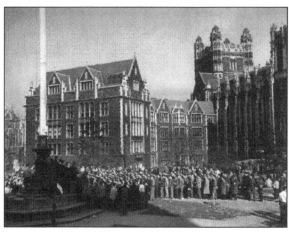

Striking students mass across from main building.

and forming a picket line a thousand strong. We chanted, "Free the students!"; "Fire Knickerbocker and Davis!"; and "Jim Crow must go!" We cheered when some students drove past displaying early editions of several New York newspapers. They all had the same headline: "Students Riot at CCNY."

Five thousand students walked out of class that day in what the New York Times called "the first general strike at a municipal institution of higher learning" in the United States. Knickerbocker resigned as department chairman and Davis was forced to withdraw from his Army Hall post and received a sharp cut in salary.

Our multi-racial unity against racism was impressive in a student body that at the time was 85% white. The strike made headlines across the country and showed the kind of struggle a united leadership of teenagers and young ex-GIs could organize. The action opened my eyes to how people could stick together and not break ranks while fighting back.

Chapter Three
The 1950s

Basketball, Racism and Karl Marx

One of the more memorable chapters in my youth occurred in 1950 when several events came together to link — in my mind — two championships won by the City College of New York's (CCNY) multi-racial basketball team, to the fight against racism and to Karl Marx.

It was the March 8, 2017, sports section of the New York Times that triggered this connection for me. Its spread on the coming NCAA "March Madness" tournament that brings together the top college basketball teams in the country included a story on Madison Square Garden and the "Heyday of College Basketball." In 1950, the Garden was considered the mecca of the sport, and CCNY's team viewed it as its home court. CCNY reached the pinnacle of the sport in winning both the NCAA title as well as that of the National Invitation Tournament (N.I.T.). At that time the latter was considered the equal of the NCAA, inviting all the leading teams to compete in the Garden for its title as well. CCNY's victory in both tournaments was an unbelievable achievement, the "Grand Slam," never accomplished before and — because of subsequent events — never to be repeated.

When the tournaments began, Kentucky's powerhouse basketball team, having won the two previous NCAA titles, was heavily favored in the N.I.T. and seeded first. CCNY, while having an excellent squad, was the last entry. In its first game, City defeated defending champion San Francisco 65-46. They then met Kentucky in the quarter finals. Kentucky's coach, Adolph Rupp, having always "resisted putting black players on his roster" (NY Times, 3/8/17), fielded an all-white team. (Rupp's first name conveniently associated him with another infamous "Adolph.")

Just before the game started, City's legendary coach, Nat Holman, encouraged his players to shake hands with their Kentucky counterparts, but the latter refused. Holman countered Rupp's racism by fielding a starting five composed of all black and Jewish players. Strikingly, in an historic upset, City demolished Kentucky, winning by 39 points! Soon afterwards, Rupp began recruiting black players.

Coach Bobby Sand standing at left

In the spring of 1950 I was in my second year at City College and enrolled in a course on American Economic History taught by instructor Bobby Sand. As it happened, Sand was also the coach of CCNY's junior varsity basketball team. (At that time the junior varsity was composed of all freshmen, preparing for promotion to the varsity team in their sophomore years.) This also made Sand the assistant to the coach of the varsity, then led by Coach Holman and viewed as a god by CCNY's fandom. When we came into Sand's class in early March, he told us right off that we would only be discussing basketball for the next two weeks. History was "off the table." That was the case until City had swept to its two championships.

At the time, I was working on a term paper based on Marx and Engels' "Letters on the Civil War." Marx had been hired by the New York Herald (later the Tribune) to analyze the war. He had made three main points on how the North could win the war: (1) that Lincoln should enlist tens of thousands of freed slaves into the Union Army (ultimately 180,000 would serve); (2) that he should put General William Sherman at the head of the Army; and (3) that he should direct Sherman to split the South's armies by moving on what became the famous "March through Georgia." Actually, Lincoln carried out such a plan (although I doubt he ever read Marx's columns). When I submitted my paper, Sand drew me aside to tell me that he agreed with Marx, both on the Civil War specifically as well as generally on Marx's economic analysis of capitalism. (He also gave me an A.)

In the fall of that year, a scandal broke that was to forever downgrade CCNY's basketball program and change Sand's life forever. It seems that several City players had taken bribes of maybe a few hundred dollars to "shave points," that is to control the margin of victory by deliberately missing shots or messing up on defense. So even though they won, it was by less than the point spread set by the bookies, helping bettors in the know to "clean up."

These events shook up college basketball. Some point-shaving players, convicted of misdemeanors, served prison terms; CCNY suspended its season when the scandal broke and the school's program was de-emphasized, placing them in a lower divisional category, never to compete at the top level of the March Madness. The National Invitation Tourney had been disgraced and in subsequent years reduced to inviting teams to the N.I.T. of a lesser caliber than those participating in the NCAA tournament.

Rupp blamed the influence on New York gamblers, saying they "couldn't touch his players with a 10-foot pole." But soon 32 players in seven colleges were implicated in fixing 86 games. And they included several leading players on Rupp's team, found guilty of similar point-shaving.

That fall, I switched to night school, having taken on a full-time day job in Manhattan's garment center, hauling bolts of cloth from a textile firm to ladies' garment shops. One day as I was pushing my 4-wheel wagon down Seventh Avenue, I spotted a familiar figure; it was my old history prof, Bobby Sand, carrying a huge flat satchel. We stopped to chat. It seems he had become a salesman, hawking dress designs to the ladies' garment shops (probably the only "Marxist" garment salesman in New York).

Apparently one effect of the point-shaving scandal was the loss of his teaching job at CCNY. Holman was suspended for one season and later reinstated. But Bobby Sand, who never had been implicated in the players' actions, fell victim to charges of "not controlling" the players, even though Holman was the head coach. Sand had been the team's top recruiter, scout and bench tactician, guiding the team to "pass to the open man, use the pick-and-roll offense" and other staples that now are featured among the leading professional teams. Sand was never offered a head coaching job at any college.

I told him it was a shame that his teaching skills were denied to City's students. "That's life," he remarked. I asked what led him to become a garment center salesman. He smiled, saying as he departed that one's "gotta put bread on the table."

Listening Is the
Key to Learning

In the 1930s and '40s, probably the all-time best-seller was a book by one Dale Carnegie entitled, "How to Win Friends and Influence People." I never read his tome but learned that lesson without his help from a group of workers who also had never read it. "Life" was their "best seller."

In 1950, when I was 20 and attending City College, I decided to switch to night school and get a full-time day job. I had a union book in the Communist-led Local 65 RWDSU (Retail, Wholesale & Department Store Union), so I went to the union's hiring hall and landed a job at Yale Fabrics, a textile shop. It was located in Manhattan's garment center in the basement of the old Metropolitan Opera building at 39th Street and Broadway. The opera's standing-room-only crowd would be lined up around the block when I would emerge from the freight elevator pushing a 4-wheeled box-like wagon filled with bolts of cloth for delivery to the area's dress manufacturing shops.

I was making 52 bucks a week, but the neat thing about the job was the necessity to wait for a freight elevator for an average of an hour on each delivery (about six trips a day) so I was able to use the time to do my homework. Since I had joined the YCL (Young Communist League) at college in 1948, and having been influenced towards Communism by my family, I now saw this as an opportunity to test my knowledge of Marxism and win these workers to see it as *the* solution to their problems.

At college in the Spring of 1949, I had been a picket captain in an anti-racist strike that had shut down the school. That summer I had volunteered as sports writer for *The Worker*. But now the time had come to "put my money where my mouth was." However, my trouble became much too much "mouth."

I figured all I had to do was explain Marxism to the workers and they'd just fall in line. On my first week on the job, I began haranguing the shop's dozen workers about my politics. I was the youngest among them, my co-workers all being in their 30s and 40s, some of them old enough to be my parents, most with families to support. Since my job was the only one that placed me outside the shop on the street, I only mingled with the workers for a short time between deliveries when picking up new shipments of cloth. I felt impelled to compress my "agitation" into those few minutes inside the shop.

After about six weeks of what was my probably insufferable behavior, Phil, a worker who was about 45 with three kids, drew me aside and said, "Wally, you're a good kid, you don't goof off, you do your work, but you've got to realize we've heard a lot of this before. We know who heads our union, but there's a lot of fear about losing our jobs, as good as this union is. Besides, you don't really know who we are, you don't know our problems, our family life, how we got here, how long we've been here. You don't know anything about us 'cause you're so busy talking that you're never listening."

"Sure, you want us to agree with your ideas. Can't say I personally agree with many of them but lots of what you say makes sense. You sound like a sincere guy. But you hardly know anything about us and why we'd be ready to accept your ideas, especially in the middle of this red scare. [It was the era of McCarthyism and the Korean War.] So settle down, cool it on the Communist stuff and let's become friends."

Wow! Was I set back on my heels. I asked Phil if everyone felt that way. "Sure," he replied, "ask Harry and Molly and the rest. They all think you're a good kid, but you gotta listen a little more, then talk."

Obviously, Phil was right. My mouth was open, but my ears were closed. I didn't really know any of these workers. How could I when all I had been doing was running my mouth for six weeks? These workers had taught me a more valuable lesson than any I had learned in 15 years of schooling.

After that "dressing down," I did an about-face. Listened plenty, "explained" less. This process was aided by the nature of the union and its organizing efforts, which I plunged into along with my co-workers. Local 65, a union with 30,000 members, was divided into many sub-locals. Yale Fabrics was in the Textile local with 2,500 members in probably 250 shops. To keep the local alive and growing, it was necessary to organize new shops constantly. But "65" was no ordinary union. Led by Communists, it involved the rank-and-file every step of the way. (May Day was a paid holiday; see story on District 65 organizing.)

Participation in these kinds of struggles brought my co-workers and me closer together. For one thing, they saw how I reacted in these situations which increased my standing among them. After I spent much more time learning about their lives, they were ready to listen to what I had to say.

Unfortunately, the following June we got word through the union that the boss was closing up the shop. We'd all be laid off but could get new jobs through the union hiring hall. Everyone received severance pay, a week for every year of seniority. Some of the older workers got 15 or 20 weeks. Me, I got one, but of course I had no family to support and lived at home, so the 52 bucks was heaven to me.

The most important thing I had gained from this 10-month sojourn at Yale Fabrics was what my co-workers had taught me — "How to win friends and influence people..."

Pages from A Working Life

In 1950, at the age of 20, I gradually learned the real meaning of working-class solidarity when I transferred to night classes at City College and went to work on a full-time day job in New York's garment center. I had been working as a part-time shipping clerk in the afternoons at the Florn Clock Company on Fifth Avenue while attending morning classes. I was one of six workers employed in this non-union shop when my brother-in-law — the assistant editor of the union paper at the Retail, Wholesale and Department Store Union's District 65 — suggested that I try to bring the place into the RWDSU, a union which organized hundreds of small shops in many different industries. He introduced me to an organizer responsible for such small warehouses.

I explained to the organizer that I had no real experience in such an effort. He pointed out that anyone could learn this trade, saying, "Here the rank-and-file are the organizers." He said he would guide me every step of the way. When I asked what would happen if I was fired for attempting to unionize the shop, he handed me a union book and replied that I had now become a member of District 65 and if the organizing attempt failed and I lost my job, I could use the union's hiring hall to obtain a new job with union wages and benefits. That seemed great to me, so I plunged ahead.

The organizer and I discussed the other five workers, trying to select the ones who might be most favorable to joining a union. I started with William, who ran the shipping department and with whom I was closest. He had been working there for several years and was wide open to gaining union benefits, as well as the use of the hiring hall for an even better job. I had numerous discussions with Ruth, the bookkeeper, who seemed to have progressive views on many subjects so I introduced the idea of a union. She said she would be willing to sign a union card. So now we had three of the six.

Ruth suggested we try Ann next, especially since Ruth said it was very unlikely Ann would tell the boss about our campaign. This took a little persuading, but after a series of lunch-hour discussions, Ann also signed a union card, so now we had a majority. The organizer then went to the boss and told him a majority of his workers were now in favor of a union, and we wanted to discuss a contract.

The boss was taken aback, shocked that all this was going on right under his nose. He said he wanted time to think about it and consult his lawyer. We didn't press him, which turned out to be a mistake. He came back to us a few days later and said that we only had three votes for a union, not a majority. It turned out that one worker had backed out, none other than Ruth, the "progressive." We figured the boss had promised her something and we couldn't convince her to change her mind. So my first attempt at union organizing had flopped. I told William I was quitting and going to the "65" hiring hall to get a better job. He said he'd think about it but I never heard from him again.

Within a week of sitting in the hiring hall, I was offered a job in the garment center in mid-Manhattan at $52 a week, more than double what I had earned at the clock company, plus receiving full benefits, paid holidays and vacations. I was to be a member of the Textile local of District 65, employed among a dozen workers, at Yale Fabrics [see "Listening Is the Key to Learning"], delivering bolts of cloth to hundreds of ladies dress manufacturing shops.

I was soon to learn, however, that delivering piece goods was only part of what my life would be as a member of District 65's Textile Local.

I BECOME PART OF A RANK-AND-FILE ORGANIZING FORCE

District 65 had its origin in the 1930s during the height of the CIO organizing drives. It was led by communists whose unionizing efforts were based on utilizing the rank-and-file as the source of winning other workers to join District 65. In my first few months I was introduced to this way of life.

The garment center's textile industry was composed of scores of small shops in numerous high-rise buildings containing anywhere from perhaps a dozen workers down to as few as one. When the union set its sights on such a non-union shop, a textile local organizer would come through the area asking rank-and-file members in unionized shops to come out on their lunch hour to organize a non-union shop. Maybe a dozen of us would proceed to that shop — in this case one with just two workers — march in, go right up to both workers and start explaining the benefits of joining District 65. The boss would suddenly yell at us, "This is private property; you can't talk to 'my' workers. Get out!"

We would simply ignore him and continue talking to the workers about the advantages of union membership: higher wages, health benefits, pensions, holidays, vacations and more. The boss was beside himself when he heard all this and retorted, "If I have to give them all this, I'll go out of business and these guys will be out of a job." Our answer was always, "If you refuse to grant these workers a decent standard of living, you don't deserve to be in business and we'll drive you out! After all, the other textile bosses who've signed union contracts seemed to have found a way to stay in business."

The workers, of course, were enjoying all this and invariably signed union cards. We then demanded the boss start negotiating a contract right then and there, similar to the rest of the unionized shops, and invariably the boss relented. In this way, dozens of shops were organized based on the strength of the rank-and-file.

But it wasn't just the textile shops that our members "invaded." Times Square was just a few blocks north of the garment center and contained three non-union Hector's restaurants. During lunch hours they would be crowded with the area's workers. So several District 65 organizers would enter scores of unionized textile shops and tell workers we wanted to organize Hector's. Then hundreds of union members would troop up to the three Hector's restaurants, order a cup of coffee or tea — then costing a nickel — and sit down at a table. Soon the place would be taken over by "patrons" whose "lunch" would net the owners a few nickels a table.

The managers would walk around frantically looking over our shoulders and gnashing their teeth over all the profits they were losing. So without even an outright strike, we were able to force Hector's to sign a union contract. And our members organizing this "lunch" proudly strode back to their textile shops with a job well done, having brought scores of non-union workers into District 65.

These experiences increased my confidence in my co-workers on whatever jobs I would have in the future, to forge solidarity among ourselves, and among workers as a class, and rely on it to collectively improve our lives.

My Connection to Rockefeller's Oil Empire?

When I was a member of District 65's textile local while working in the garment center, I took night classes at City College. Majoring in Labor Economics I had registered for a nine-credit Honors Course, six involving going to class and three devoted to writing an undergraduate thesis (without having to attend class, which I liked).

Since I was heavily active in the union [see above story, "Pages from a Working Life"] I decided to write my thesis on the union's health and welfare plan. It was quite an advanced program for that era. (Esther had been working in a '65' office when she became pregnant with Anita and received six week's maternity pay from that plan after giving birth.)

After submitting my thesis, I met with my advisor, Dr. Sigsbee, an economics professor. He told me that before he had taken this position, he had been a vice-president of personnel with Standard Oil of New Jersey (now Exxon), the center of the Rockefeller oil empire. Therefore, it was no surprise when he said he sharply disagreed with the pervasive communist politics throughout my thesis, especially given the fact that many of the union leaders in '65' themselves were communists.

However, he said my work was excellent and he awarded me an A.

As I left his office I thought back nearly 40 years to my father's escapade when he was working as a bus boy at Keene's Steak House in Manhattan where John D. Rockefeller often dined. (see story, "An 'Ordinary' Man"). During that period, amid widespread newspaper reports of bomb-throwing, bushy-haired anarchists (which matched Pop's appearance, but not his politics), by glancing intermittently and menacingly at Rockefeller, Pop scared the hell out of the tycoon.

So here was Abe Linder's son, nearly four decades later, getting an A on his communist-influenced undergraduate thesis from a Rockefeller vice-president! What goes around comes around.

From A Blind Date to a Matchless Marriage

When I reached my early twenties, I was convinced I was too shy to ever get married. Although I had gone out on dates with various women, nothing had clicked. At 24 I began seeing a young woman named Charlotte. We went out for about a year but I sensed something was not quite right — "Wally, I could never marry someone who doesn't dance," she said — leading my sister June to advise that such superficiality was not for me. "Forget her." (Ironically, the three women with whom I would spend the next six decades of my life — Esther, Toni and Vera — were all terrific dancers! In Vera's early years, she taught ballroom dancing.)

During that year I had already been working on the railroad and a comrade from my CP railroad section asked me if I had a girlfriend. "Yes," I replied, but "it doesn't seem to be going anyplace."

"Well," said Gladys, "if you break it off with her, I've got the girl for you."

"A blind date?" I said.

"Why not?" she answered.

I later did break up with Charlotte. Determined to overcome my shyness, I called Gladys for the phone number of "the girl for me." Gladys had checked for her friend's O.K. It was the first week in May, 1955, and it was then that I met Esther Chanzis.

She lived in Bensonhurst, a Brooklyn neighborhood I now visited for the first time. When I picked her up I suggested we go see a Swedish movie in Manhattan, "One Summer of Happiness." She agreed and off we went. I was so entranced with her looks and the beautiful peasant blouse she was wearing that I spent more time staring at her than at the movie.

When I took her home I asked if she liked bike riding and, if so, suggested we take a trip the following Saturday afternoon along the Belt Parkway bike path. We could start from Bensonhurst and ride to the old Brooklyn ferry that embarked from the beginning of the Belt to Staten Island. (Ten years later, when the Verrazano Bridge opened, that ferry closed down.)

The week went by and my excitement mounted. Saturday arrived; we rented bikes and cycled off in the afternoon for about four or five miles to the ferry. We decided to board the next boat and take the trip to Staten Island. It turned out to be the least expensive date I'd ever had, a nickel per person each way. But when we got to Staten Island, we decided to stay on the ferry without paying for the return trip to Brooklyn. The fare for the two of us was ten cents all told!

She had a family gathering that evening so before I left her I asked her out for the following weekend. To my delight she readily agreed. Saturday came and I took her out to dinner. By this third date we had told each other a lot about our lives. Like me, she had come from a Communist working-class family so our views on life had much in common — except that she was a great dancer.

Afterwards she invited me upstairs. She shared a tiny, box-shaped four-room apartment with her parents, Ida and Sam, both retired — two small bedrooms, an even smaller living room and a kitchen. In the course of reviewing our lives she had told me of a two-month trip she had made to Europe in 1951, going to the World Youth Festival in Berlin. She had just been laid off from her job and used the severance pay to finance the trip — traveling on the Queen Mary to England and flying home from Berlin, with stops along the way in Holland, France and Poland.

To me, who had never been further from home than the Catskills, her trip sounded positively sensational. She then told me she had written a 100-page description of the trip and gave it to me to read. For the next three hours I sat in the kitchen completely spellbound. All her descriptions were captivating: with all the people she had met on the trip, hanging out with the crew (not the passengers) on the ship, trying to figure out which of the seven pieces of silverware she was supposed to use at dinner, touring London, Amsterdam and Paris, meeting with people who had fought the Nazis during the war.

When I got to the last page it was 3:00 a.m. By then she was asleep. And I was convinced that this was the woman I wanted to marry!

For the next six weeks we recounted what kind of future we might share together. I was absolutely overjoyed over having met such a wonderful human being. As luck would have it, I had just received my driver's license the week after we had met (although I had no car). Her family had bought a two-door Chevy convertible, on the theory that she would get a license and then drive her family around. But so far she had failed two driving tests. And here I had a license. What a set-up!

The July 4th weekend was approaching and she said she had been planning to go upstate with a number of her friends, some single and some married. I said, "Let's go!" and so we did, with her car and my license. We all had a great time. My mind was agog. At the end of the weekend, and despite the fact that we had known each other for only eight weeks, I decided this was the woman I had been waiting for. When we got to her apartment I told her I wanted to marry her and spend the rest of our lives together. She was ecstatic, threw her arms around me and fairly shouted, "Yes!"

Her parents were spending the week at a resort so she immediately called them and told her mother the great news. My future mother-in-law Ida was overjoyed, especially since she thought I was "a piece of gold." It was then that Esther told me of the heartbreak she had experienced a year before. She had been going out with a guy for some time and they had decided to get married. A hall had been hired; the invitations had been sent out — Esther had a huge family, with aunts and uncles and cousins galore who were all delighted at the approaching marriage. But about a week before the wedding the guy shocked everyone. He backed out. He told her he didn't think he could commit himself to marriage.

Esther was despondent. She told me she felt her time "was over." She'd never get married. But now she exclaimed how lucky she was. "If that guy hadn't backed out, I would never have met you!"

I then said we'd have to wait until October. "Not again," she said. "No," I told her, "I'm not backing out." I explained that I had a 3A draft classification based on supporting my parents and that my next hearing to continue the deferment was scheduled for October. She was relieved. I had been sharing an apartment in downtown Brooklyn with a friend but I decided to move back with my parents in order to save up money for our honeymoon. So we spent the next four months planning the wedding and our trip.

Esther was slowly helping me shed any inhibitions, to forsake much of my shyness. I didn't know it at the time but she later told our daughter that she looked on me as "a project," as "a work in progress" that was absolutely worth taking on. Lucky for me.

We were married on October 22, 1955. At the wedding she pulled a fast one. The bandleader had announced that the bride and groom should now come out for the first dance. I was struck dumb. "I can't do this," I moaned. "Don't worry," she said. "We won't be alone." She then invited all the guests to join us on the dance floor. Somewhat relieved that everyone would not be staring at me, we started dancing. Then I looked around and realized we were the only ones on the floor. She had told everyone not to obey her invitation, which they did, and now the guests on the sidelines were laughing uproariously while the groom was "dancing."

Just made it among the bride's mass of relatives.
(That's me standing on upper right. Esther's
cousin Morris [second row seated, far right] was wounded
in the Spanish Civil War.)

We left the following week, during a snowstorm, driving cross-country in our little Chevy convertible, by way of Niagara Falls, then Chicago to visit her cousins — who owned a deli and sent us on our way with a load of food — and then for a week in the snows of Boulder, Colorado — the beginning of years of bliss that I had only dreamed about.

My next draft board hearing was a year away but by that time Esther was pregnant with our daughter Anita, which meant a new deferment. So I had escaped once again, never to be drafted.

But that's a story for another day.

The Chanzis Clan Celebrates Anita's Arrival

It was February 27, 1957; our first child had just been born and I was about to discover how Esther's family greeted such an occasion. I was visiting the new mother at the Brooklyn Women's Hospital in East New York (an institution no longer in existence). She was recovering from a Caesarean birth and in a certain amount of discomfort, but was happy to tell me that her mother Ida had called to invite me to a party at their apartment in Bensonhurst to celebrate the new addition to the Chanzis family. Little did I realize that this would be a party with a capital P.

Esther's parents lived in a 4-story walk-up. When I arrived at their third-floor apartment, I was startled to see the hallway filled with furniture. When I walked in, a huge cheer arose from the scores of relatives crowded into their tiny four-room flat. The living room was completely empty of furniture with the floor set up for dancing. I was aware of the substantial family I had now entered, having seen them at the wedding, but now was introduced to how they celebrated a new grandchild.

The music started and immediately I was being whirled around the floor by cousins and aunts. Soon the food was served, all the relatives having brought in their home-cooked dishes. There were toasts galore for the infant Anita. Somewhat later tables and chairs were returned to the living room, cards were brought out and a hot poker game ensued, a custom I was to learn was integral to the Chanzis household.

Clean-up time arrived and I offered to help. When the aunts sitting in the living room saw me wiping off stains on the refrigerator door, they were besides themselves. "Ida," they kvelled (marveled), "what a son-in-law you have!"

That little act set me up for life as part of the Chanzis clan.

A Child We Never Really Knew…
and a Son Who Ushered in a Bright New World

In the spring of 1959, two years after our daughter Anita's birth, her sister Julia entered our growing family. My wife Esther, requiring her second Caesarean birth, spent ten days in the hospital before returning home. By the third night we began to notice Julia was having difficulty breathing so we called our doctor and described this condition. He said we needn't worry and prescribed an over-the counter medicine. I hurried to the pharmacy to pick it up and we put it in her formula. We then sat on our bed alongside the baby in her crib and watched for any change. But it only worsened. Her color gradually darkened and her body appeared to stiffen so around midnight we called the doctor again and told him that the medicine didn't seem to be working, that her condition was deteriorating and asked him to come examine her. He seemed annoyed at being awakened and told us to "wait." But we couldn't wait.

We immediately called 9-1-1, explained the situation and the doctor's refusal to come to look at the baby. Soon two cops arrived bringing the doctor with them. He examined her and told us what we had feared; she had died. It was March 3, 1959.

The police told us that before burying her she had to be examined for the cause of death. They called a city agency responsible for such situations to take her away. Esther was standing at the living room window, with her back to the agency's personnel, not wanting any last look at Julia. When they left with the baby, I went over to Esther, we embraced and she agreed that the only thing we must do was to try for another child as soon as she was able.

The doctors who had delivered Julia told us she had died from a form of viral pneumonia — when the first symptoms appeared in such a condition, "it was too late"; nothing could be done to save the child.

We were extremely angry, both at the pediatrician and at the health plan to which we belonged, HIP, and discussed bringing a case against them for their sickening response. We agreed, however, that the time spent in doing that would only prolong our anguish, so we pursued the only relief open to us: to try for another child.

In early October, Esther became pregnant again. The doctors at New York Hospital told us there was no real chance of a repeat of the viral pneumonia. We assumed that she would have to endure a third Caesarean, but were told that depending on the size of the baby, Esther might be able to have a normal birth. They said this was a decision they could make at the last minute and if necessary, they could perform a Caesarean right there on the operating table.

The baby's due date was July 8, 1960, but that day came and went. On the 18th and 19th, "false alarms" brought us back and forth to the hospital. On one of those days, we were told to come back in four hours, so rather than returning home to Brooklyn, we actually went to a movie playing nearby (Hitchcock's "Psycho" of all things) to wait it out.

Finally, at 2:30 a.m. on July 20, Esther's water broke. We sped to the hospital on East 68th Street in Manhattan and at 10:06 a.m., Andrew was born, 12 days "late." As the baby was large (8½ pounds), the three doctors in attendance had decided it had to be another Caesarean. The baby was healthy, showing no sign of Julia's condition. Esther stayed in the hospital for ten days, in a room for four mothers, one of whom was the child of an Indonesian diplomat. She received great care, even including getting her teeth fixed! This time Esther breast-fed the baby.

On the 20th of July, 1960, Anita's brother, our new son Andrew, arrived home, and a bright new world opened up before us.

OUR BIRTH ANNOUNCEMENT

MOTTO: 12 can live as cheaply as two / **THE DAILY MALE** USA* / **PRICE:** Whatever you've got!

STORK STRIKE SETTLED! (finally)

Linder Baby Arrives

The strike of 17,000 storks has ended in complete victory for the union, and normal deliveries have been resumed. The Storks' leader, Mr. I. D. Liver, issued a statement regretting any inconveniences, false alarms, aggravation, and assorted aches and pains suffered by prospective parents. He reported that the storks will now receive time and one-half for all night work--that is, for all deliveries between 6 P.M. and 6 A.M. In addition, the shape-up system of hiring will be abolished, as all storks will be guaranteed a full week's pay. However, if a slow season should develop (something which would be unprecedented), all storks laid-off would be compensated at three-fourths of their daily rate.

"WOULDN'T CROSS"—ANDY

Andrew Linder came squalling into New York Hospital at 10:04 A.M. on July 20, 1960, after having stoutly resisted crossing the (post-natal) picket line set up by striking storks (see adjoining article). Andrew was the first fetus to fuss about crossing the line. His refusal to appear as scheduled on July 9th spread to scores of others, as doctors became weary at sending mothers home only to keep returning with more false alarms.

Mrs. Esther Linder, Andrew's esteemed mother (ahem), herself tropped back and forth twice on July 18, before rousing her, by now, ulcer-ridden husband at 2:30 A.M. on July 19 to make the final trip to East 70th Street.

WPB ON WORK-RULES

Thus, on the key issue of work rules, the employers gave in completely. They didn't even attempt to raise the issue of automation, which would have eliminated present methods of conception and delivery. Feelers sent out on this score were met with a demonstration of protest by 1,437,633,441, at City Hall, defying the old adage. It was reported that the Storks' Union was delighted with this show of solidarity between Labor and the public.

President Liver also stated that every union member would get

NEWCOMER WEIGHS 8½ POUNDS

It was obvious that Master Linder put the time he spent inside to good use, tipping the scales at a healthy 8 lbs., 8 oz. While his father has repeatedly denied stories that he slipped "Big Andy" half gallons of ice cream to keep him going, there are many who are disregarding his weak disavowals. However, reports that heavyweight champ Floyd Patterson shuddered when he heard the weight figure are completely unfounded, according to the usually reliable sources.

The Stork Union has presented a beautiful bouquet of orchids to Mrs. Linder in gratitude for her patience in waiting for the end of the strike while her new son was respecting the picket line. Andrew received free diaper service for twenty years, and honorary membership in the Storks' Union. And good ol' "Pa" Linder received a couple of sharp pecks from the beaks of a few scabs. He refused to make a statement to the press about the incident, although when he was overheard muttering "never again" under his breath, several storks laughed uproariously, with knowing winks.

a full month's vacation at Rocky Mountain National Park at no cost to themselves or their families.

A particular sore point, long at issue, was finally settled. Hereafter, no stork will be required to deliver its own young ones. This job will be performed by another, completely unrelated, fellow union member. The management's refusals in the past to agree to this clause was resulting in a rapid deterioration of the stork species, as many nervous father storks were dropping their own children in transit. It is believed that this fact convinced the employers to grant this demand or face eventual elimination of the work force.

CORPORATE PRESSURE TREMENDOUS

It was understood that tremendous pressure was exerted on the storks to end the walk-out in the "public interest" by the Evenflow Bottle Company and the Crib Diaper Service, both of whose sales plummetted during the eleven-day strike. However, the unexpected solidarity of the prospective newcomers themselves turned the tide in favor of the union. (See adjoining article)..

*United Storks of America

The Road I Had to Follow — How The Rosenberg Case Changed My Life

When I was laid off from the garment center in June of 1951, I went to District 65's hiring hall and got a job in a union shop, Timely Fabrics, at 1410 Broadway in Manhattan. It was a pretty lonely job, only one other worker besides me, but was enough to support myself living in my cold water flat on Thompson Street in "Little Italy."

The Korean War was raging at the time. I had a college draft deferment as long as I maintained a 12-credit schedule. However, that summer the draft board said that unless I graduated in the normal four years, it would revoke my deferment and would draft me immediately. Draftees were being given 13 weeks basic training and then shipped straight to Korea. The Chinese were in the war then and G.I.s were coming home steadily in body bags. I wanted no part of that but maintaining my deferment meant taking 20 credits that fall to enable me to graduate in four years. I was collecting unemployment insurance so I took a room in City College's only dormitory,

"Army Hall," (at five bucks a week!) and was able to complete the 20 credits.

Now to maintain that deferment I had to get accepted into graduate school. To make sure, I applied to 13 universities and was accepted in all of them. I decided on NYU at Washington Square in Manhattan. I had qualms about all this because of the cost, with only my mother working (my father was home after suffering a heart attack), but they would have none of that, saying, "We'll get by. We're not going to let them kill you in some imperialist war."

I got a part-time job and registered for the required 12 credits. I remember to this day my father handing me $191 for tuition for my four courses. It was the most money I had ever held in my hands in my life up to that time.

But my graduate school career was to be short-lived. Two weeks later my mother fell sick and was forced to quit her job, so I went to work full-time to support her and my father. This meant leaving NYU and to me the biggest crime of all was losing those $191 ("No refund" said NYU.) But my new draft status became 3A — supporting my parents. My sister's husband Ralph said I should learn a good trade, like printing, so I got a job in a union shop as a proof boy and proofreader. This would enable me to get a 4-year apprenticeship and a journeyman's card, giving me entrée into any union shop in the country. But when the apprenticeship seemed too distant, I took a job in a non-union shop on Mulberry Street in Little Italy in order to learn the compositor's trade and then go to New Jersey to a union shop and get my card there. This was a common route for many young workers at that time.

The owner of that shop might as well have been named Simon Legree. He trooped around on his wooden leg, sneaking up behind you to check on your work and screaming at you for some minor mistake. I vowed to tough it out until I gained enough experience to follow the Jersey route, but larger events were taking shape to send me in a different direction and change the course of my life

It was the spring of 1953 and a movement was sweeping the world to get "justice for the Rosenbergs." Julius and Ethel Rosenberg, parents of two sons, six and ten, had been convicted of "conspiracy to commit espionage." They were accused of having stolen atomic secrets and given them to the U.S.'s Cold War enemy, the Soviet Union. All of us on the left were convinced they had been framed and the Eisenhower administration would be executing two innocent people as part of its continuing drive to maintain a Cold War hysteria.

Worldwide protests saw tens of thousands demonstrating in the streets of London, Paris, Rome and on six continents. Even the Pope petitioned Washington for clemency — life imprisonment instead of the death penalty.

I was 23 at the time and became emotionally swept up in this movement, participating in demonstration after demonstration, in New York and Washington. I read the papers avidly every day, poring over every twist and turn in the case.

As the date of the execution drew near, Eisenhower said he would grant clemency only if they "confessed to their crime." They steadfastly refused, maintaining their innocence. They were writing to each other and to their children while in prison, a collection published as "The Death House Letters." Tension was mounting daily. Protests flooded Washington from all over the globe. It was certainly the biggest movement I had ever witnessed in my young life. I felt inextricably bound up in it.

The day before their scheduled execution, Supreme Court Justice William Douglas granted them a stay but the full court soon over-ruled him. I joined tens of thousands in Washington on the night of June 19 when the execution was scheduled for

11:00 p.m. As we marched around the White House word came that the deed was done.

All the way home on the train I had been thinking about what had gone wrong, what was absent from such a worldwide movement that prevented it from changing the course of events. I concluded that the missing link was the working class right here at home. The labor unions, in the grip of reactionary leadership, with the communists having been ousted five years earlier at the start of the Cold War, had done absolutely nothing to protest the executions. In my young mind, I figured if the mass of workers here had joined in, had threatened a general strike to stop the country — which they surely had the power to do — the Rosenbergs might still be alive.

I knew about the past achievements of the communists, playing a leading role in organizing the mass of unskilled and semi-skilled workers in the 1930s into the CIO, especially in the basic industries. During that period it produced thousands of fine mass organizers and leaders, like William Z. Foster who was the key leader in organizing the entire U.S. industrial union movement, with its tens of millions of members. This movement, in effect, set up advances that workers made in the ensuing decades. Their organizing of the unemployed, their fight against Jim Crow, their struggles for the 8-hour day and the 40-hour week — which basically established weekends off for tens of millions — were the high-water marks in the history of the U.S. working class. Stemming from the influence of my parents, I had become a member of the Communist Party from the late 1940s.

By the time we reached Penn Station, I had decided to quit the print shop and seek a job in a basic industry. There I could join with other communists and help influence my fellow workers in a direction similar to the events of the 1930s and go beyond that to a point, among other things, that could have turned around the result in a case like the Rosenbergs[1]. I agreed with the Communist Party's outlook that it was the workers in the basic industries who were the key sector of the entire working class and because of their potential power could lead our class towards workers' rule.

The execution of Julius and Ethel Rosenberg led me to spend the next decade of my life as a railroad freight handler on New York City's Manhattan waterfront.

---

[1] In a March 1997 article, Alexander Feklisov, a former Soviet KBG agent, said he met with Julius Rosenberg between 1943 and 1946 and told the New York Times: "He [Rosenberg] didn't understand anything about the atomic bomb, and he couldn't help us."

Even if one were to assume that Julius Rosenberg had tried to help the Soviet Union in its quest to develop an atomic bomb, a legitimate motivation could easily have been the fact that in 1943 the Soviets were battling 80 percent of the Nazi army — the largest army in world history — by itself on the 2,000-mile long Eastern Front. Meanwhile, the U.S. and Britain were a year away from opening up the D-Day invasion of France. U.S. officials admitted they could not have defeated the German army in western France without the Soviet Red Army engaging most of Hitler's legions in the East. Julius may well have hoped that helping the Soviets would have enabled them to survive the Nazi onslaught until the opening of the Western Front.

Even more disturbing was the conviction of Ethel Rosenberg. "She had nothing to do with this — she was completely innocent," said Feklisov. Decades later, Ethel's brother David Greenglass admitted lying to implicate his sister Ethel. For his cooperation with the FBI, he and his wife were never prosecuted.

FBI Director J. Edgar Hoover later stated the clear motive behind the prosecution of Ethel: "There is no question [that] if Julius Rosenberg would furnish details of his...activities, it would be possible to proceed against other individuals. Proceeding against his wife might serve as a lever in this matter." (Julien Bell: "The Case of the Rosenbergs"; Archive, May 2003 issue # 28)

Chapter Four
The 1960s

"I've been workin' on the railroad...."

When I concluded that the absence of the trade unions in the worldwide movement to save the Rosenbergs had allowed the rulers a free hand in executing them, I decided to leave my job in the print shop and get a job in a basic industry within which I could join others to try to move the working class towards a society ruled by the workers, who, after all, are the ones who produce everything of value.

The Communist Party's policy of industrial concentration aimed to build a mass base, especially in the basic industries, those areas which held the lifeblood of the country in their hands: auto, steel, electrical, railroad and so on. So in the summer of 1953, on the Monday after the executions, I sought jobs in auto plants, at GM in Tarrytown, N.Y. and at Ford in New Jersey, but without success. However, I did get hired at the freight-car repair yards of the Central Railroad of N.J., in a three-man welding gang. I would use long tongs to grab red-hot rivets from a portable oven and hand them to the two workers inside the freight car being repaired; they would then solidify the rivet in its proper place.

I soon learned there would be layoffs at Christmas time, so I went up and down the Manhattan waterfront seeking a railroad freight-handling job at one of the 13 railroads criss-crossing the Metropolitan N.Y. area. I was hired on the Baltimore & Ohio where I would spend the next decade. I later discovered that the CP had a railroad section comprising 65 members in 13 party clubs on 13 different roads in various crafts. Metropolitan New York's 90,000 railroad workers comprised the second-largest rail center in the U.S., after Chicago.

When my sister June heard about my decision, she pleaded with me not to "ruin" my life. "You're a New York Jewish intellectual," she said. "You'd be out of place on the railroad," in the rough and tumble world of industrial workers. I was not convinced. I felt I had grown up in a working-class home and neighborhood, none of my friends were "intellectuals," and so on. But even if she was right, I still was determined to try. Otherwise, I felt my efforts to free the Rosenbergs would have had no meaning. So began an 11-year journey among railroad workers that enveloped my life.

It was during this period that I met my future wife, Esther, got married, helped bring two children into the world, left the CP and helped organize the Progressive Labor Movement (later to become the Progressive Labor Party). As it turned out, it became among the most rewarding and exciting decades of my seventy adult years, when I started "workin' on the railroad."

I joined the country's largest railroad union, the Brotherhood of Railway Clerks & Freight Handlers, totaling a

A railroad "float" of freight cars we loaded and unloaded.

quarter-million members. Our work was essentially to unload freight from trucks and trailers backed up to railroad piers on Manhattan's West Side waterfront, and then load the freight into railroad cars resting on barges (called "floats") tied to the piers. Tugboats then towed these barges laden with perhaps a dozen fully-loaded freight cars across the Hudson River to Jersey City freight yards, where they were coupled together into trains hundreds of cars long to be moved westward to their destinations. Similarly, we would unload the freight cars towed over from Jersey containing eastbound freight and load that into trucks and trailers, manned by Teamsters, who would then deliver the freight to Metropolitan NYC destinations.

Our role as CP members was to organize mass, militant, rank-and-file struggles, possibly become local leaders, but as we were instructed, not tell anyone we were communists "because that would isolate us from the [brainwashed] workers." It was past the era of the mass, open communist organizing of the 1920s and 1930s, and heavily into the Cold War period when the CP had beat a hasty retreat from its leadership days. (I started on the railroad during the Korean War, at the height of McCarthyism.) In all my years on the railroad I never once directly told a co-worker that I was a communist, although I later learned that the company knew, the union officials knew, and so did the mass of workers!

Our Party club among the B&O freight handlers started slowly, by becoming involved in very low-level struggles. My first challenge to the bosses occurred when I was part of a gang unloading a refrigerator car. We were forced to work ankle-deep in melted ice water without protective boots (which we knew to be a rule violation). I discussed it with the rest of the gang and we told the foreman we would refuse to work without boots. I was immediately summoned before the station agent who told me I "couldn't refuse to work." That was "insubordination." I told him the company was being "insubordinate" in not issuing us boots. Did he want us to get sick and not report to work? He smiled and told the foreman to give us boots.

This story spread around the 26th St. Freight Station. (The B&O freight operation comprised Piers 20-23, 39-40, 63-66, a pier on Staten Island and the 26th St. Station, involving about 1,000 workers.) Because of that incident, workers on my shift (7 PM to 4 AM) began approaching me with grievances. We had no steward; the local's leadership was centered downtown at Piers 20-23. My co-workers petitioned the union to appoint me to be a steward on that shift. This was at the end of my first year on the B&O.

Sanitary and health conditions on the railroads were abominable. One example: the "bathroom" on the end of one pier consisted of an iron bar on the edge of the pier. One would drop one's pants, sit on the bar and crap into the Hudson River. We had no locker rooms and very few lunchrooms. This was true of most railroads in the NYC area. So our Party railroad section proposed the idea of starting a movement to get a law passed in the two state legislatures guaranteeing minimum sanitation and health facilities on all railroads in the area.

In addition to this was a struggle that became known as the weekly pay campaign. Railroad workers were paid three times a month, every ten days. While seemingly meaningless to workers paid every week or every two weeks, it wreaked havoc on railroad workers. Some pay periods would include six working days, some seven and others eight. It made it very difficult to budget one's pay, especially when rent time rolled around. Railroad workers were always bitching about being paid so irregularly. So our Party section seized on this apparently universal complaint, which cut across all road and craft lines — there were 23 different craft unions on the railroads at that time — in an attempt to organize a movement that would build rank-and-file unity among the tens of thousands of rail workers in the area.

Joined together as the Campaign for Weekly Pay and Health & Safety, it caught on among thousands of workers. It gave our Party section a chance to involve all 13 clubs in one unified effort around what we felt was a winnable reform. Of course, the union leaders weren't blind to this development. Finding it difficult to veto something that would guarantee a flush toilet on a railroad pier (among other things) — and not wanting it to be a rank-and-file initiative — they took it over as their own. As it turned out, both state legislatures passed laws essentially granting our demands and forcing the railroads to institute minimum health conditions, lunchrooms and pay us regularly, every week.

FIGHTING RACISM IN THE UNION

Rail workers were very pleased at the outcome, and knew who the organizers were, despite the leaderships' claim that they had done it. We had taken some issues that really got under every worker's skin and combined them into a mass campaign which had involved thousands of workers throughout the area. Simultaneously, we had exposed the railroad bosses, putting them a bit on the defensive when they were in the midst of a defamatory campaign of their own, painting workers as "featherbedders," in an attempt to lay off hundreds of thousands. It also involved the unity of black and white workers on the railroads, historically a racist industry in which the bosses restricted certain crafts as "white only." In fact, at that time there were still several craft unions that barred black members altogether!

(It was our CP section that had broken the lily-white craft of brakemen on the Pennsylvania RR. The PRR had never hired a black worker as a brakeman — a generally higher-paid, operating craft job — in its first 120 years. When we saw a Pennsy ad for brakemen, we sent down two black comrades, who were not hired. Then we sent two white comrades the same day, who *were* hired. The black comrades took their case to the State Commission Against Discrimination and the white comrades who were hired testified on their behalf. The Commission ruled that the Pennsy had discriminated and ordered them to hire the two black comrades. Within the year, the PRR hired 200 black brakemen for the first time in its history.)

This racism was prevalent throughout the industry. While there were many black freight handlers and some clerks, most had been hired for the first time during World War II when there was a labor shortage. Our union constitution barred black members, so the black workers were placed in "auxiliaries." They took their case for "first-class citizenship" to court and won a ruling awarding them full membership. The international asked them if they wanted to join the all-white locals or have their own locals. With good grounds for suspicion of the white locals' leadership, they opted for their own all-black locals. So it was that 150 such locals were created around the country.

This was the situation we faced in 1953 among the B&O freight handlers in NYC, where among the 1,000 workers, 600 were in the black local and 400 in the white local. We worked on the same platforms in the same gangs, under the same foremen, under the same union contract, but were in separate locals. Most workers, white and black, saw this as a disadvantage, if not outright wrong, and favored one multi-racial local. But few were active in the union. No one organized for it. This situation enabled the company, obviously, to play white against black. Merging these two locals, with a multi-racial leadership, became a top priority for our Party club, which had members in both locals. (As the civil rights movement grew nation-wide in the late 1950s, a small number of young, newly-hired black workers chose to join the previously all-white local, and were admitted, thus breaking its lily-white character. But the main goal remained: to merge the two locals.)

As a steward, I had developed ties among some other stewards, both black and white, among whom I raised the idea of both black and white stewards representing any worker whom the company brought up on disciplinary charges. This meant that black and white stewards would be representing both black workers and white workers for the first time in the union's history. Based on painstaking studies of previous cases, and our newfound unity, we began to win virtually every case.

We demanded that the foreman present the company's case first (this was in front of the railroad station agent who was judge, jury and executioner.) Then we, both black and white, would cross-examine the (usually) white foreman. This hadn't happened before, either. Usually we would so wipe the floor with him, exposing all sorts of lies and contradictions in his story, that the boss was forced to end the hearing before the defendant worker ever testified. Workers were winning thousands of dollars in back pay. In addition, we would bring up five or ten workers to testify in the hearing, on company time. This also got under the bosses' skins (and ate into their profits). Soon the number of hearings dropped to a trickle.

This result had a marked effect on the rank-and-file, especially on the black local's leadership. For the first time they saw white stewards whom they could trust. And the fact that we were winning cases led to white workers increasingly supporting the idea of one multi-racial local with a multi-racial leadership.

RANK-AND-FILE, ANTI-RACIST SLATE

At that point, our Party club proposed that I try to develop a rank-and-file slate in the predominantly white local, running on a platform of rank-and-file militancy and multi-racial unity. I approached one worker who seemed somewhat active in the local and critical of the current leadership. His first question took me unawares: "I hear that you're supposed to be a communist." I managed to squirm out of the conversation without ever answering it directly. In effect, I "ran like a thief." But it was the first inkling I had that I was known to be in the CP. As I learned later, the FBI had told the railroad, which told the union leaders, who told the workers.

So all along the workers figured I was a communist, but never really baited me about it (probably because I did a good job as a steward). So I just left well enough alone. Predictably, our Party club never discussed how we could turn this situation to our advantage. I can't remember ever having a discussion about actually recruiting anyone to the Party, not until my last year on the railroad after I had quit the CP to join in starting the Progressive Labor Movement.

We decided that I should run against a weak union officer. The local's vice-president was an assistant foreman (they, and foremen, were allowed in the union) and a blowhard at that, generally disliked by the rank-and-file. I was elected easily. Now the present leadership had to contend with a rank-and-file-supported officer whom they knew to be a communist.

I didn't confront them directly but rather made suggestions that contained elements of unity. I proposed we have a local paper of which I would become the editor and that all the officers write for it. They agreed, never realizing what a weapon for class-consciousness such a paper could and would become, eventually helping to turn them out of office. Some examples:

During national negotiations, workers were very dissatisfied with the demands and with the long, drawn-out course they were taking. (RR labor negotiations sometimes went on for two to three years!) The question became how to point out the international's inadequacy in the local paper without confronting them So we made a series of contract proposals and won a vote at a union meeting to send them to the international. Of course, we expected an answer, one that we figured would be very wishy-washy at best. It was. Then we proceeded to print both letters in the Local's paper — ours and their answer. The contrast was self-evident, without any comment from the editor.

At another point, the railroad began a "speed-up" campaign. They sent efficiency men from Baltimore to monitor our every move and tried to order us around. We took the position that the contract said we only took orders from the foremen. This frustrated them, since they were forced to issue orders through the foremen. The latter didn't like that either, which tended to drive a wedge between them and these "outside" bosses.

We printed a cartoon (drawn by my nephew Alec) depicting three men in suits and ties sitting on a platform wall watching one freight handler pushing a hand truck, and entitled it "Efficiency." This drove the railroad wild. They sent a vice-president up from Baltimore to meet with the Local Chairman and the Grievance Committee (which I was on) to tell us that if these "disparaging" descriptions of the railroad continued, it would lead to shippers dropping the B&O's business and this in turn would lead to layoffs. "Do you want to lose your jobs? The railroad is already losing money." "How much?" we asked. "$31 million last year," was the reply. "O.K.," we said. "We're making $68.84 a week. You're losing $31 million a year. Let's change places. You take our job and make $68 bucks a week. We'll take yours and lose the $31 million."

The guy went nuts, saying, "Do you realize that $16 million of that $31 million is going to Chase Manhattan Bank as interest on 'our' debt?" Oh, we figured, so that's where it's going. In the next local paper, we printed a report of the meeting, with the headline, "Chase Manhattan Made $16 Million in Interest Profit

Off Our Labor!"

In this way we were able to report events without putting ourselves in a position of bringing down the full wrath of the international on our heads too soon. When the paper came out every month and was distributed through the stewards on all the piers, work virtually ceased on the platforms as everyone, black and white, stopped to read the paper. We had a lot of cartoons and "personals" in it as well. The workers loved the paper and wrote to it and for it.

This was not lost on the leadership of the black local, who were somewhat nationalist but didn't know what to think about what we were doing. We approached them and asked if they wanted to write various columns for the paper. They agreed. We proposed in our (mostly white) local that the paper become a joint effort of the two locals. The black local voted the same. So the move for merger into one multi-racial local got a big boost as the paper became the one voice of the two locals. In this way, the paper was building both class-consciousness and anti-racist, multi-racial unity.

CHALLENGING THE WHITE LOCAL'S LEADERSHIP

By this time, we figured we had built up enough strength, through the winning of hearings, grievances and the influence of the paper, to not only challenge the established local leadership, which was generally opposed to any militancy, but to beat them handily. We organized a slate for four of the top positions — president, vice-president, treasurer and recording secretary. I was nominated for president. (We didn't feel quite strong enough to run someone for Local Chairman, who is also head of the Grievance Committee, and the most powerful position in the local.)

We ran a real campaign, giving out leaflets, putting up

posters with our pictures at all piers (many of us worked at different piers every day, on a shape-up basis, and workers could more readily identify us by our pictures than by our names). We held lunch-hour meetings with all shifts at all piers (the company operated 24 hours a day, seven days a week). This bewildered the incumbent leadership. They had been in office a long time and had never been challenged at all, much less by such a "high-powered" campaign. Their only card left was red-baiting, which they started in a veiled fashion, but centered at their base downtown and in Staten Island (where the B&O had a small operation). Since our base worked at all piers, they were able to deflect this attack based on the militant work I had done over the years. However, the worker on our slate running for vice-president approached me and said, "I hear you're supposed to be a communist. But don't tell me, I don't want to know!" My reaction was, "Whew, another obstacle overcome!" When it was discussed in the Party, the reaction was similar, and "keep up the good work." There was no attempt made to discuss communism with that worker, who was obviously sympathetic to me, or to turn the incident into a Party-building effort.

The leadership of the black local watched this contest from a distance, but many black workers openly campaigned for us among their white co-workers, especially because they knew we stood for a merger of the two locals on a multi-racial basis. The election took place at the union hall, and we won by an overwhelming 2-to-1 margin.

FIGHTING THE COMPANY

Within a year of that election, the company came down hard on the efficiency campaign again to eliminate "featherbedding." The new leadership discussed it and decided to go on a slowdown. But on a railroad freight platform, a slowdown rather quickly has the same effect as a strike (the latter was "illegal") in the sense that the platforms become so choked with freight that nothing can move — gridlock. And after a few hours, that was exactly what happened. The bosses went wild but could do little to unlock the gridlock. So they did the next best thing; they called the international union which sent down one ot their bigshots to "settle it."

We realized that this guy was coming to undercut us. I estimated that we didn't have enough strength to oppose them. Subjectively, I thought to myself that I couldn't be a part of what would inevitably be a sellout. So I called a meeting of all the workers in a park near the 26th Street Station and laid out the situation as I saw it, ending with my decision to resign as president rather than be part of a sellout. It was then that the workers taught me a good lesson in the responsibilities of leadership.

Both black and white workers were involved in this slowdown/strike, and were present at this meeting. One young black worker rose to challenge me. "Who the hell do you think you are, resigning? You're here as our leader, helping us to fight the railroad. Win or lose, we're in this thing together. We know the international rep is here to sell us out. You're not. We've got to work it out together. We won't let you resign!"

I was taken aback. All the workers had cheered this worker's criticism of my decision. I told the workers I was wrong, I was retreating when it was unnecessary, so I would stay as president and would try collectively to fight the international. Although we had to end the slowdown, we won the respect of hundreds of workers, and forced the railroad to sharply tone down its "efficiency" drive. And the unity we established in that action would hold us in good stead for a much bigger battle to come.

Challenging the
Central Labor Council

It was now the fall of 1960 and something else occurred which demonstrated how the mass strength built up in a local situation can spread far beyond the local, and into the political sphere. The Kennedy-Nixon Presidential campaign was in full swing. Labor was full-scale behind JFK. The NYC Central Labor Council, which at that time represented 2,000,000 members, was backing Kennedy. Coincidentally shortly before that, I had raised the idea of our local electing a representative to the Council. Theoretically, all railroad locals were supposed to send someone, but most, including ours, never did. The Local Chairman, who was part of the old guard and figured I would be running for his position in the next local election in December, saw this as a move by our slate to consolidate our strength even more. He said we should first get the O.K. from the international. We agreed, figuring they would be hard-pressed to oppose such a move, since they publicly favored participation in central labor bodies. Sure enough, the answer came back that we should elect someone. And everyone said I was the logical choice.

In addition, a black comrade in our Party club who raised the same proposal in his black local was then chosen to be its rep. So here were the two of us coming to the Council's September meeting, with maybe 1,000 or more local delegates from unions all over the city in attendance, and the leadership, headed by Harry Van Aarsdale, determined to endorse Kennedy.

We had no illusion that we could defeat that, but we figured we should stand up and oppose it. The first point on the agenda was this endorsement. Various hacks fell all over themselves slobbering "we needed a change" (sound familiar?) and "Kennedy is our man." The vote was called and hundreds of delegates raised their hands in favor. When "opposed?" was called for, our two hands shot up. Van Aarsdale tried to ignore us and announced that the vote was unanimous. "No! No!" the two of us shouted, and a number of workers yelled to Van Aarsdale while pointing to us raising our hands in opposition. (Many of them had simply not voted at all.)

At this point Van Aarsdale was forced to recognize our votes. One of his henchmen then jumped up and made a motion that the vote be unanimous. Again we yelled, "No, you can't do that; we're voting against endorsement. It's not unanimous." There were various murmurs throughout the hall crying out, "That's right, you can't. These guys are against it." So the vote was finally recorded as a thousand or so for endorsement and two opposed. A lot of delegates came up to us afterwards and shook our hands. But, of course, our real victory emerged when we both returned to our respective locals and reported on our action. Again, it helped to build unity between the locals and confidence that we can stand up to the powers-that-be.

When the Local Chairman election arrived, the incumbent saw the handwriting on the wall. We were running a slate again, with me for Local Chairman and our current VP for President. So the current Local Chairman simply withdrew from the election and took a management position. (All local officials worked on jobs for the railroad; none were full-time paid union officials.) The company later put him in charge of answering the grievances we would submit, since they figured he knew more about the rules than any of them. Our slate swept the election, but before installation in January of '61, our biggest struggle in my ten years on the railroad erupted.

We Shut Down the Waterfront (and Beyond)

The railroads owned the tugboats that towed the "floats" carrying the loaded freight cars back and forth across the Hudson between Manhattan and Jersey City. In a money-saving effort, they dieselized the tugboats. This operation now required fewer workers to run the tugs. They wanted to lay off two-thirds of the 660 tugboat workers. The latter were members of the Seafarers International Union (SIU), ruled by Paul Hall, among the most right-wing of all the union leaders in the U.S. Negotiations had been dragging on for 14 months past the contract expiration date. The railroads were finally set to lay off the workers, who were now in position to legally strike.

Traditionally, railroad workers always respected the picket lines of other crafts. But this strike, more than any other, absolutely depended on the solidarity of the freight handlers and the Teamsters. (The latter was not a rail union.) The railroads figured they could circumvent the strikers by having the freight handlers load and unload the freight in and out of trucks and trailers, and the Teamsters would then haul the freight back and forth through the tunnels under the Hudson River and over the bridges

121

to and from the yards in Jersey. This was a strike not only against the B&O but also against all the other large roads in NYC, the NY Central and the Pennsylvania being the two biggest, richer than the B&O.

Our own union negotiations were dragging on at the same time. We in the Party saw this as an opportunity to not only organize a general strike of all the railroads in the NYC Metropolitan area, but as an action that would unite all railroad workers across all craft and color lines. It had never happened before. We pointed out to our locals (and to those on the NY Central where Party members were also among the leadership) that if we allowed the railroads to pick off the tugboat workers, small though their number, we would be next in their anti-"featherbedding" efforts. We campaigned up and down the waterfront, held union meetings, and called for respect for the tugboat picket lines, if and when they occurred. Most workers agreed, although many were worried; they had never been in an all-out strike on the railroad before. They were also nervous about how long such a strike would last, and how many paychecks they might miss. The railroads seemed like an all-powerful force to them. Who were we to oppose them in such a high-stakes battle?

We had several things going for us. All the work we had done for eight years had been embedded in the consciousness of hundreds and even thousands of workers. In our own locals, especially, the monthly newsletter had constantly embedded class-conscious ideas in the minds of the workers. Secondly, railroad workers were covered under separate laws. The railroad unemployment insurance law, under which railroad workers collected benefits, stipulated that, in the event of a legal strike, railroad workers were eligible for unemployment insurance benefits from the first day of the strike. Rail strikes were few and far between. The last big one in 1946 was broken by President Truman in four days when he moved to draft all the workers into the army and then court-martial them if they refused to work! (Again this showed the potential power of this basic industry.) The bosses felt they had had little to worry about because of the threatened use of that law. However, it gave us a little edge: we could respect the tugboat workers' picket lines and receive $51 a week, a goodly share of our regular net pay.

Finally, the most important factor in our favor was something that might seem intangible and hard to estimate. It was the feeling of power that could develop when the workers saw they had actually shut down these powerful corporations for whom many had worked all their lives and hated their guts. This was something we did not understand completely going into the strike but came to realize as it occurred, as will be seen.

On the morning of the first day, B&O freight handlers showed up at the first shifts, 5:01 and 6:00 A.M. There were no pickets, so they went to work. The striking tugboat workers appeared around 7:30 A.M., about two to a pier, since there were so few of them and they had hundreds of stations in the NY area to cover.

As soon as we saw them start walking with their picket signs, we ran up on the platforms and the "floats" and yelled to the early shifts, "There's pickets out there! We've got to walk!" Most workers didn't hesitate. They fairly ran off the platforms, happy to be sticking their fingers up at the billion-dollar company. The pickets were amazed and delighted. As the rest of the shifts began arriving hourly, they saw the freight handlers gathered in front of the pier and realized the strike was on. Not one single worker crossed the line. This was true up and down the entire waterfront on all the railroad piers. The railroad end of the strike was complete. Within 24 hours, we had shut down the entire rail freight operation in the biggest city in the country. We were amazed ourselves.

Next came the Teamsters. Freight had already begun collecting on the platforms. The Teamsters who drove the trucks and trailers (and could drive them through the tunnels and over the bridges to circumvent the tugboat operation) did not work for the railroads. They were employed by freight-forwarding companies which operated as middlemen between the railroads and the consignees. These freight-forwarding companies would solicit the business of, say, General Electric or all the small garment manufacturers in the garment center, to ship their freight and truck it to the railroad piers which those businesses would pay for. Then the railroads would charge the freight forwarders to ship their freight by rail, employing us to do the loading and unloading.

One of the big freight forwarders who operated via the B&O was ABC Freight Forwarding ("ABC" = Arthur Brown Co). Herein lies a tale of real class-consciousness. The B&O freight handlers never saw the railroad president who was in Baltimore, and headed a two billion-dollar outfit. But every day they did see Arthur Brown being chauffeured to work in his Rolls Royce, which was parked near the platform on which many of us worked. The railroad workers concluded that Brown was really the power behind the throne, that he, this richest of the rich in his Rolls Royce, told the railroad what to do. We told workers that Brown was really small potatoes, his $25 million company really being subordinate to the railroad. But they were hard to convince.

When some of the workers pointed out that the Teamsters were scheduled to start taking out their trucks and trailers at 8:00 A.M., we acted quickly. (There were no pickets in front of the ABC platforms, only at the railroad piers across the street.) We told one of the two pickets in front of Pier 63 to come with us across the street on 24th St. to the ABC platform, explaining to them that if this freight went out, it could be trucked to Jersey and circumvent the strike. The tugboat strikers, seeing what we had done for them so far, figured we knew what we were doing, so one of them set up his one-man picket "line" outside the ABC platform. A few hundred railroad workers who had been gathering in front of Pier 63 followed us and stood across the street from the platform, watching. It was like street theater.

We yelled to the Teamsters on the platform getting ready to take their trucks out that there was a picket out front. These were workers who we knew quite well, having worked alongside them loading and unloading trucks for years. They immediately called a meeting on the platform right under their bosses' noses and discussed the situation, with the railroad workers watching from across the street. They took a vote and decided unanimously to respect the lone picket. To a man they walked off the platform, their ABC trucks loaded but with no one to drive them. It had taken five minutes to shut down this $25 million-dollar outfit, Rolls Royce boss and all. The railroad workers cheered. In that moment, they realized more than ever before the collective strength of united workers. Our unity was sky-high. This was to be, we thought, the final nail in the coffin for the divided freight-handler locals, the final step on the road to one united multi-racial local.

BROADENING THE STRIKE

Having drawn the Teamsters into the strike, the shutdown was complete. But the railroads were not through. The NY Central bosses figured out another way to undercut the tugboat operation: bring freight trains over railroad trestles across the Hudson River way upstate, then pull them down the east side of the river into the Mott Haven yards north of Grand Central Station in central Manhattan. They began hauling scab freight into and out of Manhattan. But again we had an answer, based on workers' solidarity and the militant leadership of Party members.[1]

One of our 13 Party clubs included the electricians on the NY Central. There were 1,000 workers in that IBEW local, the largest railroad electricians' local in the country. Our members were part of that local's leadership and active among the rank-and-file. The local president knew he was working with communists and respected them (although he was never recruited). He also respected the idea of union solidarity. Our Party members raised the fact in the local that scab freight was being

---

[1] Unknown to us in the Party railroad section at the time, the strike (and our leadership of it) had big repercussions inside the CP leadership. At that time, Milt Rosen (who later became chairperson of the PLM and PLP) headed the trade-union division of the NY State CP. He was already pretty wary of the sellout nature of the Gus Hall leadership. It was pretty well known among the city's trade union leaders that communists were heavily involved in leading the strike. When the press began ranting about the strikers "holding the city for ransom," Hall called Milt in and ordered him to tell us (we were part of the industrial division Milt headed) to "call off this goddamn strike or we'll all be thrown in jail!" Milt said he thought the strike was a good thing; he asked Hall what he meant. Hall replied, "You know what I mean; they're going to blame the Party for the strike."

Milt said, "How can I tell these comrades to stop doing something that represents the workers' interests?" Hall said he didn't care, "just do it." So the outlook of winning workers in basic industry had degenerated into selling them out, abandoning even a militant reform struggle. (Of course, Milt never told us to do any such thing.) The strike continued. A year later, the nine remaining members of our railroad section voted to quit the CP and join the PLM, predecessor of the Progressive Labor Party. We aimed to draw on what had been positive in the CPUSA's activities in the 1930s while avoiding its later accommodations to the capitalist profit system as well as its avoiding the open advocacy of communism.

hauled over NY Central tracks into Mott Haven in the Bronx and even into Grand Central Station. They said that if pickets showed up in front of Grand Central Station on 42nd Street, the electricians should respect the picket line. The electrician's local president agreed.

Our electricians' Party club relayed this information to the freight-handler clubs on the B&O and the NY Central, and again we directed some tugboat pickets across town to Grand Central Station. As soon as two of them appeared, the NY Central electricians shut all the electric power on that road and walked out. The Central (the country's second largest railroad) was shut tight. But this didn't just affect freight. All the commuter trains from Westchester and from Fairfield County in Connecticut, which carried 90,000 commuters a day into and out of New York City, couldn't operate either. In a matter of days, the NY Central was shut down as far west as Cleveland.

It was then that all hell broke loose. All the daily papers in NYC (and there were about ten of them then) began screaming for our scalps. We were "holding the city for ransom." Soon "starvation will set in. There will be no fuel," and so on. The editorials were calling for Kennedy (who had just taken office) to pass a law (à la Truman) to call out the troops and break the strike.

But the walkout was gathering momentum. Many workers around the city realized the power of solidarity, and the great potential of a general strike. We received tremendous support. So Kennedy, probably not wanting to have one of his first acts in office labeling him a strikebreaker, was not quick to break the strike directly. He sent his Secy. of Labor, Arthur Goldberg — the lawyer who was the architect of the expulsion of the communist-led unions from the CIO in 1948 and later became a Supreme Court justice — into NYC to mediate the strike. He proposed that the workers return to work, that the railroads not lay off anyone at this time and that negotiations resume. Both sides accepted this and, after ten days, the strike was over.

As it turned out some time later, the SIU agreed to the layoff of "only" half (not two-thirds) of the tugboat workers, who each received $10,000 severance pay, about $100,000 in current dollars. While not achieving the goal they had sought, they won more than they would have through this militant strike.

The International Convention and Fight for Job Security

Following the tugboat workers' fight for their jobs, we were now confronted directly with our own job security struggle on the B&O. Our progress towards uniting the black local with the mostly white local was advancing. We didn't realize how threatened the railroad felt about dealing with one united, multi-racial local with a multi-racial leadership, and communists involved to boot. It could set an example for the 150 segregated locals nationwide. The company was developing a plan to contract out all our work to the freight forwarders, who were the middlemen between the shippers and the railroad. This would lay us all off permanently, thereby wiping out both our locals completely. We later found out that they were fed up with what they called "that element in New York." Meanwhile, the national union negotiations were dragging on.

We wanted any new national contract to include situations like ours. There were already established agreements to protect workers laid off due to railroad mergers and acquisitions, but they didn't specifically include the threat of contracting work out to freight forwarders. The protected workers were offered either comparable jobs elsewhere or $10,000 severance pay (now worth upwards of $100,000). Such coverage would make it much more expensive for the railroad to get rid of us.

The union's international convention was approaching, slated for Los Angeles in June 1963. We figured that was where we could make our last stand. Our city-wide struggles and the tugboat strike had put us in touch with other locals on the NY Central and Pennsylvania, which were facing the same mass layoffs. Our Local's leadership called together rank-and-file leaders from six locals, all of whom would be delegates to this convention. All six submitted identical resolutions to the convention dealing with the threat to our jobs. We planned to make a floor fight on this issue. We figured that most of the 1,300 delegates would be in the hip pocket of the international's machine. Were we surprised!

When our resolution came up on the first day of the convention, all six delegates in our caucus took the floor to speak for it. The bureaucrats were somewhat taken aback at this. Their Resolutions Committee had recommended rejection, since they were not about to add such a demand to their national contract negotiations.

A couple of hacks spoke against us. Then the chair called for a voice vote. The international president — who had been in office since 1928! — was half blind and couldn't see to count a hand vote; therefore a voice vote was called. We had expected this and had prepared some friends and spouses attending as guests in the balcony to yell like hell with us on the floor when the voice vote came up. We hadn't counted on the fact that there were many locals facing their own job security problems and would vote with us on general principle (and probably were affected by our impassioned speeches).

Our resolution clearly carried on the voice vote. The president was flabbergasted. He called for a second vote (amid cries of "No! No!"), figuring the machine would get the hint and yell louder the second time. But the fact that the first vote was being arbitrarily over-ridden seemed to anger a lot of delegates. The second vote produced an even larger margin favoring our resolution.

At that point the chair entertained a motion to send the resolution back to committee, to be brought up later in the week. That passed and we knew what it meant: they'd bring out their big guns, buy off a number of delegates and squash it the next time around — which is what happened. This whole fight had tied up the convention for nearly half a day. Afterwards, many delegates, including a number of black delegates, came up to us and thanked us for raising this issue on the convention floor.

As it turned out, more issues presented themselves to our 6-delegate caucus and we seized upon them. The leadership was intent on pushing through a dues increase. A lot of delegates were opposed to it, especially the Canadians, who had always felt they were second-class citizens in this union. So we chimed in on that one, asking why the nine Vice-Grand Presidents needed another $150 a week to add to their already enormous salaries. (Their salaries were more than triple the average freight handler's.) The leadership's answer was that the railroad vice-presidents, whom they faced across the bargaining table, earned ten times what they did; therefore they needed higher salaries "so the railroad executives would respect the union negotiators!" That brought a big derisive laugh. The vote was taken and the dues increase passed narrowly.

RACISM REARS ITS HEAD

Then one of the more explosive issues emerged (something which I learned about for the first time at this convention). It directly involved the issue of racism. Many of the 150 all-black locals (formed after the 1948 court decision) were from the South. One after another, black delegates rose to speak on the racist oppression they suffered based on collusion between the white-led locals on their properties and the railroads in the South. Black freight handlers (the lowest-paying jobs) were not allowed to bid on openings for higher-paying receiving clerk jobs, even if they had seniority. Junior white workers were awarded these jobs. And it appeared this question had been raised at previous conventions, to no avail, always slapped down by the lily-white racist international leadership.

This somewhat shocked our 6-delegate caucus since here in New York seniority was pretty strictly observed among all workers. We had a hurried discussion within our caucus (only one delegate was black) and decided we would take the floor and support our black brothers. We made fairly militant speeches, saying that this kind of racism directly contradicted the idea of a union and would eventually destroy us. (Remember, this was June of 1963, two years into the sit-ins and freedom rides, and two months before the Civil Rights March on Washington.)

Big cheers arose when we sat down. The leadership was put somewhat on the defensive and agreed (it seems for the first time ever) to "look into the situation," with the participation of the black locals involved. (We never found out what happened because, for most of us, it was our last convention.) Afterwards, the black delegates approached us to thank us for our support. They said it was the first time that white delegates had ever supported them on this issue.

It was then that I realized the importance of working in reactionary unions. Starting from the lowest-level struggles in one local, our forces had reached a position from which to influence possibly thousands of others far beyond our little bailiwick in NYC, on a nationally important political issue like racism. Who knows how far we could have gone had we been able to hang on in the industry?

Upping the Convention Struggle

When that day's session ended, our 6-delegate caucus returned to our hotel and compared notes. While we had gone to the convention only with the idea of raising our own job-security issue, we now realized that we had had an impact far beyond our expectations: on the dues issue, on racist job segregation and on the jobs issue itself. We posed the idea, supposing one of us was to run for one of the nine Vice-Grand President offices? Not because we expected to win, but to see how many forces we could draw together in opposition to the corrupt leadership.

There were three groups from which we could draw strength: those who had favored our job-security fight, those opposed to the dues increase (especially among the 200 Canadian delegates) and the delegates from the all-black locals. We agreed on who would be nominated, a brother from the Pennsy local.

The next day we nominated him from the floor. By then most delegates knew who we were and many even applauded the nomination. The leadership went crazy. Obviously there were rarely, if ever, any nominations other than the leadership slate — especially nominations representing principled fighters. When we went back to our hotel, we got a call from none other than the hack who had been handpicked to become the new Grand President. He said he'd like to meet with us. We knew why: he would want us to withdraw the nomination.

We suddenly realized how weak these sellouts really were. Here was a group of six delegates at a convention of 1,300, run by a tightly-controlled machine that had been in office for 41 years, worried about a nomination of just one of us, at the last minute, for one of nine VPs, with no chance of being elected. Suppose we were elected? How much could we really accomplish? This act had scared the hell out of the seemingly all-powerful machine! Suppose we really had made plans to "take over"? We figured that was what the leadership was thinking: if we got one leg up the ladder, even assuming we wouldn't win the position, the idea of anyone other than those chosen by the machine being in the race was too much for them to stomach.

The incoming Grand President came to our room and really soft-soaped us, congratulating us on our participation in the convention, and asking us why we wanted to run. After all, we stood no chance of success. Then he said, "Why don't you boys go to Las Vegas and have a good time?" We looked at each other, wondering what he had up his sleeve. Then he said, "I'll charter a plane for you and your spouses and you can spend an evening there, and forget about this election stuff. How about it?"

We were shocked, never realizing how important we had become in their eyes. We said we'd talk it over and get back to him. After he left, we had a good laugh. It was clear that none of us wanted to withdraw our nomination. But a few guys did like the idea of going to Las Vegas. Someone suggested suppose we take him up on it, fly on his plane to Las Vegas, return and then go ahead with the nomination anyway? Everybody got a charge out of that, so we called him back and said, "Yes, we'll take the Las Vegas trip." He probably felt this implied we would withdraw the nomination when the elections were held two days later. Meanwhile, we plotted our campaign.

That night we wrote a campaign leaflet, incorporating all the issues that we and others had raised at the convention. The next day we took it to a printer, where it would be ready early the following morning. That night we went to Las Vegas (the worst flight I ever experienced, the charter having a 20-seat non-pressurized cabin which nearly burst our eardrums).

We arose early the next morning, picked up the 1,500 campaign leaflets and raced to the convention hall to be there when it opened. We then dropped a leaflet on the seat of every delegate. When the hacks walked in and saw we weren't withdrawing the nomination, they were furious. But there wasn't much they could do about it; we had met every requirement for our nomination, which they had already accepted.

Our candidate's contest was the only one on which the leadership had any opposition, so there wasn't much counting to do. When the ballot totals were announced (by the leadership's election committee), our guy had received over 500 votes from the 1,300 delegates present, an astounding total given the circumstances. A lot of delegates congratulated us on the campaign.

We had no illusion that we'd win. We did realize that with long-range planning we could develop a much bigger influence in the union. But if that happened, the machine would mount a much bigger attack on us, go all out. They (and the U.S. ruling class) would never let us simply take over the largest railroad union in the country. Unfortunately, those of us in the Communist Party had not functioned with a strategy that would use such a campaign (and many others) to tie such union struggles to revolutionary ideas. That was not to come until the Progressive Labor Party had 15 years experience under our belts. But it gave a glimpse of the potential that comes from functioning in a mass way in an important union. Think of all the friends and contacts we had made in the course of these ten years, and what could have been accomplished in terms of building a true communist party.

The Jobless Fight Back — From City Hall to the White House

Our struggle for job security at the union's International Convention won a lot of support, but it was an uphill battle. In the

Photo by June Linder

summer of 1963, all our jobs on the B&O were contracted out without even a whimper from the international, but we refused to take this lying down. Our campaign touched big shots from New York City's mayor to Kennedy's Secretary of Labor to rail baron Cyrus Eaton and his buddy Nikita Khrushchev.

I was now part of the newly-organized Progressive Labor Movement (PLM) and intent on keeping many of these laid-off rail workers together to reap some benefits from our decade of struggle. We discussed the idea of a Railroad Workers Unemployment Council to sue the railroad for severance pay (which the union had refused to negotiate), and charge the union with collusion as well, for failing to represent us. Our actions would involve demonstrations and picket lines exposing everyone we perceived to be our enemies or those who stood by and did nothing.

The idea caught on. Over 200 former B&O workers — black and white — agreed to join. We formed an official organization, with regular meetings, dues, officers, a newsletter and so on and discussed all our plans and activities at each meeting. We elected two black and two white workers from our rank-and-file to comprise our four leading officers (with me as president) and hired lawyer Conrad Lynn to sue the B&O for severance pay and to charge the Brotherhood of Railway Clerks and Freight Handlers with collusion. After years of trying to merge the separate black and white locals — the International had 150 of these segregated units — we finally had our multi-racial, merged "union."

Our first demonstration was directed against the Chesapeake & Ohio RR (C&O), which had bought out the B&O. It turned out that the C&O was headed by none other than Khrushchev's buddy in the U.S., Cyrus Eaton, who had become the darling of the Communist Party for his championing trade with the Soviets (from which he expected to make a pile). We figured we would add a little political spice to the situation. We sent out press releases and about 100 of us picketed the C&O building in lower Manhattan with signs such as "Cyrus Fired Us" and "Cyrus and Buddy Khrushchev Are No Friends of the Workers." (My sister took pictures.)

Our plan was to march from the C&O building to City Hall and picket the Mayor (Wagner, at the time), demanding the city do something about the firing of 1,000 black and white workers. This, remember, was a time of heightened civil rights action; the famous March on Washington led by Martin Luther King (in which our Council had also marched with our signs) had just taken place.

In 1963, workers' picket lines like these were not particularly common. When City Hall got wind of our plan to picket them, they tried to head us off at the pass. The Deputy Mayor called my house and told my wife to tell me we didn't have to picket; they would meet with us; "Tell him to call it off." "Too late," Esther gleefully told him, "they're already on their way." As we circled City Hall, the Deputy Mayor emerged to "greet us," saying he would meet with our committee on behalf of the Mayor. The TV, press and radio were going crazy around us. "Who the hell were these workers?" We went inside and met with this hack for half an hour. He "pledged" that the Mayor would "see what he could do." Our Council members were hip enough to know that this meant zilch, but were happy that we had at least made them uncomfortable and publicized our cause.

That night, interviews with me ran on seven TV and radio stations and we were in all the papers the next day. I linked the government with the railroad and Eaton with the sellouts in Moscow as one big bunch not interested in helping workers at all.

ATTACKING THE SYSTEM

Our next action was outside Grand Central Station a couple of weeks later. Our press releases brought out NBC hotshot Gabe Pressman to interview us. I began explaining our grievances and between sentences brought up the connection to the government allowing this to happen. I said that a government representing the bosses was no damn good as far as we were concerned, and that we needed to destroy that kind of system in favor of a workers' system. Suffice it to say, we didn't get one second on that night's TV news. Maybe we learned a lesson about not depending on the bosses' media.

Shortly afterwards the Council organized a demonstration at the White House which taught us another lesson: as all-powerful as the government and rulers might seem, they are scared as hell of workers. Since our severance-pay suit legally involved regulations related to the Interstate Commerce Commission, we decided we should picket the federal government in an attempt to draw attention to its role in our being denied justice. In the fall, we mobilized 80 of our members to drive to Washington in a 20-car motorcade to picket the White House.

As we started marching with our highly-charged political signs directed at Kennedy, we discovered he was at his compound in Hyannis, Mass. This incensed a lot of these unemployed workers. With no particular goal in mind, I said, "Well, the Labor Department is walking distance from here, why don't we go over and picket there as well?" Everyone agreed, so in a Saturday-deserted Washington, we trooped a few blocks and "set up shop" again. Barely 20 minutes had elapsed when an official-looking guy appeared and asked us what we wanted. We asked him who he was and he said, "Under Secretary of Labor." This surprised us a little, but we proceeded to relate our case. He then said, "Wait here; I'll be right back."

Five minutes later, he returned and, to our amazement, said, "Secretary of Labor Wirtz will see a five-person committee." We couldn't believe our ears. But the best was yet to come. The Under-Secretary escorted us upstairs and ushered us into Wirtz's office, a huge conference room with a score of empty chairs around a long conference table, covered with a lot of notebooks and half-filled water glasses. Obviously, some meeting had been going on.

Kennedy's man Wirtz then explained that the national railroad labor negotiations (to which we had originally directed our convention resolutions) were taking place and when he heard about our plight he had asked the union representatives of the 23 railroad crafts and the representatives of the nations' railroads to retire to adjacent rooms while he talked to us! We couldn't believe it. Here we were, 80 rank-and-filers who had come to march at the White House and by sheer accident we had picketed the Labor Department. Now we were holding up the national negotiations because somehow we seemed to represent some hitch in the plans they were cooking up. Imagine if we had had the strength to organize 5,000 railroad workers to picket the place, or, better yet, invade it!

After explaining our case for about half an hour and getting the usual reply of "I'll see what I can do," our Council members were happy to feel that our trip to D.C. had resulted in what they interpreted to be a little recognition. And a few months later, when Kennedy was assassinated, most of our members' reaction was, "So what? He didn't do anything for us."

It was during some of the picketing actions that fall that an article appeared, written by the nationally syndicated anti-labor columnist Victor Riesel, in the now-defunct N.Y. *Journal-American* (a Hearst paper). The article "exposed" PLM as an agent of China and Che Guevara, out to start guerrilla warfare in the U.S. Among other examples cited was the "fact" that ten years ago I had been sent to "infiltrate" the railroad and was a threat to the national security in this industry vital to the country's "defense." Most of the Council members had seen the article, and rather than cowed by it were incensed. I had already told them about PLM and had shown them *PL Magazine (Challenge* — PL's weekly newspaper in English and Spanish — hadn't started yet), some with articles about our struggles. Their immediate reaction was to want to go picket the *Journal-American*, but that never came to pass. Some of them began to think that maybe capitalism wasn't the best system after all.

FINAL LESSONS

The following year our suit finally went before a millionaire judge. (It was in the course of this trial that word came out inadvertently from one of the company lawyers that the railroad had moved to contract out its N.Y. freight operation because of "that element in N.Y." It was from this that we concluded that they just didn't want to deal with a multi-racial union led by communists.) The judge actually questioned the union lawyers about why the union hadn't even negotiated with management for the protection we had demanded. We were also charging the union with collusion.

The union lawyers were flustered and couldn't drum up too much of an excuse. This exchange led many of us to think we might actually win something from this judge. But those hopes were soon dashed when his decision came down that, "unfortunately," the company was within its rights to do what it did, without compensation. "Better luck next time," he said.

This was probably the final blow to our Council. It gradually dissolved after that, our demand (which had been holding us together) having been defeated. Most of the workers had found other jobs, at GM in Tarrytown, Ford in Jersey, the Transit Authority, Otis Elevator and so on. But it left the door open for me to point out about how rotten this system was, and that we needed "a workers' system."

The gravity of the mistake I had made in the ten years of not trying to recruit any of these workers hit home. Had I recruited a few of them, they would now be working in some of the places mentioned above, and thus the railroad bosses, by laying them off, would have helped us spread "ready-made" communists horizontally throughout the industrial working class.

By '64, after *Challenge* started in June, some of them were reading the paper. For any progress on my part, however, at the level we were at in PLM at the time, it was too little and too late. However, the highest level of political expression of all my years on the railroad was soon to take place. [See story on Harlem Rebellion.]

Confronting 'Savior' Jimmy Hoffa

It was odd how the fight to save our jobs on the B&O RR became interwoven with the Teamsters' Jimmy Hoffa and the Cuban missile crisis. In 1963, after our caucus had fought unsuccessfully at the International Convention to save our jobs [see story on Convention], we returned from Los Angeles knowing our days were numbered. We felt that after our 1961 shutdown of the New York City waterfront in the tugboat strike, we had done everything we could to fight for our jobs.

The previous fall (of 1962) we had actually pursued the idea of signing up with the Teamsters. This process is worth describing if only to demonstrate the crass business nature of the U.S. trade union movement.

We had been speaking to a lawyer friend about the immediate threat to our whole roster. Previously, he had successfully prevented the International from voiding the election of one of our delegates on the Central. This lawyer represented the Teamsters' huge over-the-road trucking local in NYC, and asked us what we thought about asking the Teamsters to step into the situation. We told him if they could help us, we could easily convince a majority of the freight handlers on the B&O and the Central to switch unions. He said he would arrange a meeting with Jimmy Hoffa. (Hoffa, still the president of Teamsters at that time, was then on trial in Tennessee on charges of trying to bribe a juror in a previous government corruption case.)

Hoffa agreed to meet with Andy Hagen — the Local Chairman on the Central — and myself, head of the B&O Local. I spoke to our officers on the B&O about this possibility and they urged us to pursue it. The two of us flew to Nashville, all expenses paid by Hoffa, including our hotel rooms.

We met Hoffa late in the afternoon, following that day's trial session. As soon as we entered his hotel room, Hoffa told one of his entourage to switch on the TV to see reports of that day's trial proceedings. But lo and behold, what should come on the screen but pictures of Soviet missile bases in Cuba! It was October 1962, just as the Cuban missile crisis was reaching its height. It was then that we got a taste of how crazy some of these union officials could be.

Hoffa hated the Kennedy brothers with a passion because they had prosecuted him. When the reconnaissance photos of the Soviet missile bases were shown on TV, Hoffa started ranting and raving about how stupid JFK was, and how Khrushchev was "tricking" him into thinking that these bases were real when they were actually structures "made of balsa wood!" All his yes-men nodded in agreement. Hagen and I looked at each other with wide eyes, as if to say, "This is the guy who's going to save our jobs?"

Over dinner — the best steak I'd ever eaten — we discussed our job situation. Hoffa asked us how many jobs we might lose between the two railroads. We told him at least two-thirds. "Well," he said, "those two thirds are gone. But I can get something for the remaining one-third." (!)

So this was our big "savior." To Hoffa, this was strictly a

146

business proposition. He calculated how much he could spend for how many workers, that it wasn't worth the investment to fight for ALL the jobs, but that he could net a tidy sum from picking up the pieces after the main damage was done. We told him we would report back to our respective local committees and decide what to do. But we already knew that Hoffa was as bad as the union we belonged to now; obviously nothing would come of this.

However, it reinforced the lesson that dependence on rank-and-file struggle, not on businessmen running the trade unions, would be our only path to progress, and that depended on how much strength we could mobilize at any one time. Unfortunately this was not that time. The understanding gleaned from later organizing in the PLP, to tie these mass, class struggles to the necessity for revolution, led us to conclude that rank-and-file trade unionism was not enough to free the working class from capitalism.

Launching the Progressive Labor Movement

In December, 1962, I was among over two dozen members who had quit the moribund Communist Party (CP), and met to discuss the formation of a new organization dedicated to the communist principles that had been abandoned by the CP and wanted to lay the groundwork for a new communist party. PLM's core beliefs included fighting racism and its source, capitalism (which reaped billions in profits from the super-exploitation of Black workers); basing ourselves among the workers in the basic industries; and fighting imperialism's attacks and wars on the world's working class.

Our efforts began in January, 1962 with publishing *PL Magazine* and then in July, fifty workers and youth gathered in New York City to form the Progressive Labor Movement (PLM). Over its three-year history, it organized a series of militant struggles on many fronts — which reflect the principles above — some of which are described below:

- In the winter of 1963, backed the Hazard, KY. rank-and-file miners' wildcat strike, organizing the Trade Union Sol-

148

idarity Committee (which I proudly chaired) to collect truckloads of food and clothing nationwide to send to these embattled industrial workers; [See "Which Side Are You On..."];

• In the summer of 1963 formed the Railroad Workers Unemployment Council, a group of laid-off black and white rail workers who has been denied severance pay, and organized protests throughout New York City and then Washington, D.C., where we picketed the Kennedy White House and forced the interruption of the national railroad contract negotiations to plead our case. [See "Jobless Fight Back — From City Hall to the White House"];

• Supported the 1964 Harlem rebellion in which PLM's new publication *Challenge* became the flag of the uprising and was read by thousands; we were the only group to view it as a rebellion against a racist system. [See "Arrested for Supporting the Harlem Rebellion"];

• Formed the May 2nd Movement opposing the U.S. invasion of Vietnam when the PLM chairperson addressed a Socialist conference at Yale University to call for the first nationwide demonstrations against that war on May 2, 1964, demanding the "U.S. Get Out of Vietnam";

• In late 1964, distributed a *Challenge* flyer to another group of industrial workers (striking longshoremen), exposing the impending sellout by the Scotto/Mafia mis-leadership, leading the rank-and-file to reject their contract and go back on strike; [See "Challenging the Mafia, Its Control of the Docks, and Anti-Communism"];

• Broke the Kennedy travel ban on travel to Cuba, sending two groups of students and workers there; ten PLM members (Esther was one) unfurled the first "Hands Off Cuba" banner during the UN debate over the issue;

• Organized mass picket line demonstrations outside the anti-Communist hearings of the House Un-American Activities Committee (HUAC) in Washington protesting its attack on the those who broke the ban on travel to Cuba (and who refused to "take the 5th" telling HUAC they "were proud to be communists") and organized 1,500 more in Buffalo when HUAC was attacking PLM'ers in that city's industrial plants. That protest was supported by thousands in that city, including the University of Buffalo Student Senate and various mass groups. Clerics joined the picket line. These actions completely disrupted the hearings and HUAC fled town. These and later mobilizations led to HUAC's demise as a Congressional committee.

"Which side are you on...."

One of the earliest struggles of industrial workers involving the Progressive Labor Movement (PLM) was a solidarity campaign to support a wildcat strike of black and white rank-and-file miners, centered in Hazard, Kentucky, during the winter of 1962-63. The miners were striking against brutal working conditions and receiving only a $25 weekly wage. Attempting to break the strike, the coal barons and their hired thugs, cops and bought-and-paid-for local officials launched violent attacks on the miners. But 500 armed miners answered back, blowing up scab mines and dynamiting bridges.

PLM, seeing the example being set by these miners for the entire working class, formed the Trade Union Solidarity Committee (TUSC) to support the miners. At the time, I was the Local Chairman of my railroad freight handlers' local [See "Workin' on the Railroad"] and became the head of the TUSC. We brought the miners' struggle to unions and working-class communities nation-wide and workers contributed food, clothing and holiday gifts for miners' children. Truckloads were shipped to Hazard, along with PLM's publication *PL Magazine*, bringing communist ideas to the strikers.

The mine bosses and their cronies went nuts. A front-page 8-column banner headline in the *Hazard Herald* screamed, "Communism Comes to the Mountains!"

We organized a mass meeting in Manhattan and nearly 1,000 workers and students came in zero degree weather. It was addressed by the rank-and-file's leader Berman Gibson and myself, representing the TUSC. Gibson invited me down to Hazard to meet with the miners. Growing up in Brooklyn, I was not prepared for what I encountered in Appalachia.

Gibson and his fellow strikers met me at the Lexington, Kentucky, airport and drove me south to Hazard. On the seat between Gibson and myself was his rifle, which was as close to one as I had ever been. The other miners in the station wagon were all armed. "It's to protect us from the cops and thugs," Gibson told me, as we passed scab mines. It was flood season in the area and as we approached Hazard the waters had submerged the entire center of the town, which was shaped like a bowl. I stayed in a miner's home in which the floors and rugs were soaked from the rains. The miners and their families greeted me warmly and thanked the TUSC for the food and clothing we had shipped to them. It was a humbling experience for me. The expressions of working-class humanity have stayed with me my entire life.

The picture of an inter-racial group of armed miners rebelling against the coal bosses, and united with communists, scared the Kennedy Administration. They pulled out all red-baiting stops and sent their union henchmen into the TUSC to eventually take us over. Initially, the miners resisted this anti-communist attack but soon retreated, and their strike faded.

The whole struggle taught us that the bosses will use anti-communism as a crucial weapon, alongside violence, to break workers' rebellions; that workers will arm themselves to fight such armed attacks by the rulers; and that they will respond to bold, communist leadership.

As the old miners' song asks, "Which side are you on?" Obviously, the working class and PLM chose the miners' side.

Challenging the Government, the Mafia, Its Control of the Docks, and Anti-Communism

On October 1, 1964, 60,000 members of the International Longshoremen's Association (ILA) from Maine to Texas struck against the shipowners' demand to cut half their jobs in the union struggle against containerization. The newly organized Progressive Labor Movement (PLM) and our newspaper *Challenge* unexpectedly played a significant role in the outcome of this movement, despite the Mafia's control of the Brooklyn local, the ILA's largest.

While we had no members in the ILA, we did know one old ex-CP'er who worked on the docks and had become disenchanted with the old Party. He agreed to talk to us about a sellout contract that was in the works. I interviewed him for an article in *Challenge* which revealed the following: this industrial strike was crippling the East and Gulf Coast waterfronts. The government wanted to end it "in the national interest." It told the ILA leaders that a grand jury was being convened to indict them for their alleged Mafia ties, racketeering and wholesale corruption, and would end up throwing them in jail if they didn't get the rank-and-file to return to work.

I wrote a front-page *Challenge* article — headlined "Dockers Resist Sellout, Bosses See Red!" — exposing the contract. It was then reprinted as a four-page *Challenge* flyer to be distributed to the strikers. The latter itself was a dangerous activity, given the Mafia goons threatening to beat up anyone seen giving them out. But enough copies reached the ILA members to worry the head of the Brooklyn local, Anthony Scotto, himself a "made" member of the Mafia's Gambino family, and intimately tied to the leaders of the Democratic Party.[1]

He called an emergency meeting of the local to ratify the sell-out contract. Over 2,000 dockers attended. In his attempt to get the members back, Scotto used old-fashioned red-baiting, claiming that communists were attacking the union. Our contact inside the ILA and present at the meeting told us that Scotto denounced the "red lies" in the *Challenge* flyer and proceeded to read it in its entirety word for word!

A big mistake. It had exactly the opposite effect. Upon hear-

---

[1] Anthony Scotto, son-in-law of former ILA boss "Tough Tony" Anastasia, controlled the Brooklyn waterfront and was not only a well-known Mob figure, but also had intimate ties to the Democratic Party hierarchy. He was a delegate to the 1972 Democratic Convention, was a friend of Robert Kennedy, raised money for Mario Cuomo's 1974 campaign for lieutenant governor and was named as a possible candidate for Secretary of Labor by President Jimmy Carter. When he was later convicted of bribery and racketeering in 1979 and faced a 20-year prison term, at sentencing the judge said he was "influenced" by requests for leniency from New York Mayors Wagner and Lindsay. Scotto received a five-year sentence and served only 39 months. Early on he had been billed as a new breed among mobsters, having been sent to college and studied law. After release from prison, he became a lecturer at Harvard.

ing the details of the government's strike-breaking effort, and the ILA leaders' readiness to go along with it, the rank-and-file became enraged and refused to fall for the anti-communist red-baiting. They voted overwhelmingly to defy Scotto and continue the strike.

Immediately, New York's eight daily papers — which had lauded the contract — launched an anti-communist barrage. A front-page headline in the NY World-Telegram shouted, "Red Hand Seen on the Waterfront." The ILA leaders blamed communists for the rank-and-file rebellion. Notorious anti-labor columnist Victor Reisel accused "Chinese revolutionaries" of "spreading unrest on the docks."

A new contract added some crumbs. But while a majority of the working longshoremen rejected it, ILA officials used the votes of other trades in the union and retired workers to get it passed. Thousands of jobs were lost from the containerization provisions in the contract.

The ILA leaders were never indicted.

The fledgling PLM, barely two years old — following its goal of concentrating on winning workers in basic industry — helped these workers to defy the bosses, their government and the Mafia, by refusing to succumb to anti-communism in fighting for their class interests. The lesson for the PLM was that to win such workers, we had to be embedded among them, rather than working from the outside.

Becoming An Electrician —
But My Past Catches Up
With Me

In the summer of 1963 the B&O RR laid off our entire roster, so for the first time in 11 years I joined the army of the unemployed. My $51-a-week unemployment checks plus wife Esther's part-time job could keep us going for a short while, but those checks would run out after 26 weeks. So where to look for another job?

Then I remembered my contact with Russ Homiak, president of the railroad electricians' Local 817, International Brotherhood of Electrical Workers (IBEW) on the New York Central. We had first met in the rail workers' struggle for weekly pay and later during the tugboat workers' strike that had shut down the railroad operation on the West Side waterfront. When the Central tried to move scab goods through the tracks leading into Manhattan, we had moved a tugboat picket to Grand Central Station and with Homiak's support and the actions of CP members in his local to respect the pickets, shut off all electrical power on the Central, as well as tying up the railroad's commuter lines.

All these ties with Homiak held me in good stead when I became jobless. Homiak had seen our local union paper on the B&O (of which I was editor) and confided in me that if I "ever needed a job, come see me and I'll get you hired and you can edit our local union paper." So off I went to see Homiak, and sure enough he got me hired as an apprentice electrician. This job actually had a far better future than working as a railroad freight handler. Once you serve a four-year apprenticeship, you get a journeyman's card, and can get a job as an electrician anyplace in the country. After 60 days, I would become a regular employee on the Central and a certified union member in the IBEW.

Soon I was learning the trade, working alongside a journeyman, installing electrical pipe, wiring ceilings in the company's main building on Third Avenue in Manhattan and fixing electricity breakdowns. But there was one hitch: when I filled out my job application, should I state that I had worked on the B&O? Once the railroad sent my wage records to the Railroad Retirement Board, the latter would notify the Central that I already had a railroad retirement number, having worked on the B&O. While I knew the Central would then contact the B&O seeking my work record there, if I lied about my years on the B&O (and was forced to manufacture eleven years of alleged employment), once the Central found out, I could be fired for lying on my application. So my Party club decided I should take a chance and tell the truth about B&O employment.

Before my 60-day initiation period was up, the Central contacted the B&O and got the whole story: local president, strike organization, probable CP affiliation and so on. So the Central let me go, saying I had "failed the physical," even though I had been working for at least 45 days with no problems. In fact, my foreman had vouched for me as a "good worker." But the railroad was not required to provide any evidence of physical ailments.

So my career and promising future as an electrician was over. I was back on unemployment benefits and seeking still another job. It was then that my sister's husband Ralph convinced me to try to become a union printer, another trade in which once you served an apprenticeship, you'd get a union card and entrée into any print shop in the country. But that's a story for another time.

Workers Salute
Challenge-Desafio with
"The Internationale"

In June, 1964, the Progressive Labor Movement decided to print an eight-page weekly newspaper; *Challenge-Desafio* was born. Our search for a printer led us to an outfit in Trenton, N.J. After laying down a deposit, the printer looked at the first issue and told us that would be the last one he'd print.

We called up the Harris offset press manufacturer and asked for a list of newspaper printers to whom it had sold web offset presses. That's how we found the Sun Publishing Co., located in the Chinese community on Manhattan's Lower East Side. We showed our first issue to the owner, Mr. Chan, and he agreed to print our newspaper.

His wife and kids helped with various tasks. Milt Rosen, PLM chairperson, and I packed the papers into boxes for pick-up.

As it happened, later that month the Harlem rebellion erupted, during which the rebels were holding the front page of *Challenge* as their flag while marching [see Story and photo in "Arrested for Supported the Harlem Rebellion"]. This prompted the NYPD Red Squad to visit Mr. Chan and warn him that if he continued to print our paper he would be in for trouble. Chan told them he was within his rights to print any newspaper brought to him. "What about freedom of the press?" he shot back at the cops' threat. He was not about to abandon his only account.

Years later, when Mr. Chan retired, our search for another printer led us to Brooklyn and Ballan Printing, a company that printed many small community and campus papers — and a huge number of pornographic ones that had spring up since the 1960s. (The Mafia, in collusion with the owners, had coerced the workers into a local union it controlled.) But neither the owners nor the Mafia counted on the workers' rebelliousness.

The workers read our paper and saw the various exposés we wrote about the lousy working conditions that profit-hungry bosses were pushing on workers throughout the country. When we went to pick up the paper, the workers showed us the horrible condition of what passed for their bathroom and asked us to write about it. Our editor Luis Castro wrote an exposé for the next issue, which the workers read with enthusiastic approval.

When the bosses saw the article, they went wild. They told us it was all lies and one-sided and challenged us to print their side, "the truth." We told them that there was only one "truth," the "workers' truth," which made them even crazier. From then on, they would scrutinize every issue.

Soon afterwards, the owners renovated the bathroom into a half-way decent condition. The workers attributed that improvement to the article we had written.

When a pre-May Day issue had come out, we had printed the words of the workers' anthem, "The Internationale." When we went to pick up that issue, suddenly a pressman leapt up the two flights of stairs to the top of the huge web press and in a clear, loud voice began singing "The Internationale." As the strains of the final words, "the International working class shall be the human race," drifted across the pressroom, the workers spontaneously burst into applause.

We never found out how this worker knew the song's tune, but news of the performance soon traveled to the far reaches of Brooklyn. We are now in our 55th year of publishing *Challenge*, and have never missed an issue.

Arrested for Supporting the 1964 Harlem Rebellion

In June, 1964, a New York City cop fatally shot a 15-year-old black student. The murder touched off an uprising of thousands of Harlem workers and youth, protesting racist police brutality, and heightened by their age-old victimization in employment, housing, schools and health care.

I was a member of the Progressive Labor Movement — PLM — part of a group that in 1962 had quit the old Communist Party, which we concluded had abandoned its Communist principles. We were determined to organize a new, truly communist movement. One of PLM's core beliefs was the necessity to fight racism, whose foundation we traced to capitalism, which reaped super-profits from its racist exploitation of black workers. We saw the Harlem Rebellion as a working-class uprising against this racist system and therefore PLM went all-out to support it. (As it turned out, over the following decade, scores of such big-city black-led rebellions were to spread across the country.)

In the course of this initial uprising, PLM's newspaper *Challenge* was read by thousands and became its flag as anti-racist rebels displayed its front page at the head of their marches on the

162

streets of Harlem. We printed posters with the killer cop's picture atop a headline, "WANTED FOR MURDER! — Gilligan the cop" and pasted them up all over the city. (Two PLM members who printed that poster were later jailed.) We organized support rallies in the city's boroughs, the only group to do so.

Workers displaying *Challenge* and the Gilligan poster, march in Harlem, 1964

The government placed an injunction against PLM, banning us from gathering anywhere between mid-town Manhattan and the Upper West Side. We then defied this ban and organized a support rally in the center of Harlem. This led to the arrest of the PLM speaker and others in PLM's Harlem chapter and to the convening of a grand jury to "investigate PLM as the fomenters of this 'riot.'"

Solidarity messages denouncing the attacks on PLM came from notables from around the world. Bertrand Russell said, "I wholeheartedly condemn the shocking persecution in New York of those who speak up in behalf of the oppressed...in Harlem." Jean Paul Sartre and Simone De Beauvoir said, "We strongly protest [this] persecution" as did Cheddi Jagan, president of the Progressive Party in British Guiana.

Soon afterwards members of the NYPD's "Red Squad" came to my apartment door to question me. While my wife Esther and 7-year-old daughter Anita were sitting on the living room couch watching, I told them I had nothing to say to them and shut the door.

On January 18, 1965, I was among five members who were called before the grand jury — a number that eventually was to swell to more than 40 others. We had all agreed we would not cooperate with this witchhunt. Prior to the day any of us were scheduled to appear, we would call on friends, classmates and co-workers to protest on our behalf by coming to picket the state court that day. I contacted my workmates in our Railroad Workers Unemployment Council — a group formed after we had all been laid off by the B&O Railroad — explaining the issues to them and tying the Harlem workers' fight against racist unemployment to our struggle against the mass layoff we had been hit with the previous year. Sixty percent of our members were themselves black, many of them residents of Harlem.

On the day Joan Sekler, Bill Turner and I were scheduled to appear, over 40 laid-off railroad workers assembled outside the court building, carrying signs linking our layoffs and fight for severance pay to the issues in the Harlem Rebellion. Previous picket lines had been composed mostly of students who were able to take the day off to participate. The appearance of these workers floored the cops in the Red Squad, who were busy taking pictures of the demonstration.

On January 20, 1965, the Red Squad appeared again with a warrant to arrest me for "criminal contempt": refusal to cooperate with the grand jury. Daughter Anita remembered them, turning to Esther to say, "Mommy, those are the same men who came here before to question Daddy."

Two other comrades and I were arraigned in New York State Court in Manhattan. We all pleaded not guilty to charges of "fomenting" the Rebellion. A letter I wrote to all my friends asking for donations to help pay for our legal defense brought in over a thousand dollars. We hired civil rights lawyer William Kunstler to represent us. He told us we'd have a better chance to defend ourselves in federal court so he moved to transfer the case out of state court.

The nature of this grand jury inquisition and its manufacturing of evidence was somewhat revealed in the fact that now, 54 years later, we've yet to hear from the federal court.

Launching A New Communist Party

The struggles led by the Progressive Labor Movement (PLM) set the stage for the formation of the Progressive Labor Party (PLP). PLM had organized among industrial workers (the Hazard miners, the 1964-5 longshoremen), fought racism (the Harlem Rebellion), fought against imperialist war (the May 2nd Movement) and the government's anti-communism (smashing the House Un-American Activities Committee, aka HUAC).

My first clue of the CP's abandonment of communist principles — which I didn't realize at the time — was perhaps symbolized by a discussion in my family in 1944 when I was 14. My 24-year-old sister June, a CP member, had just come home from a mass meeting attended by 20,000 in New York's Madison Square Garden called by Earl Browder, the head of the CP. He proposed the Party's dissolution and replacement by a political association. June was all aglow with this news. My father listened intently. With his insightful understanding, he asked her one question: "How can you make a revolution without a communist party?" June thought about this for a moment and said, "You've got a point there, Pop."

After some internal struggle, the CP was re-established a year and a half later, and I joined it at CCNY in 1948. I was a member for 13 years and witnessed the Party's abandonment of communist principles and cozying up to the liberal wing of the Democratic Party. I did not really understand this, however, until the Party adopted a new constitution in 1960, which advanced the idea that socialism could be established in the U.S. by voting for a constitutional amendment that would, among other things, abolish private property.

My experience with the government's and bosses' attack on our tugboat railroad strike in early 1961 [see "Workin' on the Railroad"], and the attempt to challenge the NYC Central Labor Council's endorsement of Kennedy in the 1960 presidential election (along with the CP's own veiled endorsement of JFK), had left me open to some of my CP comrades' convictions that the likelihood of the CP leading a revolution against capitalism was zero. Would the corporate rulers of the country ever allow a peaceful change abolishing them? Hardly. So when a small group of CP industrial section leaders and others invited me to a meeting to discuss organizing something new, I was ready. The product of that meeting in December 1961 was *PL Magazine*, and the July 1962 establishment of the PLM [See "Launching of the Progressive Labor Movement"] and three years later, the PLP.

There were numerous communist principles advanced by PLP at its inception and later in its development that the CP had either forsaken or never really fought for. These included:

- The necessity for answering capitalism's violent repression of the working class with armed revolution;

- The abolition of the profit system's wage system, which divides the working class;

• Opposing individualism and the cult of the individual leader, advancing the idea of collective leadership;

• Fighting racism as the key to revolution and fighting sexism, both capitalism's weapons to further divide the working class and profit from it;

• Later, through PLP's experience, the advocacy of a mass Party — "everyone can become a communist";

• One international Party, one class, not various individual Parties' "roads to Socialism" in "their own" capitalist country;

• Answering capitalism's assault on immigrant workers by refusing to recognize even the concept of "immigrant" with the slogan "Smash All Borders!" — borders created by capitalists, mostly by wars;

• Recognition that the industrial working class is crucial to a communist revolution;

• Understanding from the experiences in the Soviet Union and China that socialism, in retaining many features of capitalism (like the wage system), leads directly back to full-blown capitalism, and therefore we must fight to win over the working class directly from capitalism to communism.

• And crucially, using the science of dialectical materialism as the method for the empirical study of social processes, to understand how society functions and consequently how to advance the struggle for communist revolution.[1]

Based on many of these and other principles, PLP carried out thousands of class and anti-racist struggles:

- Occupied Chrysler's Detroit Mack Avenue auto plant in 1973 over discriminatory health and safety issues, the first sit-down strike since the communist-led Flint auto strike in 1937;

Pickets mass in support of sit-downers.

- Led an estimated 100,000 workers and youth for over five decades in attacking and routing KKK and neo-Nazi rallies, protected by the police and the bosses' concept of "free speech" —we say, "no free speech for racists";

- Mounted a city-wide campaign to support the Stella d'Oro bakery workers in the Bronx, NY, striking for equal pay for women workers;

---

[1] A detailed understanding of the Laws of Dialectics and its Categories can be gleaned from a PLP pamphlet entitled: "JAILBREAK! Dialectical Materialism: The Key to Freedom and Communism."

It explains the three laws of dialectics: Unity and the interpenetration of opposites; the passage of quantitative change to qualitative change; and the negation of the negation. It also analyzes the categories, including: appearance and essence [see example in story, "Don't Jump to Conclusions"]; form and content; potential and actual; relative and absolute; finite and infinite; contingency and necessity; general and particular.

• Led a 6-day wildcat strike of thousands of Washington, D.C. transit workers in 1978, defeating the bosses' attempt to deny them a wage increase;

• Demonstrated international solidarity in supporting workers' struggles worldwide: the British miners' 1984 strike against the Thatcher-led rulers, refrigerator and beer factory workers in Colombia, striking teachers in Mexico, as well as numerous anti-racist struggles in Palestine-Israel, Pakistan, East Africa and Haiti.

• Helped organize the International Committee Against Racism (InCAR), a mass anti-racist, multiracial group, as well as the Workers Action Movement (WAM), both of which led many of these struggles;

• Organized among the Black youth and workers in Ferguson, Missouri, and Baltimore, Maryland, against the racist police murders of Black youth;

• Mobilized 2,500 anti-racists on May Day in 1975 to smash the racist/terrorists ROAR (Restore Our Alienated Rights, nicknamed Racists

Boston, 1975: Thousands of May Day marchers answer racists.

On A Rampage) in the fight against school segregation, integrating formerly all-white beaches and escorting Black children into formerly all-white schools;

169

• Organized May Day marches of hundreds and thousands in scores of U.S. cities, beginning in 1971 (after they were

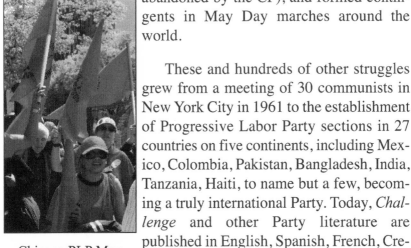

abandoned by the CP), and formed contingents in May Day marches around the world.

These and hundreds of other struggles grew from a meeting of 30 communists in New York City in 1961 to the establishment of Progressive Labor Party sections in 27 countries on five continents, including Mexico, Colombia, Pakistan, Bangladesh, India, Tanzania, Haiti, to name but a few, becoming a truly international Party. Today, *Challenge* and other Party literature are published in English, Spanish, French, Creole, Arabic, Hebrew, Dari, Urdu, Bangla and Mandarin. I've been on the many multiracial staffs of editors of *Challenge* — Latino, Black, Latina and Bangladeshi.

Chicago PLP May Day marchers invade Nazis' turf. (I'm in center, near front.)

The fight to free the world of the exploitation and wars engendered by capitalism is a lifelong struggle. One can only be proud to have been part of this movement, in a Party whose goal is, as my father said seven decades ago, "to make a revolution."

The 1936-1937 Great Flint Sit-down Strike Against General Motors

This memoir has touched on historical events only insofar as they have been the backdrop for the lives of my family members and myself. However, since I wrote an article — later published as a pamphlet — of probably one of the most significant actions in the history of the U.S. working class, I feel it is incumbent upon me to include it in this memoir. The pamphlet came out at a time when the Progressive Labor Movement (PLM) was laying down roots among industrial workers. This focus on the basic industries inspired me — in 1965 — to research and write the story of the Great Flint Sit-down Strike. It was one of the more widely circulated pieces of PLM/PLP's literature; has appeared in two collections of U.S. labor history; been republished by Amazon (without permission, I might add); has been ordered by a number of college professors to use in their classes; and has gained some notoriety in academia.

What follows are only brief excerpts from the pamphlet. For the complete story, see [PLP.org].

171

THE GREAT FLINT SIT-DOWN STRIKE
AGAINST GENERAL MOTORS

The sit-down strike and occupation of the GM Flint, Michigan, auto plant for 44 days and nights — from December 30, 1936 to February 11, 1937 — demonstrated the power of workers in the basic industries, a central outlook of the three-year-old Progressive Labor Movement, and later the Progressive Labor Party.

The sit-down strike is one of the more unique actions workers can take in their battle for a decent life. By occupying the means of production, it prevents the bosses' use of scabs and is harder to attack than an outside picket line. It forces the company to think twice about any frontal assault since that would endanger millions of dollars' worth of machinery. While not a revolutionary act, it is completely controlled by the rank-and-file, although the press and GM labeled the Flint sit-down as "Soviet-style tyranny." GM CEO Alfred Sloan called it "revolutionary in its dangers and implications," possibly because communists played a central role in its organization and leadership.

The city of Flint was arguably the most company-controlled town in the U.S. Every city official — the mayor, the city manager, the police chief, the judges — were GM stockholders, company officials or both. GM spent nearly a million dollars on company spies to be used against union organizers, including hiring the infamous Pinkertons, and had ties to the U.S. Justice Department and Navy Intelligence. GM organized the Black Legion, a terrorist group that beat, tarred, feathered and murdered active unionists.

All this was to protect Flint, the nerve center of GM's world empire. Three-fourths of GM's cars were dependent on the chassis produced in Flint. One million Chevrolets were assembled in Flint's Chevy # 4 plant. Eighty percent of the city's population was directly dependent on GM for a living, including the 45,000 who toiled in its plants. Their average monthly take-home pay was $900, far below the $1,600 minimum that the government determined was needed for a decent living.

The workers suffered the most intense speed-up on GM's assembly lines, often unable to climb the stairs when they got home. Many think it was speed-up that organized Flint. The workers were determined to slow it down and smash the open shop. This was occurring during the Great Depression, with millions unemployed, the company using the threat of layoffs to enforce its speed-up. This became a driving force to establish an industrial union that included both the unskilled and skilled, a rarity in unions at that time.

The workers were fighting for union recognition, a 30-hour work-week, time and one-half for overtime, abolition of piece work and slowing down the line. They organized the most effective strike apparatus ever seen, completely controlled by the rank-and-file. A mass meeting elected a stewards committee and a strike strategy committee of seven, six of whom were communists, led by Walter Moore, with left-wingers Wyndham Mortimer, Bud Simons and Bob Travis among the main organizers and leaders.

Rank-and-file committees were established governing food distribution, police, information, sanitation and health, a "kangaroo court," entertainment, education and athletics. Two mass meetings of 1,200 — the supreme body — were held daily.

A Special Patrol of 65 in the police committee made a 35-minute inspection every hour, 24 hours a day to check on any problems, "rumors," and disruptions.

Every worker served six hours of duty — on 3, off 9, every 24 hours.

A daily cleanup occurred as tens of workers moved through the plant in waves, leaving it spic and span.

Strikers' children were hoisted through the windows to visit their fathers.

Labor history and writing classes were organized.

Charlie Chaplin donated his film "Modern Times" for workers' viewing.

A "Living Newspaper" was established for workers to act out the events of the day.

Women workers and strikers' wives constituted Brigades armed with 2X4 clubs to guard the plant from the outside against police attacks and potential assault by the National Guard. The women defeated the cops in one battle in which the strikers on the inside sprayed water from hoses on advancing cops. It became known as "The Battle of Bulls Run" — the Bulls ran.

An even bigger battle ensued in the capture of Chevy Plant No. 4 that up to that time had not been struck, where its 14,000 workers churned out GM's biggest money-maker. With a military maneuver, strikers led by Joe Sayen, feinted an attack on Plant No. 9, drawing company guards there, only to find out that a strikers' attack was supposedly being launched on Plant # 6. While the guards raced there, leaving Chevy No. 4 defenseless, the latter — the real target — was captured by the strikers and its 14,000 workers joined the sit-down, something which the leader of GM's security thugs, a Hitler sympathizer, vowed was "impossible."

With the threat of a looming attack by the National Guard, which had been ordered into Flint, Sayen addressed the victorious workers, asking, "What if we were to be killed? We have only one life, so we might as well die like heroes than live like slaves!"

After that decisive battle, GM, fearing destruction of its machinery, capitulated, especially in light of 40,000 workers from four nearby states marching into Flint and surrounding the struck plants, ready to defend the sit-downers.

The workers ended up winning union recognition for the CIO's United Auto Workers, a 40-hour week (which led to weekends off for tens of millions of U.S. workers), overtime pay and a slowing-down of the assembly-line speed-up. It was this kind of monumental organization which defeated the attacks of the world's largest corporation.

The effect on the country's working class was electric. In less than two weeks, 30,000 workers were sitting-in in a variety of industries. U.S. Steel, the world's largest steelmaker, and General Electric saw the handwriting on the wall and signed up with CIO unions — WITHOUT A STRIKE. Women in the million-dollar Woolworth chain were sitting in. Within the next four years, five million industrial workers had joined the CIO. Industrial unions were born.

Communists in the Communist Party had played a fundamental role in this development. As historians noted, "Had it not been for the Communists, there is serious doubt that the forces of industrial unionism would have lived through this period"; "The Communist Party [made] a major contribution in organizing the unorganized for the CIO."

However, there was also a major flaw in the CP's outlook. They did not link this huge reform struggle to the need to win workers to the real solution: revolution. They did not expose the relationship of state power to the ruling class. In fact, they spread illusions in government as being some "neutral" institution in the battle between classes. They did not explain the class nature of the law. The CP essentially backed Roosevelt in the 1936 presidential election, even though it ran its own candidate.

Trade unions are a defensive weapon for workers; any reforms that are won eventually are taken away by the rulers because they have state power and control the government. This first great reform victory for the UAW saw it decimated to a shell of its former self. Capitalism is a worldwide phenomenon. Reform victories like these are undercut by capitalists moving their plants to low-wage areas. Today GM produces more cars in China than in the U.S., not to mention the U.S. auto industry's presence in South Africa, Vietnam, and Eastern Europe.

The only answer to this contradiction is overthrowing the system of capitalism — along with its government — a profit system which will always seek to exploit workers wherever it can, pitting one group against another.

As one striker noted as he left the Flint plant, "The first victory is ours. But the war is not over."

Chapter Five
The 1970s

Appearance and Essence:
Don't Jump to Conclusions

A good lesson on the importance of not jumping to conclusions occurred when a comrade, Fred Mendez, and I were engaged in our weekly sale of *Challenge* outside the Long Island College Hospital in Brooklyn. This was in association with a comrade, Kathy, who worked as a nurse there. [This is an example of one of the categories explaining dialectical materialism; see story on the Progressive Labor Party.]

We were also distributing a leaflet from the anti-racist International Committee Against Racism (InCAR) while outside the workers' entrance, adjacent to the hospital's parking lot. An official-looking uniformed employee wearing a military-style hat and white gloves was directing cars in and out of the lot. He suddenly walked over to me and asked to see a leaflet. I was sort of wary of his request, thinking that once he read it he would try to kick us off the property — especially if he noticed *Challenge* "the revolutionary communist newspaper."

He carefully read the leaflet and then exclaimed, "Oh, InCAR! I remember when I was down in Washington testifying on behalf of Vietnam War vets who had been victimized by

Agent Orange dropped by U.S. aircraft and I met up with InCAR pickets."

I quickly recovered from my initial shock and then engaged in a highly political discussion with my white-gloved parking-lot attendant, who also bought a *Challenge*. The *appearance* of someone who I thought was about to tell me to stop leafletting masked his *essence*: an anti-war, anti-racist and potential friend with whom I exchanged contact information.

Wally Meets Red China

After PLP had just exposed the Soviet Union as having become a capitalist power — long before anyone else recognized
that fact — we then saw the Chinese Communists as the main
revolutionary hope for the future. The Party had built ties with
the latter, partly through shipping them nearly 1,000 copies of
every issue of *Challenge*. The official Chinese news agency
would begin every article on events in the US with, "U.S. *Challenge* says…"

At that time the Party decided to have more direct contact
with Chinese Party officials. It was proposed that I travel to
Geneva to talk with China's ambassador. (When PLP's vice-
chairperson Mort Scheer later visited China — to get a second
opinion on the heart attacks he had suffered here — while sitting
in his hotel in Beijing, then called Peking, he said everyone in
the lobby was reading our paper.)

This was quite a few years before Nixon had established relations with the Chinese, and was what later led PLP to conclude
that China was going the way of the Soviet Union, becoming
what is now the world's second biggest capitalist economy. My
trip, of course, had to be a secret one, even from my own family.
How to tell my wife Esther that I would be gone for a week doing

Party work? I told her I had to meet with our comrades in San Francisco. I then wrote three letters which contained news on my "meetings in California," along with personal questions about how the kids were doing, and so on. Every few days one of these letters would be mailed by Frisco comrades to Esther, presumably leaving the impression that I was there.

Meanwhile, I flew to Paris and took a cab to the train station to travel to Geneva. After renting a hotel room near the Chinese ambassador's residence, I walked there to meet their officials. (I assumed that the CIA probably had stationed itself in a room across the street from their consulate to photograph anyone entering.)

In any event, I was greeted by the ambassador and first sat down to a delicious seven-course meal of Chinese dishes, ones that I had never encountered in Chinese restaurants in Brooklyn. Afterwards, the ambassador asked me about my experiences as a communist in the U.S. I told him about my eleven years on the railroad [See articles on "Workin' on the Railroad," on the International Union Convention, and on the R.R. Workers Unemployment Council] and answered questions about the Party's ongoing activities. I told him we wanted to have closer relations with the Chinese Party; the ambassador said he would send a packet reporting our discussions to Peking and would get back to me soon. He then suggested I rent a car and become a "tourist" for a week or so before returning to get the answer from Peking.

This was my first trip to Europe, or even anywhere beyond the U.S. and Canada. I decided to drive over the Alps to Italy, arriving in Milan and took in the sights, especially the debates going on outdoors in the central square, and ate some delicious Italian food. I then returned to Geneva to receive the reply from Peking, which I would take back to New York.

(Of course, by the time I got back to Brooklyn two weeks had elapsed, though I had told Esther I would be back in a week.)

By the eighth day of my trip, she was getting concerned about what was happening "in San Francisco," so she asked our chairperson Milt how to get in touch with me. Somehow he convinced her he couldn't phone me because I had gone down to Mexico to exchange experiences with the famous painter Siqueiros, who had strong ties with Mexico's railroad workers. Esther was dubious about that, but had no choice but to accept the reason why I was gone longer than the original week planned.

I took the train from Geneva back to Paris, and because I couldn't get a flight for New York right away, did a little sightseeing in that beautiful city. When I arrived back in Brooklyn, I went immediately to our apartment. Finding no one home, I realized Esther and the kids would be in our neighborhood park. As I started walking there, the kids came running toward me screaming, "Daddy! Daddy! Daddy's home!" Trailing behind them was their mother with as a mean a look on her face as I had ever seen directed toward me. I apologized and, of course, went with the Mexico story (still keeping the Geneva trip a secret) and soon things got back to normal.

Later that spring, however, Esther was gathering clothes to take to the cleaners when lo and behold, she plucked my passport out of an inside jacket pocket. Opening it, she found entries for Paris and Geneva. She confronted me with a nasty look, demanding, "What's all this?" Now that it was all over, I felt obliged to explain the whole business. At first she was suspicious, but then she relented. Her last words were, "Why couldn't you take me with you?"

Seeing Is Believing — Or Is It?

It's curious how a combination of events can play tricks on people's minds and lead them to imagine something quite contrary to reality. But that's exactly what happened on the day that my good friend and comrade Gracie Moreno married her husband Jeff Coplon in Schenectady, New York.

Early that morning when my wife Esther and I were getting ready to drive the three hours from Brooklyn to attend their wedding, I received an anxious phone call from the groom asking me if Esther and I could fulfill a father's role and walk her down the aisle. I was puzzled until he told me that Gracie's brother in Texas slated to perform that role would be unable to get to the ceremony in time. Of course we agreed, so that was how Esther and I acquired a "second daughter," one whom many in attendance were convinced Esther had mothered.

When we arrived we were filled in on the imminent proceedings. Then as the strains of the wedding music echoed throughout the hall, Gracie took the arms of Esther and me as we slowly advanced down the aisle to the position in front of the minister where Jeff assumed the groom's stance.

Once the ceremony was over, everyone settled in, eating and dancing and generally enjoying the festivities. Then came the

moment for Esther and me to join Jeff's parents in accepting the congratulations of all those present. We were instructed to stand next to his parents as the crowd passed down the line in front of the four of us. Of course, all of Gracie's friends and comrades from New York and New Jersey, who knew Esther and me, knew we were not the mother and father of the bride, but Jeff's relatives and friends were seeing us for the first time.

Walking down the aisle.

I smiled dutifully as I shook the hands of all, hearing the chuckles of our knowing friends. As Jeff's side of the crowd extended their hands to Esther and congratulated her, virtually each and every one commented how remarkable was the resemblance between her and her "daughter." Esther played her role as mother flawlessly, smiling as she shook each hand and acknowledged their good wishes.

So it was that imagination trumped reality — and a good time was had by all.

Sweet 16 Re-creation

This Sweet 16 story is more of a re-created one. When I was at an Elder Hostel (Turning Memories into Memoirs Workshop) as a "lesson" we were asked to compose (manufacture?) a dialogue between family members, I chose this "argument" between my children. Actually some of these exchanges and attitudes were factual but much of it I dreamed up in accordance with our teacher's instructions on writing dialogue. I enjoyed doing it. Hope you enjoy reading it. [No offense, Anita and Andrew]

SWEET (?) SIXTEEN (1973, BEFORE CELLPHONES)

"Daddy," said daughter Anita, "you want to know what I *really* want? You know when you pick up the phone to make a call and you hear me talking to Roberta on the extension? How angry you get, waiting and waiting for me to get off? And you certainly can understand how I feel when I'm dying to talk to Marla and I pick up the phone and you're on the extension going on and on with Milt or Morty about some article?

"Well, Daddy, this all could be solved in one neat package by me having my own phone! That's not asking too much, is it?

My own phone — I'm sixteen now, Daddy. I'm a young woman. What a beautiful gift for your daughter!"

Gifts galore.

"What?" screamed son Andrew. "You're giving her her own phone? Why should she have a phone? She's already got the bigger bedroom. You and Mommy have got me in that tiny cubicle at the other end of the house. If anyone needs their own phone, it's me!"

"But, see," he went on, "I'm not even asking you for one. Why do you always favor her? She's having this big sweet sixteen party with all her friends and she'll end up with a pile of presents. And her own phone on top of that?

"You didn't have your own phone when you were sixteen, and neither did Mommy. Sure, then when I want to call Alan, and I pick up the phone and you're talking on the extension and I have to wait, and she's got her own phone and doesn't have to wait her turn — it's *not fair!*"

"Sure, I want my own phone," retorts Anita. "I deserve it. I'm sixteen. A 16-year-old can't wait around for her father to get off the phone."

"Your own phone!" exclaimed Andrew to Anita, raising his voice. "You've got a helluva nerve! You already have the bigger bedroom. Besides, you're right near the kitchen extension with that long wire. That wire never reaches my hole-in-the-wall at the other end of the house!"

"Well," Anita replied, "Did you figure that if they give me my phone now, when you're sixteen there's a lot more chance you'll get *your* own phone? Did you figure that, huh? Besides," she announced triumphantly, "when Daddy or Mommy's on the phone and you want to talk to Alan or anybody, you won't have to wait. I'll let you use my phone!"

"Fat chance," Andrew shot back. "At the rate you talk to Marla or Roberta or god knows who else, my talking on your phone is pure fantasy!"

"Well," said Anita, "I'm only showing you how this is for your own good. And," she continued, "When I'm not home, you can use my phone anytime. No waiting then."

"Yeah, it all sounds oh so neat," replied Andrew. "You've got it tied into a cute little package. But they're always favoring you, and you know it. If anyone should have their own phone around here, it's me. I always get the short end of the stick. But I'm not even asking for one. It's about time things were equal in this house…"

As it actually turned out, Anita and I compromised; she didn't get her own phone number ("too expensive" I said) but she but did get a princess color phone.

(Anita won this one. Andrew moved into her bigger room the day after she left home and up went the Pink Floyd poster.)

How I Lost My Sister

When my sister June took her own life at the age of 52, I wondered if our relationship had played a role in her decision.

She was born on June 6, 1920, ten years before my birth. In

my early years, she was the ideal baby-sitter. When I was 13, she married a Brooklynite named Howard Gruber. At that time he was serving in the U.S. Army during the Second World War. I thought he was a great guy, and he probably was. (He later became a psychology professor.)

Then one day, when I was 15 and returning home from a summer job in Monticello, N.Y., my sister met me and said, "Let's go for a walk. There's something I've got to tell you."

I suspected bad news. She told me she and Howie were getting divorced and explained why. I really didn't listen too closely, but I just felt lousy. I couldn't figure out why they were unable to solve whatever problems they had. After all, I

Sister June, 22, at Brooklyn College

reasoned, our parents had fought like cats and dogs but they were still married.

Soon afterwards I was rummaging through a table drawer and came across a few pages obviously written by my sister. It wasn't a formal diary, just some thoughts she had put down on paper. Essentially she said the reason she had married Howie was to get away from our mother. I was momentarily stunned, but then recalled the many violent arguments that had erupted between our mother and my sister. I hadn't realized how deeply this relationship had affected her.

It was one of the first times in my life that I understood that there are consequences for everything we do, some of which result from our relations with others. I had always respected my sister and knew her as a person with many talents — as a painter, photographer, clothing designer, among others. I was impressed that she possessed the honesty and courage to conclude that her marriage had been a mistake and had the strength to act on that understanding.

Several years later, after June had married her second husband Ralph, my wife Esther and I visited them and noticed she seemed very depressed. She was about to follow Ralph's wishes and move 2,500 miles to El Paso, Texas, near Ralph's family. (They were later to move twelve times during the course of their marriage.) Ralph seemed to be always looking for the "greener grass on the other side of the road." I told her I thought it was crazy to make such a move. She said she thought so too, but felt there was nothing holding her here in Brooklyn. She said she had no real friends and, in fact, had always wished that I would have been a real friend to her.

I was taken aback and immediately tried to rationalize to myself that we all have friends who are not necessarily family members. But I really didn't want to think about how, as sister and brother, we could and should have been close friends.

As it turned out June couldn't stand the desert sands blowing in on El Paso from New Mexico. Within two months she, Ralph and their son Alec began moving again, to Dayton, Ohio, to Westchester, N.Y., to Connecticut, then back to Brooklyn — where she became a librarian — and finally ending up in the village of Vergennes in a very poor area of northern Vermont. There she landed a job which she came to love, as a librarian in what was known as a reform school. She introduced scores of students to reading, was lauded by their parents and written up in the local paper.

But Ralph — who had been hired as an advertising copywriter at a Middlebury newspaper — came up with still another idea. He said they should start thinking about providing for their retirement and proposed they open up a fabric shop, given her talent in clothing design. Ralph would go to New York City to scout out fabrics and she would display them in their store. The venture was a huge financial success, but when Esther and I visited June, she appeared quite unhappy. She had never sought to be a "business woman."

Shortly after our return to Brooklyn, Ralph called to say June had taken an overdose of sleeping pills and was on life support in an Albany hospital. I knew this was no accident. She had always had trouble sleeping and had been taking sleeping pills for years. She had exact knowledge of the dosages and knew the amount to take to sleep. Obviously, she had taken enough to end her life.

I raced up to Albany. She was in a coma and never regained consciousness. It was May 16, 1972. I later found out from my nephew Alec that she had left a note explaining her decision, a note which Ralph refused to show him. As it turned out, Ralph remarried six months later, to a woman he had previously introduced to June.

I was stunned that my dear sister had taken her own life. I

later wondered if our mother's quarrels with her had laid a terrible groundwork. Or if her husband's nomadic existence had led to all this? Or if June had any suspicions about Ralph's relationship with this woman friend and that had played a role? Or had our own too-distant sister-brother relationship left her so bereft of someone to lean on that it had became the final straw?

I'm not sure if I ever knew who my sister really was.

PHILLIP "Kap" — 1957–1976

The adage that nothing's more sorrowful than when a parent outlives a child hit home to me in a very personal way with the accidental death of the 19-year-old son of my dear friends Gertie and Gus Kaplowitz. Phillip's life was intertwined with my own family's, from his birth until the day he died. He was my own son Andrew's closest buddy from early childhood into their teenage years and was virtually a second son to me.

Our two families were a tightly-knit group. In 1956, the "Kaps" (as Andrew later called them) and we moved into apartments in the same building in Brooklyn's Crown Heights. At that time my wife Esther and Gertie were both pregnant. My daughter Anita was born on February 27, 1957, and a week later Gertie — after an arduous pregnancy — gave birth to Phil. He was born six weeks premature and very small. He had an unusually high forehead and initially we all worried about what that might mean for his normal development. However, he eventually seemed to outgrow it, although he always remained small for his age. Andrew, born three years later, grew to the same size as Phil, another characteristic that enabled them to play sports together and gave them a brotherly appearance despite not looking alike.

Our families rarely had to hire a baby-sitter since, living one floor apart, it was easy for us to baby-sit for each other (Phil had a sister, Rena, two and one-half years older). In 1966 both our families moved to the Ebbetts Field houses, site of the old Brooklyn Dodgers stadium on whose land this 5,000-resident, seven-wing building had been erected. Our three-bedroom apartments gave the children their own rooms, a principal motivation for our move. Four years later we bought a two-family house together in the Sheepshead Bay neighborhood. Friends warned us against it, saying that buying a house together often led friends to become enemies. But we scoffed at this. Having known each other quite intimately for 25 years we felt we could overcome any differences that might crop up. As it turned out, we were right; we lived together in that house for 36 years. Beginning in 1963 we began taking annual camping vacations together, often packed into the same large station wagon, pulling a U-haul with our gear stashed inside.

All these moves should indicate how the four parents and four children were linked into an inseparable "family" and, among other relationships, laid the basis for Phil and me to become like father and son. Often, our two families would spend Sundays visiting various sights around the city. I particularly remember one jaunt to the Bronx Zoo, which vividly illustrated the unpredictable and independent sides of Phil's personality. As we strode through the zoo checking out the various animals, we suddenly realized Phil's absence. The four parents became frantic, calling his name and searching all over for the three-year old tyke. Suddenly Rena spotted him. Where? Just what one might expect from Phil — riding on top of a camel, in between its two humps, holding the reins, all by himself! Why a zookeeper took the liberty to hoist little Phil onto the camel, without his parents present, and allow him to ride around was something none of us could fathom. Unpredictable Phil!

Another example: returning on a camping vacation from Great Smokies National Park, we stopped at a convenience store for some items and then returned to the station wagon, where the children would play in the back. We had driven a few miles when someone asked, "Where's Phil?" Everyone thought he was with someone else. When we realized he was missing, we turned around, sped back to the convenience store and there was Phil, sitting on the stoop in front of the store, figuring, no doubt, when we'd notice his absence we'd return to fetch him.

Given Phil's small size, Gertie and Gus took special pains to enable him to be "part of the gang," to put him in a position to develop friendships. Growing up, sports were a big part of this, which Gus recognized and took special care to ensure that Phil became proficient at playing ball. When Phil was a teenager, Gus would come home from a hard day's work, eat dinner and then he and Phil would grab a bat and their baseball gloves and go out to the lot across the street where they'd bat and catch an old baseball.

Somehow Phil really got into roller hockey and joined a team in a neighborhood league. All of this influenced Andrew to follow in Phil's footsteps. Andrew joined the league, became a lifelong hockey enthusiast and, to this day, a rabid New York Rangers fan. When our two families went on camping vacations together, I developed a baseball routine with Phil and Andrew: we would form a triangle, with Phil at "shortstop," Andrew at "second base" and me "covering first base." I would then throw the ball to one of them, he would then toss the ball to the other at second base who would then whirl and throw it to me at first, thus completing the double play. What really got them going was the fact that I would also be acting the announcer while we played, simultaneously reporting the action: "short to second to first."

When our two families had bought the two-family house together, Gus and I set up a small "office" for me in the basement where I wrote articles, away from the hubbub upstairs. Every so often, Phil would come down to do his laundry and while waiting for the washer-dryer to finish, he'd come over to me and ask what I was writing about. This was the era of the Vietnam War. Phil thought it was senseless and wrong and said he would seek a way to avoid being part of it. He was developing an awareness of injustices around him and had developed close friends based on their worth as human beings, not on their skin color or having similar prejudices. Interestingly, he had attended a junior high across from our Ebbetts Field apartment house in Crown Heights and was one of only four white boys in the school. He made some good friends among the black students who "protected" him — being on the small side — from any attacks by the bigger boys. This was borne out from the multiracial crowd that honored him at his funeral service.

In July, 1976, Phil died at 19 during a holiday weekend outing with friends, drowning while swimming in a reservoir near Boonton, New Jersey, as a friend tried but failed to save him.

While some might have viewed Phil as shy, this did not prevent him from developing these friendships, somewhat belying that characterization. Others might have thought he was reckless (the camel ride), but actually Phil loved life too much to be reckless about it. Those who were close to Phil as a friend, as a relative, as a son and as a brother had their lives enriched. These relationships were what Phil's life was all about.

SAM CHANZIS - 1891–1981: "I have to help because I'm here…"

In recalling the life of my father-in-law, a lasting impression is his constant concern for those around him. Even in the old-age home where he spent his last three years, he was always helping his roommates, making sure they awoke for dinner or calling someone when they messed up. When we saw how agitated he was about such things, we'd tell him, "Pop, don't aggravate yourself; leave it to the nurses." But his reply was invariably, "I have to help, because I'm here."

People who knew him, even only slightly, recognized this quality. My mother, bedridden in the same old-age home for a short time, told me how he would check on her to see if she was all right.

When he walked the streets of his neighborhood, his arms were constantly in the air, waving to all who knew him. He was known as "the Mayor of Bensonhurst."

His concerns were not limited to those he knew personally. Every time we would pass the Waldbaum supermarket in our neighborhood, he would curse those responsible for the fiery death of six firemen — due to skimping on safety precautions — victims of the greed for money. Sam's care for humanity reached the wider world: I was told how he sat glued to the radio during the Second World War, following the battles of the Red Army on Europe's Eastern Front, fighting against the Hitlerites to save the world from fascism.

Not long after he arrived in this country from Russia, he became a presser in Manhattan's garment shops, a career that lasted four decades until he retired in 1945. All that time he was wedded to the ocean. From May to October, he would race through his work every day so he could leave by three o'clock in order to arrive at Coney Island, where he rented a locker, changed into his trunks and enjoy hours of swimming before dinner.

The ocean was embedded in his bones. On weekends when Esther and I would bring the family to the beach, and I would attempt to dry myself upon emerging from a swim, he would scold me, "Drop that towel! You need to let the salt water sink into your bones!"

He was intent on instilling this idea into his grandchildren. He was never prouder than the day he took my son Andrew into the steam room — the "schvitz" he called it — to insure that my three-year-old received its "health" benefits. And when our two families drove upstate to the Arrow Park Resort in the Catskills, he would revel in dipping six-month-old Anita into the lake. "Careful, Pop," I would warn him, but he only laughed, saying, "She's got to learn to love the water!"

Sam was tender enough to cringe when he heard a baby cry, but virile enough to be swimming in the ocean at 75.

His children always used to say, "The man has nine lives." He had smoked since he was ten years old, so when he began to develop a periodic cough in his late eighties, his doctor said, "If you've gotten this far, and you enjoy it, why stop now?" The surgeon marveled at the fact he even survived the operation he underwent to try to prolong his life.

During those last few years, on weekends, we would take him to our house to spend some time with our family. I had to make sure we had his favorite snack, pumpernickel and herring — I guess something he never tired of since his boyhood days eating "the black bread of the Ukraine."

Some might say Sam Chanzis was a throwback to an earlier, simpler world, but he was actually a vision of what the future will be when the world is not based on the thievery that leads to the tragic deaths of working people — as happened to those firemen in the Waldbaum fire — but instead a world where men and women will be guided by the rules that governed Sam Chanzis's life.

If he was a "simple man," remember, eventually the world will be re-made by such people as Sam Chanzis, and that will be no "simple" task. Sam Chanzis was really not so simple after all. He was the stuff of which life is made.

Wherever people gather to talk about those among us who can be described as "the salt of the earth," bear in mind, Sam Chanzis wrote the book on that one.

"I have to help, because I'm here." If an epitaph was needed for Sam Chanzis, that was it.

[What follows is a memoir drawn from a eulogy given at Ida's funeral service.]

At our wedding: Momma Ida and
daughter Esther dancing up a storm.

IDA CHANZIS:
A Remarkable Human Being

One measure of the ninety years encompassing my mother-in-law Ida's rich and wonderful life is the fact that the 23 years I knew her were only those after she retired. I only heard about the previous six decades from others, about the struggles marking those years: carrying Esther in her womb when in 1926 she marched to protest the murder of Sacco and Vanzetti; the confidence she had in working people; how she brought the ideas of a socialist world to all she came in contact with.

Recognizing her leadership qualities, her co-workers in the millinery shop elected her shop steward. And she would bring her ideas and her CP newspaper, *The Daily Worker*, to Brooklyn's waterfront, fearlessly mingling among the longshoremen and among the bus drivers in her neighborhood bus depot.

In her waning years, when she was no longer politically active, I would explain to her why we organized PLP. She understood, would smile and, periodically, hand me a contribution.

Yet the truest measure of Ida was her ability to translate these ideas into her relations with all those surrounding her. While to many, a world free of exploitation seems utopian, when one knows such a person as Ida, one can get a glimpse of what that world should be and can be like.

While knowing her personally only in her so-called waning years, and although seeing her progressively losing a step with each succeeding year, she never lost an inch where it counted — in her mind and heart. If anything, there she grew.

The remembrances are legion. One sticks out in my mind. Shortly after Esther and I were married, I had to work nights and Ida worried that I wouldn't get any hot meals. So she had me over in the afternoons before work and cooked potato latkes for me. No one could make latkes like Ida! She served me one helping after another and marveled at my capacity to consume them. She got pleasure from giving me pleasure.

I will never forget an image from a vacation trip Ida and Sam took with Esther, me and our 15-month-old Anita out West. It was 1958; we were touring Mesa Verde National Park in southern Colorado and came upon the cave dwellings constructed centuries ago by Native Americans. Rooms were dug out within the caves, and to get to them, wooden ladders had been erected. And there was 68-year-old Ida scrambling up the ladder to peer inside the "apartments."

Another memory which I only heard about but made a deep impression was the way she related to her older daughter Jean and Jean's husband Joe. Just after the Second World War, during the housing shortage, Ida and Sam took the couple into their tiny apartment for a year and a half. And although being in tight close quarters, Ida never interfered in their lives, never got in their way, never told them what to do, never became entangled in their decisions. Anyone knowing the size of that tiny apartment would appreciate that feat. Comedians are always making jokes about how bad mother-in-laws are; if they depended on Ida for their material, they would have gone broke long ago.

When we think of genius, an Einstein or a Beethoven may come to mind, but Ida's quality of helping people change their lives for the better is the real genius, for which most of us can only strive. In all the years I knew her, I never heard her say a harsh word. Not that she couldn't be stern and express what was on her mind, but only in a way that would help, not hurt.

I knew that her husband Sam could only be broken up by her death, but in days when couples sometimes look cross-eyed at each other and it was grounds for divorce, sixty years with Ida put him way ahead of the game. Would that all of us could spend six decades with such a wonderful person.

Ida could never be forgotten. She lived on in all of us, especially in the way she touched the lives of her grandchildren, Howie, Pauline, Mindy, Anita and Andy. Being a parent, one does not get the chance to choose a grandmother for one's children. But never in my wildest dreams could I pick one as great as Ida.

While every breath we take is important, in the whole scheme of things — in the thousands of years that humans have walked the earth — each one of us is but a mere dot in the eye of history. Yet that makes it all the more important what we do here, in the short time that we have, to change ourselves, to change our friends, to change the world.

In these terms Ida certainly was "a tough act to follow." But follow we must, for our beloved Ida wouldn't have it any other way.

My Treasured Sister-in-Law Jean

What is a person's life but a collection of remembered stories? Mine began sixty-two years ago on the 15th of May, 1955, at the end of my second date with Esther (we didn't "hang out" in those days; we had actual dates). I had just entered the tiny apartment on Bay 25th Street in Brooklyn's Bensonhurst neighborhood, where Jean and her sister Esther were raised by two wonderful parents, Ida and Sam. I immediately saw a little four-year-old boy sitting on the living room easy chair, sizing me up, this stranger whom he had never seen before. Hiding behind him was a toddler, a tiny girl, barely a year old. That's how I first met Howie and Pauline.

Soon, striding into the room came someone who appeared to me to be Howie's older sister. She shook my hand and said, "Hi. I'm Jean, Esther's sister." I couldn't believe that this teen-aged-looking young woman was a mother of two! Jean always had the vigor of youth about her, even later into the seventh decade of her life. Years later Esther was to tell me that when Jean took her 14-year-old Howie to buy shoes on Flatbush Avenue, the salesman asked the boy how come his "kid sister" was telling him what to buy.

Not that Esther looked any older. (She was actually a year-and-a-half younger.) While each was an individual in her own right, in many ways they were similar. So much so that when Jean's husband would see them talking to each other a mile a minute, comparing notes about anything and everything, he would exclaim, "There's the two sisters, at it again."

In 1983, at the memorial service for Esther, Jean drew a vivid picture of these "two sisters." She described what the May Day celebration was like when they were six and seven years old. Momma Ida would dress them in their very best finery, preparing for the workers' march down 8th Avenue in Manhattan into Union Square. "She made us proud to be daughters of the working class," explained Jean.

I recall that story because two months before her death, Jean called to tell me that although she wasn't feeling too great, she was itching to go to that year's May Day March, if only someone could drive her to the bus and she could get a ride during the march. I was elated and told her, "No problem." Then in her sixties, Jean was still going strong.

I remember Jean's strength through the trauma of her sister's sudden death. She had been standing alongside Esther when it occurred, and had been thrown into a snow bank herself. She arose at the service for Esther to tell her decades-long story to 250 people. I doubt if Jean had ever spoken to more than a roomful of people before, but this was something she felt she had to do.

I will never forget that for an entire year after Esther's death, Jean and her husband Joe would call me up virtually every week to make sure than if I had nothing to do on Saturday night, they'd come over. They didn't want me to be alone.

These were feelings she had learned from her Mom and Pop. They were very evident in how she handled her daughter

Pauline's relationship with her boyfriend David. It seemed like these two must have been going together since they were two years old. Actually it was somewhere around 13 or 14. It was something Joe found difficult to get used to. He had been taught that David, not being Jewish, was "not our kind." Jean patiently re-taught him, employing a lot of subterfuge and trickery to do it. Gradually, Joe changed and came to admire and love David. This was all Jean's doing. It was not something she learned in books, but was part of the very fiber of her being, something she had absorbed growing up in the household of Ida and Sam. It had become part of the principles that guided her life. Thus, by the time Jean's daughter Mindy's husband Frank rolled around, Joe didn't think of him as "from a different kind," praising Frank to everyone. Yes, Jean was quite a piece of work.

It always amazed me that when after son Howie graduated high school at 18, he went off to Schenectady on his own, made his way in a strange city, got a job in the General Electric plant while going to school, and lived with a GE family he had never known. All that was not something he had learned on his own, but the upbringing he had received from his mother.

With whatever differences that may have existed between Jean and her children (as in most families), she created a certain respect within her family. However, Jean enlarged the concept of family and was concerned about everyone's kids. Symbolically — although probably not with any preconceived plan — she got a job involving the safety of other people's kids, as a school crossing guard. However, Jean's concerns were to spread far beyond that.

In the mid-1970s, Esther gradually introduced Jean to the world of fighting not merely for one's own kids but for her whole class, the working class. She went to meetings and rallies and demonstrations, leading her to join the Progressive Labor Party. Jean became a Communist. It was, as the great W.E.B. Dubois said, "the logic of her life." She became immersed in the Party's work, especially in selling its newspaper *Challenge-Desafio*. Everyone knew that if someone was needed to help sell the newspaper, "make a sale" as they put it, or give out a leaflet, to call Jean. She wanted to spread these ideas to as many working people as possible. And, in fact, that was exactly what she and Esther were doing when tragedy befell her sister, hit by a car driven by an unlicensed driver.

This step Jean took in joining the Progressive Labor Party unleashed a whole new life for her, greatly expanding her horizons. She had a new and independent role to play. Talk about women's liberation!

The "two sisters" and their husbands began vacationing together across the country, from New England to the Northwest;

Jean and Toni in the
Pennsylvania Dutch country.

from Michigan to the Canadian Rockies. Increasingly, Jean revealed just how vibrant she really was. I remember how excited she got when my daughter Anita and I, having driven a van to Calgary, Alberta, Canada, went to meet her, Joe and Esther — who'd flown in from New York — at the Calgary airport. Jean had always been deathly afraid of escalators. When everyone else rode, she always took the stairs. When she saw us one flight below, she unexpectedly hopped the escalator, I guess to get to us that much sooner. I was about to yell to her, "take the stairs; they're right next to you," but by that time she was at the bottom, and only then realized what her excitement had accomplished.

The active side of Jean's nature was never more evident than in her permanent state of readiness to walk, and walk for miles. A cult had been built up, I like to think, by "the two sisters," to walk the length of the Coney Island boardwalk, from Sheepshead Bay to Brighton Beach to Coney Island to Sea Gate, and back, at least every Sunday. And this was after Jean had dragged her husband to first walk the thirteen blocks from their Avenue N apartment all the way to our house at Avenue Y, just for warm-ups. Jean was no slouch!

Thus, when the side effect of chemotherapy set in, causing a loss of feeling in her legs, it was a mortal blow to Jean. A big piece of her life was cut off when she could no longer walk from her house to wherever she wanted to go — to the "Y"; to baby-sit for her grandchildren; to visit our friends Gertie and Gus or cousin Ruthie. Ironically, it was not the disease itself that did it but the side effect of that treatment, one that she eventually called a halt to.

When Jean wasn't outside, she was inside with her books. Jean was a voracious reader. Esther, Anita and later Toni would always be lending her books and she would devour them, along with her favorite newspaper, *Challenge*.

Above all, Jean was a fighter. She was an eternal optimist, which meant that it was not easy for her to hang out with Joe, who somehow would always see the glass as half empty until someone like Jean pointed out that it was also half full. I think it was her optimism about the future that carried her as far as she went after discovering cancer in the mid-Eighties. This fighting optimism probably did for more for her than any doctors did or could do. Virtually every time we would talk — and I mean *every* time — she would invariably exclaim that "you gotta keep fighting, and do what you gotta do; you can't give up; you've got no choice."

For nine years she fought this dreaded disease, never giving up. She never seemed despondent, at least outwardly. Maybe in the privacy of their own apartment, she would let it out to Joe. But to others, she was always a picture of boundless optimism, which greatly encouraged those around her.

I think Jean was a victim of a disease with more social and political causes than mainly physical ones. I think she felt that when a society could be built that eliminated the profits to be made from pollution and processed foods, from tobacco and toxic waste, only then would we have the chance to *prevent* cancer, not restrict ourselves to just searching for a cure after the fact. That was certainly one of the reasons Jean fought as hard as she did for her Communist principles.

While one might not describe Jean as an intellectual, her life reveals that she had plenty of intellect. The obituaries in the newspapers concentrate on reporting the lives of those considered to be "successful" — government officials, corporate bigwigs, diplomats, and so on. I've yet to see an obituary about Joe Blow or Jane Doe who was a machinist or a waitress and "all they did" was to raise kids, help their brothers and sisters and share what little they had with others in the same boat. These characteristics rate pretty low on the so-called "success" chart.

Jean's list of accomplishments wouldn't make it to the New York Times, but they made it to where it counts — into our hearts and minds. Working people like Jean are not considered geniuses but are viewed as "ordinary." However, when combining the strength of millions of such *ordinary* people, you can produce the *extraordinary*, creating a future in which true equality exists, in which the hardships that beset working people will disappear. Too many think this is impossible, but it is the Jeans of the world who turn the impossible into the actual.

Remember Jean as a fighter. This is her legacy, as a wife, a mother, a grandmother, a comrade and a friend. As the Bard once said of those departed, "the good [they created] is oft interred within their bones." Jean's spirit lives on. The good she created is interred within *our* bones.

My Friend Gus — A Man for All Seasons

During the 47 years of my enduring friendship with Gus Kaplowitz, I came to know him as an   accomplished cook, carpenter, gardener, fisherman, hunter (of sorts, but more on that later), a creator of ceramics and stained glass, a voracious reader (he loved Westerns) and world traveler, aside from being a loyal and loving husband and father. In a real sense Gus was as extraordinary a person as are millions of others, if we examine their lives closely.

I have a treasure trove of memories of Gus, enough to fill an entire book. In fact, my family always urged me to write such a book, along the lines of something like "The Egg and I." We even picked the title: "Gus and Us." Unfortunately I never did; maybe a task for the future.

I first met Gus in 1955 when he lived with his wife Gertie and two-year-old daughter Rena in a small apartment in the Brownsville section of Brooklyn. My wife Esther had been close friends with Gertie for a long time before that, even before she met Gus. When they saw our spacious apartment on Brooklyn Avenue, we helped get them one in the same building, where both of our families lived for 11 years.

Interestingly, when they met with the landlord, they told him we had recommended them for a vacant two-bedroom apartment. The landlord immediately asked them if they were members of the Communist party! Somewhat taken aback, they replied, "No." (They didn't mention that they had been members some time before that but had left.)

The landlord then explained that the FBI has visited him and told him to ask any prospective tenants if they were CP members. He said there were already 13 of the 70 residing in the building. In any event, they got the apartment.

Then, in 1966, we all moved to the Ebbetts Field Apartments, and finally four years later bought a two-family house together in the Sheepshead Bay neighborhood where Gertie and Gus spent the next 32 years.

My kids and grandkids grew up alongside Gus for large parts of their lives. Our two families vacationed together from 1963 to 1976, mostly camping. We all seemed to be part of the same extended family.

To Gus, life was a challenge. He loved to learn and loved to teach. He took adult education courses at night, in cabinet making, Chinese cooking, ceramics, stained glass-making and other things I probably don't remember. He then turned around and taught. He helped my son Andrew become a cook in his own right and often took him fishing. (Gus was an avid angler.) When we bought the house together, I — having lived in a rented apartment all my life — viewed it as a chore to take care of, while Gus looked on it as a toy to enjoy. He taught me plumbing and painting, as well as how to work with joint compound and sheet rock, and how to mix cement — you name it, Gus was there to fix it.

When I mentioned that with all the hubbub in my house, it was difficult to concentrate on writing and editing work, I raised the possibility of building a small office cubicle in the basement to hold a desk, a typewriter and some file cabinets, with a window opening for a fan, Gus's eyes lit up. I said I'd pay for the materials but Gus waved me off, saying, "We don't need to buy anything." From scraps of wood (of which we had plenty) and left-over sheetrock from other projects, we constructed this "office" on what Gus said proudly was "90 cents worth of nails." Without spending a penny, we made a new door from my living room to the back stairs to replace the one in the kitchen.

When friends heard our two families were buying a house together, they warned us "that's the way friends become enemies," but we disproved that adage. If anything, our two families drew closer. For a solid year following Esther's death, I was invited upstairs every Sunday night to share a dinner prepared by Gus to talk over the week's events. It helped me through my sorrow.

When some repairs had to be done in the house, we would hold a meeting to discuss it and then vote on the proposal. People would ask me, what if the vote was 2 to 2? But strangely it always came out either unanimous or 3 to 1. Who was the one? Gus! When we had to get the roof fixed, Gus said he and I could do the job. But Gertie, Esther and I had visions of Gus falling off that roof, so it was 3 to 1 to pay a roofer. And so it went for 32 years.

Gus was also a collector. Any visitor to our basement quickly recognized that. Periodically, Esther would get frustrated at what she and I viewed as junk (like 150 plastic containers) but which Gus saw as "something we'll need some day." Every so often Esther would say, "It's clean-up time," and Gus would grit his teeth but agree to throw out some of his beloved junk.

Two of the places Gus spent his lunch hours were what we called Alexander's Junk Shop as well as "Job Lot" in lower Manhattan near Gus's job in the wholesale shoe market. He knew

Gertie wouldn't approve of all these *tchotchkas* and bargains he loved to buy, so he would come home with something he'd picked up and rather than carry it upstairs to their apartment, he would circle around to the backyard and set it down near the basement door. Then he'd go around to the front, go upstairs, have supper and afterwards tell Gertie he had to go to the basement or to water the garden. Then he'd open the basement door to bring in his latest purchase and show it off to me if I was working in my basement cubicle.

Once he came in with a briefcase which he showed to me. "Gus," I asked, "since when do you need a briefcase?" "I don't," he replied, "but it was such a bargain, I couldn't resist it, only $2.69, so I bought it — for you!" I used it for years until it fell apart. ("Thank god," said Esther. "Now you can get rid of those stupid shopping bags.")

Gus, the boy from the Bronx and son of a housepainter, always had this dream of becoming a farmer. He would actually drive upstate searching for a plot of land to call his own. It may have been a fantasy, but to Gus planting things was very real. He had a forest of plants covering half his front room, the largest in their apartment. So when we bought the house, Gus looked at the postage-stamp-sized back yard with a gleam in his eye. He persuaded us to allow him to expand the 3-foot-wide soil part to six feet wide and then gathered old tires and pails onto paved areas in which he planted still more.

He would spend all winter setting things up, tending to seedlings, collecting all our egg shells and orange and grapefruit rinds for mulch and then proceed to spring "plowing" and planting and then harvesting in the summer and fall. He would always stop at our first-floor apartment, carrying his little basket filled with whatever he had gathered that day to present us with fresh tomatoes or peppers or whatever had just ripened.

Of course, Gus was forever searching for ways to improve

his crop, which sometimes led him into some unique situations. The one that sticks in my mind the most occurred a few years after we had moved into the house. On a pleasant Sunday afternoon in April in the early Seventies, Gus strode downstairs where his teenage son Phillip, my son Andrew, 12 at the time, and I were watching a ball game on TV. As Gus stood there twitching, I immediately knew something was on his mind.

"What's up?" I asked. He drew me aside and began his story. "You know the horse stables along the Belt Parkway?" he said. "I was looking for a way to enrich my soil. They've got this great manure out there, so I just took my wheelbarrow [yes, he had a wheelbarrow on his 'farm'] and bought three 100-pound bags, but I couldn't haul more than one bag at a time back here."

These stables were about four miles from our home. I had this image of Gus straining to pull his wheelbarrow across the Belt Parkway, dodging cars speeding along at 50 miles per hour, huffing and puffing on the four-mile trip home. I knew what was coming: "Could we take your station wagon and pick up the other 200 pounds and bring them back to the garden?"

What choice did I have? I knew if he had to, he'd make two more 8-mile roundtrips. If he didn't have a heart attack, there was a good chance of his being hit by a car. So I said, "Let's go." The two boys pleaded to come along. I said O.K., but under one condition: not one word to their mothers.

We took off for the stables and pulled up where Gus had left the other two bags. He loaded them onto the rear of the Chevy wagon and we sped back home, with the windows wide open and our noses pinched closed. I backed into the driveway and Gus hopped out to unload his precious cargo. The boys scrambled out and ran in the opposite direction.

When Esther and I retired for the night, I noticed her nostrils twitching furiously. Then I realized I had forgotten one salient fact — our bedroom windows opened out to Gus's garden, and the aroma of 300 pounds of horse manure. "What did you eat tonight?" she demanded. "Same as you," I replied. "Well it sure affected you differently than me," she said. "I think you'd better spend the night on the living room couch."

I realized that this wouldn't solve the problem, so I broke down and told her the story. "And you helped him!" she exclaimed. "Well," I said, "it was between risking a heart attack or Gus becoming road kill." Frustrated, she slammed herself down on the bed and stuffed a pillow over her head. I rose to close the windows. That was the earliest we had ever turned on the air conditioner.

[I wrote this story up at an Elder Hostel I attended that year on "Turning Memories into Memoirs" and gave it to Gus when I returned. Gertie said when Gus read it, he couldn't stop laughing.]

Then there was the time Gus's farming inspired another tale. We were camping at the North Rim of the Grand Canyon when Gus got into a conversation with a rancher from Nevada, while Esther and I stood nearby. Picture this: Here's Gus in his boots and dungarees, with his trusty camping knife (which he always carried, at home or away) hanging in its holder from his belt, wearing a cowboy hat and shooting the breeze with his "landsman," this Nevada rancher. Gus would always start up a conversation at the drop of a hat with anyone he met.

Anyway, the rancher was describing his tract of land as something like "20 by 30," by which we assumed he meant 20 by 30 miles (or at least acres). Gus then hitched up his pants, put his fingers on his belt and casually mentioned that he, too, had a "spread," a little smaller perhaps, something like "6 by 10." He neglected to mention 6 by 10 *feet*! At that Esther and I couldn't restrain ourselves and burst out laughing. When the rancher left, we asked Gus, "How come you didn't tell him '6 by 10 *feet*'?" Gus smiled sheepishly and said something like, "a little fudging never hurt anybody."

Gus's imagination was so vivid that he could foresee things to do, invent or construct that would never cross anyone else's mind. Once when we were camping for a week in Yellowstone National Park, Gus saw all these dead birch trees lying on the ground. Knowing that the general rule in the National Parks was not to disturb anything in its natural surroundings (and Gus had a great respect for nature), he gingerly asked the Park Ranger if he would be allowed to collect these dead trees. Much to Gus's surprise, the Ranger replied, "Go ahead."

I assumed Gus wanted these huge limbs for firewood. (Gus was a great firemaker; he would keep one going from 6:00 AM to midnight when we were camping and he taught me how to make one — "like the Indians used to," he would say.) Anyway, it turned out firewood was the furthest thing from Gus's mind. He pulled out his toolbox — he always brought one on camping trips — and proceeded to construct a forest full of birchwood patio furniture: chairs, tables, loveseats, you name it. Then our two families would sit on that furniture around a campfire, to the admiring glances of neighboring campers.

And then there was Gus the hunter — of sorts. If animal lovers and gun control advocates wanted a poster boy of a certain kind for their causes, Gus was their man. Every November when the three-week deer-hunting season began, the city boy from the Bronx and Brooklyn would take out his trusty rifle, all shined and greased, and take off, usually with a hunting buddy and other times by himself, for a weekend of hunting in the wilds of the Catskills. Gertie, of course, would be duly nervous, worried that some other hunter's errant shot might hit Gus or that his own rifle would go off accidentally and he'd shoot himself in the foot. She needn't have worried. In all those years of so-called hunting, Gus never pulled the trigger once on a deer, much less hit one. In fact, he only took one shot all told, and that one at a rabbit — and missed. But Gus loved to go hunting. He was a hunter — of sorts.

Gus had other distinctive characteristics. He was ever ready to "show you how to do it," from replacing a washer in a faucet to cutting a cantaloupe. Sometimes he would get on my nerves, when he would see me trying to hang a picture or nail something together and would say, "Not *that* way, Wally, *this* way." Once I exploded at him and yelled, "Let me do it my way, Gus, and make my own mistakes." He backed off with a grin and was more careful after that.

Sometimes, this "showing you how" would backfire on Gus, leading to unintended consequences. Once when we were on a four-day camping trip upstate, Esther, Gus the four kids and I went rowing on a lake while Gertie relaxed in her beach chair on the shore. When we finally docked the boat and the kids scrambled out, Gus watched Esther as she tried to maneuver herself out of the boat and onto the dock. Gus stood there, shaking his head, and couldn't contain himself. "Esther," he said, "that's not the way; here, I'll show you. First you lift one foot out like this, brace yourself, then swing the other foot this way," and at that moment Gus plopped right into the lake, clothes and all, while Gertie laughed uproariously from the shore.

Of course, Gus took all these things in good spirits. He could laugh at himself as easily as he could at others. And what a laugh! It was not a "ha" or a guffaw but more like a rooster's cackle, and a loud one at that. I remember when he came back from seeing the movie "Quest for Fire," which was right up his alley for it told the story, among other primitive tales, of how humans discovered fire and carried it with them wherever they went, not allowing it to go out. When Gus heard I hadn't seen it, he offered to take me, just so he could see it again.

We went and whenever there was some humorous situation in the film, a titter of laughter would be heard from the audience. But not from Gus. He would break out into a loud cackle that would sweep through the theater; heads would turn to see the source of it. Of course, that wouldn't disturb Gus whose eyes were glued to the screen.

Gus's life was not all peaches and cream. No one's is. When he was in the Navy in World War II, he was sent home after both of his brothers were killed in action. The rule was that if someone was a sole surviving son, he had to be discharged.

Gus had a hard job in the wholesale shoe market, sorting and carting around boxes each containing 48 pairs of shoes. There were layoffs, small shops going out of business and periods of unemployment, but Gus always managed to get another job through the union hiring hall, and made it to 62. He always said he wouldn't wait until 65 to retire with a full Social Security pension like some of his fellow workers "who would then have a heart attack a week later." And Gus was right, then spending 18 enjoyable retirement years traveling the world — to China, Japan, Russia, Australia, New Zealand, Alaska, Spain, Portugal, Morocco, Italy and Sicily, Yugoslavia and Canada, not to mention most of the National Parks from Maine to the far western United States.

Probably the greatest tragedy in Gus's life was the accidental death of his son Phillip at 19 who drowned in a reservoir near Boonton, New Jersey, during a holiday weekend with friends. I told Gertie that as awful as it was for me to lose Esther at 55, there was nothing worse than a parent losing a child. It's not supposed to work that way. Gus took special care of Phillip, who had always been short for his age. He overcame this by becoming very proficient at sports. It was from Phillip that my son Andrew gained his love for hockey. I remember when Phillip was a teenager, Gus would come home from a hard day's work, and go outside to play catch with Phillip.

Of course, as all kids do, Phillip would get on Gus's nerves sometimes. Gus would lose his temper and bellow something fierce. But Phillip learned how to handle the situation, remaining quiet until Gus was all bellowed out and then silently saunter away, unlike Gus's daughter Rena who would bellow right back.

Gus took great pride in his cooking. Before he retired, he would usually prepare the family meals on the weekends. He did almost all the food shopping and after he retired I think he took over most of the cooking, besides doing the heavy cleaning and periodically re-painting the apartment, a skill he had learned from his father.

I remember all this household work he did used to irritate our late friend Selma, whose husband would rather listen to a Puccini opera than wash a dish. She would see Gus defying the usual conventions in performing the tasks society had reserved for women and would tell Gertie she was a very lucky lady.

Gus was also a strong union man. While the average attendance at union meetings in this country was somewhere around three percent, Gus was always part of that three percent — although in his union the percentage was much higher. Gus was always ready to participate in the fight for decent contracts, and to strike if necessary. In his earlier years, he marched with his union, Local 65, on May Day and later on in the Labor Day parades.

When my granddaughter Eli visited Gus after he came home from a rehab center following a heart attack, she later told my daughter Anita that she "felt sad to see Gus looking so weak, and wished he didn't have to die," which set her thinking about wishing her Grandma and Grandpa didn't have to die either. Eli was expressing what many of us feel, emotions that are very understandable. Life, I guess, is a journey, a long one sometimes, but rather than dwelling on its ending, it's what we experience in the course of that journey, and the impact we have on others, that really counts. Gus's life was full of just that — *life*.

Gus's 80 years were certainly full ones. No one could say he was shortchanged. If he was not necessarily a "man for *all* seasons," he was certainly a man for many.

It's often said that our dear departed ones live on in our memories of them. While Gus is gone in body, he certainly created enough memories for him to live on in our hearts and minds forever.

Chapter Six
The 1980s to 1990s

My Life With Esther

The spring of 1956 ushered in a milestone in the lives of Esther and Wally: Esther became pregnant. With family life on the horizon, Esther continued working at her job at a travel agency in Manhattan for the first six months, so we banked her pay until she quit. On February 27, 1957, Anita, our first child, was born. Esther made it through a Caesarean birth. Anita was a colicky baby, but our pediatrician assured us it would only last three months. Sure enough, the colic disappeared on the 90th day! One way we were able to put her to sleep was to drive around for a while, the rocking of the car helping her to doze off.

As a union member in Local 65, Esther received six weeks maternity pay. Prior to this, we had lived off my railroad wage, but now it was three making do on my weekly take-home pay of not quite $60. Soon Esther insisted she bring in some money, working at home part-time. A proficient typist, she landed a job typing transcripts in our apartment while caring for Anita. I prepared the formula and fed the little one at night until she began sleeping through.

We knew we wanted more children so soon Esther became pregnant again and our second daughter, Julia, was born in late February of 1959. But this birth turned into a tragedy. After we brought her home, it seemed she had developed a form of viral pneumonia in the hospital which, when the symptoms appear, it's too late to treat. Julia died in the house on March 3. [See story "A Child We Never Knew."]

We felt the way to deal with our grief was to have another child as soon as Esther was able. And sure enough, on July 20, 1960, our son Andrew was born. [See story "A Son Who Ushered in A Bright New World"]

At that time, Esther and I became involved in a neighborhood campaign to elect a black State Assemblyman in this predominantly black district. It was there that we developed a friendship with one of the more active members, Stokely Carmichael. He told us that he would be leaving Brooklyn for Alabama to join the Civil Rights movement in the South. He felt that was where the real struggle was occurring. We tried to convince him that he was really needed here, but to no avail. He became the leader of the Student Non-Violent Coordinating Committee (SNCC) (and Esther and I failed to alter the course of history?).

Throughout this period I had become involved in intense struggles on the railroad to save our jobs, including a strike that shut down the waterfront, as well as my election as local union president. [See "Workin' on the Railroad"] Esther was busy holding up the home front while giving me advice. Case in point: when I discovered that the company and the union leaders were told by the FBI that I was a communist, I came home scared as hell. "So?" she said. "So I could lose my job!" I said. She calmly responded, "So, you'll get another one." In my panic that thought had escaped me. But of course she was right.

Alongside the activity in the union, I was part of the movement in 1962 to leave the Communist Party and establish a new real pro-communist organization, the Progressive Labor Movement (PLM). Soon afterwards Esther joined and became a stalwart member. When in June 1964 we started publishing an

English-Spanish newspaper *Challenge-Desafio*, Esther not only became one of its leading sellers but a militant champion of PLM.

When the Harlem Rebellion erupted that June, PLM organized support rallies throughout the city. One was in Brooklyn's Bushwick neighborhood; Esther got right up on the ladder, holding a bullhorn and speaking to a gathering crowd. (I stood alongside the ladder, having her back.) She had a knack for grabbing people's attention by picking out one person among those listening, talking directly to her or him and explaining the issues. It caught on in the crowd and soon there was plenty of handclapping and cheering.

When PLM evolved into a new communist party, the Progressive Labor Party (PLP), Esther joined immediately and eventually became a club leader. While much of my time was taken up with chairing the Party's trade union section and taking trips three times a year to meet with members in nine Midwestern cities (Minneapolis, Madison, St. Louis, Kansas City, Chicago, Detroit, Cleveland, Columbus and Pittsburgh), Esther was a sparkplug in Brooklyn party activities, particularly around the sale of *Challenge*.

Throughout the Seventies our family also took travelling vacations [See "Parking Through North America"] and Esther's joy showed through on many occasions; she loved camping out, sleeping in a tent and cooking outdoors. When we were in Acadia National Park, we met the lobster boats coming in with the daily catch and bought two large ones to cook in a huge pot on our camp stove. I left it to Esther to seize the live lobsters and transfer them from their box to the pot's boiling water. When I asked her, "Why do they keep popping their heads up?" she replied, "Wouldn't you if I put your head in boiling water?" Enough said.

LOX AMONG THE LUMBERJACKS

When we arrived on Vancouver Island from Washington State, we heard there was a lumberjack tournament starting up nearby. Never having seen one, we drove to the site and were quite impressed. The participants were climbing up tall poles, balancing themselves on swiveling logs floating in a pool, and so on. The price of admission included a lunch of fresh salmon.

Esther sauntered over to an outdoor cooking area where the chef was turning over huge fresh-caught salmon, readying them for the lunches. Esther watched as he cut off the heads and the tails and began throwing them out. When she asked him, "Why are you doing that?" he replied, "We don't serve those parts. Why? Do you eat them?" She replied, "Back in Brooklyn, we eat all of the lox." "Lox?" he asked, what's that?" When Esther explained, the chef then loaded up all the heads and tails and presented them to her to gorge herself on later.

Brooklynite garners some Lox

Esther was expert at playing a role as a "substitute mother" as when she walked our comrade Gracie Moreno down the aisle at her wedding. [Full story, see "Seeing Is Believing"]

This mother persona helped Esther get her first job outside the home when she applied for a position at the Williamsburg Y as an assistant nursery school teacher. There were seven other applicants, all of them fresh out of college. The interviewer was impressed with Esther's experience raising children, something lacking in the other seven. She got the job. [Full story, see "How Esther Went to College — or Did She?]

More of her "mothering" emerged in her job as secretary to the teacher of a medical technical course at Bellevue Hospital. The forty students were mostly in their early twenties, many of whom had boyfriend and girlfriend problems. They regarded her as their mother and would come to her for advice. Having had long years of experience, this "mother" responded with loads of tips and suggestions, much to their satisfaction.

In recounting our marriage, it might seem as if all our interaction was free and easy, but of course, no marriage can be without conflict. This was true of ours. In my memory, the toughest time occurred in 1963, soon after I was laid off from the railroad. The two of us developed a plan: while I collected railroad unemployment benefits and stayed home to care for the kids, Esther would get a full-time job outside the home. Meanwhile, I'd take some education courses at night. (I had already acquired a bachelor's degree.) The goal would be for me to eventually land a job as a college teacher. But my comrades in PLM had other ideas.

They sat me down and said we needed to have our own printing shop, to be able to publish a bunch of literature at lower cost. Two other comrades, experienced pressmen, signed on as officers, to operate our printing press at night. (They were later convicted during the Harlem Rebellion for having printed our "Wanted for Murder" poster and served six-month prison terms. I "escaped" since I was collecting unemployment benefits and was not signed on as an officer.) But we needed to have someone to run the shop full-time to "solicit outside business." That "someone" would be me.

Initially I rebelled. I explained the plan Esther and I had

worked out. Furthermore, Esther had applied for a job in the Brooklyn Library, despite the fact she had no college degree. Somehow she tortuously manufactured a resumé that was accepted by the library and was hired. We were overjoyed.

"Well," said my comrades, "You'll just have to explain to her the importance of what PLM needs you to do."

I was shaking when I went home. She was all aglow about having gotten this job when I shocked her by responding that she'd have to forgo it in lieu of what I had agreed to do. Naturally she was enraged. Then silence reigned. She didn't speak to me for a week, but finally decided what I was being asked to do was important. We survived, mostly due to Esther's efforts. It was then that she sought the nursery school job at the Williamsburg Y (with some shenanigans on my part — see story, "How Esther Went to College — or Did She?")

Two other incidents are relevant, although not quite as fractious as the one above, but nevertheless exposed a weakness on my part. One day when I was sitting at the kitchen table, our teenage daughter Anita was watching me as I was balancing our checking account and asked, "How come momma is not going over those finances with you?" Esther was listening and commented, "I'm not much good at figures." Anita shot back, "Oh, so women aren't good enough for such a task?" I was flustered but agreed there's no reason why we shouldn't be doing this together. So from then on wife and husband checked finances jointly, as Esther became "good at figures."

Another similar episode occurred one day when I was painting one of the rooms. I had always done such jobs myself. Esther suddenly challenged me to participate in this job. I was taken aback, never having considered this to be anything but "my job." At that point, I agreed to help set her up to join me in painting our apartment. From then on this became a joint endeavor of wife and husband.

My role in exclusively performing such allegedly "male jobs" was a reflection of the sexist nature of capitalist society and my conforming to such "rules." In this case, it limits the contributions that both spouses can make to a successful partnership, and especially that of the wife. (A conversation that I had with Progressive Labor Party's chairperson, Milt Rosen, highlighted how such limitations affect the advance of our Party's fight for revolution — see footnote on page 222.)

It is ironic that Esther's passion for selling PLP's newspaper *Challenge* is what led to an accident that caused her death. In February, 1983, Esther was a member of a Brooklyn PLP community club. At their Saturday meetings, they would have a topical discussion and then would go out to a nearby corner to sell the paper. Many of the buyers were steady customers. Esther noticed that when the club discussion was over, a number of the members would leave for some other appointment and would beg off from participating in the paper sale. So Esther came up with a proposal: "Let's meet on the corner *first*, sell *Challenge*, and then regroup at the meeting place to have our discussions." All agreed, so on the 19th of February, the members met on the four corners of Flatbush Avenue and Lincoln Road, where the sale always took place.

Soon afterwards, on the corner where Esther and her sister Jean were hawking *Challenge*, a car appeared out of nowhere, apparently out of control, hurtled up on the sidewalk and smashed into Esther. A group of men standing nearby rushed over and together lifted the car off her and pulled her out. But it was probably too late. It seemed she may have already been dead. An ambulance was called and took her to Kings County Hospital. I was elsewhere at the time and a member called me. I rushed to the hospital ER, met by the Party members. I spoke to a doctor who told me she had probably died instantly. But I wanted to see her. A comrade, Derek, guided me over and I bent down and kissed her good-bye.

What was my first thought? That she would never see her first grandchild whom Anita would give birth to in July, a grandchild she had looked forward to for six years.

We later learned this tragedy was no accident. The operator of the car was driving illegally. She had epilepsy and had a seizure, causing her to lose control. The law states that a person with such a condition must be certified by a neurologist to be free of seizures for seven years before receiving a license. But it turned out that when she had applied for a driver's license, she neglected to tell the Motor Vehicle Bureau she was epileptic. (And therefore, of course, her auto insurance was invalid as well.)

Shortly afterwards I called the District Attorney's office to inquire about any criminal proceedings. I was told they had to find her guilty of breaking two statutes and so far they had only one. I tried to follow up on this for a year, but with no result. I went to a hearing on suspension of her license; she didn't show up and, of course, the license was revoked.

The thought kept running through my mind that "*if* my dear wife hadn't made that proposal to change the club meeting's agenda, and had been on that corner *after* the club discussion, she wouldn't have been standing there earlier, at the time that car careened onto the sidewalk." However, life is full of "ifs."

My family and comrades helped me get through my immediate grief. Son Andrew stayed at my house for the first month. I had to concentrate on the 28 years of happiness that Esther and I had together. And that soon I would be a grandfather, and would share the memories of Grandma Esther with our grandchild. I would enrich my grandchildren with my memories of her, so that they would come to know how wonderful she had been. And that is one of the main reasons I am writing such stories and have adorned my apartment walls with the images depicting our life together.[1]

---

[1] In a discussion with Milt about advancing women in the leadership of PLP, he noted that capitalism, through the subjugation of women, forces the latter to face additional problems in life not confronting men: lower wages for the same work; unpaid labor in their role as the main ones who raise the children who provide the future workers to be exploited by these same capitalists; as well as the physical and verbal attacks on women encouraged within a sexist society. In overcoming these problems, it enables many women to develop talents and abilities to use in giving leadership to struggles that face the entire working class in general.

Therefore, in the course of developing women to lead the Party, we benefit from the special contribution they can make, drawn from overcoming the problems forced upon them by capitalism's inevitable drive for profits. Thus, it was no accident that some years ago a woman became the chairperson of the Party — and in this case a woman from a Latin background, having been forced to deal with even the additional problem of racism. Furthermore, when the Party decided at our last convention to advance from having one person as the leader to one now having a four-person collective leadership, it was a natural outgrowth to have three of these four leaders be women, including a woman as editor of *Challenge*.

What You Do Counts

Throughout one's lifetime, we are often unaware of the hundreds of people who cross our paths, how our interactions with them may very well influence their lives in a myriad of ways and how our encounters can actually help change the course of events around us. This was certainly true for my wife Esther. In the days after she died I received ninety-one letters from a multitude of people — friends, comrades, some whom I never met — describing what Esther meant to them.

In reading the previous story — "My Life with Esther" — one can see many of the facets of her life, whether "mothering" colleagues at work; speaking on a bullhorn from a ladder to marshal support for the 1964 Harlem Rebellion; raising two wonderful children; transforming me; surviving the death of an infant child; using *Challenge* to spread the ideas of communism; and fighting to change the world into one which liberates the world's working class.

I wish I could print these ninety-one letters in this memoir (possibly the contents of a volume by itself?) but I have chosen one, a poem written in her honor that expresses many of the sentiments of these letters. Hopefully those whose paths Esther crossed — as well as her grandchildren who never met her —

will draw inspiration from her life and carry forth the ideals she exemplified.

Truly, what you do counts.

FOR ESTHER

We grew up and you were always there.
From our first meeting in the 60's
Over the years
Seeing you at demonstrations,
May Days, picnics
Weddings and showers
Always the fast-talking Brooklynite,
Always with the ready smile
And high energy.

Some of us last saw you
Dancing at Gracie's wedding in May,
Kicking up your heels yet another time,
Oblivious in your joyful abandon,
But not unaware of the delight you spread.

That is how we will remember you
A dancer, uninhibited by life,
Dedicated to people, to finding good,
A surrogate parent to so many of us,
Modeling marriage at its best,
No better comrade or friend.

Barbara W. Batton
2/20/83

How Esther Went to College — or Did She?

If you read the story about my wife Esther being hired as an assistant nursery school teacher, you might have wondered how she did it without having the required two years of college. Well, here's how.

As you would have read, she was competing against seven other applicants who were in their early twenties, all of whom had four-year college degrees. Having been the only one with the experience of raising children, Esther still had to present evidence of at least two years of college.

I figured I had to compose a college transcript to display courses totaling 32 credits. I knew a friend who had been to the University of California at Berkeley. I asked her if she still had a course catalog and a transcript of her own career. She did, and gave them to me.

I looked up the names of the appropriate courses that would fit a nursery school teacher. I then whited out all her course names and typed in the required courses Esther would need, as well as her name and address, birth date, etc. Then I made a copy of the new transcript and fortunately the outline of the white-outs

233

didn't show up on that copy. But there was one more problem. The original transcript had the seal of the college embossed on the page, making it official. I had to acquire such a seal.

I went to the printer of PLP's newspaper *Challenge* and asked him if I could borrow his corporate imprint/stamp. He said why not (we were his biggest account). I then slipped Esther's transcript into the printer's corporate stamp and squeezed it hard enough so that it would show up as an imprint but not too hard, preventing one from reading the identifying Berkeley name. We now had a transcript in Esther's name with the required two years of courses for an assistant nursery school teacher which she presented to her prospective employer at the Williamsburg Y. My handiwork was accepted. Voila! This experienced child-raiser beat out the competition and was hired.

She did such a good job that when she applied for another job at Brooklyn's Brighton Y, she got a great reference from her first job and, presenting her transcript, was hired there. But a few years later, a new problem arose. The Brighton Y now wanted their assistant teachers to get a regular 4-year degree, and were willing to pay for those additional two years' tuition.

Esther was in no position to take those extra two years, not having taken the first two years. She thanked the Brighton Y for their offer and gave an excuse why she couldn't follow through. Off she went to a secretary's job in downtown Brooklyn.

Don't think they will prosecute an 89-year-old law-breaker...

Is There A Job Harder Than This?

In the late 1980s, I lived in the same house with my daughter and my three grandchildren, ages 2, 3½ and 5. I was able to watch first-hand the problems of raising three kids so close in age. Anita was taken up with caring for them 24 hours a day, seven days a week. I particularly remember a "simple" chore such as driving to the local Citibank on a winter day to make a deposit.

Picture this: she had to put their winter clothes on one after the other: coats, leggings, boots, gloves, hats. Then there was setting them up safely in the car, driving to the bank, finding a parking spot, getting them out of the car and hauling them to the bank. Once inside, there was having to handle the money while watching them, with, of course, one (or more) of them insisting they make the deposit. Then it was back to the car, tucking them in, driving back to the house, parking, getting them out of the car and into the house, and undressing all three, one at a time.

And this was just one part of the 24/7 tasks involved in raising three kids so close in age. It dawned on me then and there that such a job was about the hardest one could have, more dif-

235

ficult than any other I could imagine, even an auto worker on an assembly line. The latter, I'm sure, is tough, but it doesn't involve the stress of being responsible for constantly looking after the lives of three small human beings hour after hour, all day and night. But she did it, and raised three wonderful children (and gave me three wonderful grandchildren, for which I've been eternally grateful).

Life's Strange Twist
Led Me Down the Path of A
Wondrous 14-year Love Affair

Little did I realize that before I met Toni Ades — who was to become my second wife — that she and my first wife Esther had known each other before I met either of them!

One day Esther came home from work and said, "Guess who I met today on the subway, Toni Ades, whose husband Stanley was in the same YCL club [Young Communist League] with me years ago." (Stanley had died of cancer over a decade earlier.)

It didn't particularly register with me until a few months later when I was scheduled to address a PLP forum. Andrea, Toni's daughter — whom I knew at the time from having worked on PLP's newspaper *Challenge* — had brought her mother Toni to the forum. Esther spotted them and brought me over to introduce her, saying, "This is the woman I was telling you about who I met on the subway."

Following Esther's death in February 1983, after such a wonderful marriage I was anxious over the thought of being alone for the rest of my life. In March of the next year, I remembered

Esther's friend Toni. I called up Andrea and asked if her mother was seeing anyone. "I don't know. Maybe," she replied. "Why don't you just call her and 'hang out'?" With me it was still "dates," not "hanging out." "Could I have her phone number?" I asked. "Sure," answered Andrea with a trace of excitement in her voice.

So it was that I called Toni for a date, not to just hang out. She lived in a beautiful apartment overlooking the Brooklyn Bridge and the Manhattan skyline. We went out several times and exchanged our life's experiences. After about three months, things seemed to be clicking. We were talking about spending a weekend together in the country when Toni said, "There's something I must tell you first." "What?" I asked. "I contracted breast cancer sixteen years ago," she said, "and get annual check-ups to detect any recurrence." I guess she wanted me to know this before we got any deeper into a relationship. I thought this was very honest of her to tell me this. In my mind — and heart — her honesty outweighed any concern I might have had over continuing to see her. She was able to survive another cancer attack in 1992 when the breast cancer cells moved to the shoulder area, partially immobilizing her right hand, but she overcame this as well.

Soon we were to meet the other members of our respective families. That was how I gained two more grandchildren, 6-year-old Isa and year-old Anton, and two sons-in-law, Zak, Toni's son, and later Jerry, Andrea's husband. For the next seven years I would spend weekends and Wednesday nights at Toni's, until I finally moved into her magnificent apartment in November of 1991. During that time I was to devour Toni's marvelous cooking — both Italian (her family background) and Middle Eastern (her husband's background). I learned how to make chicken soup and lasagna, spent holidays with our families together and was tricked into a surprise 56th birthday party that Toni devised and included many of my friends, as well as a visiting British miner.

Meanwhile, I discovered how much Toni was wedded to traveling, an aspect of our lives which tied us at the hip. A year after we met, I was looking through a Thursday paper and saw an ad for one of the early low-cost airlines, People's Express. It had one stop in Europe, Brussels, Belgium — round-trip fare $298! I figured from Brussels we could take those fast Euro trains to Amsterdam and then to Paris. Without asking Toni, I immediately booked two tickets for the following Thursday and phoned Toni at her job at John Jay College. I said, "What about flying to Europe a week from today? I just booked two round-trip tickets." Breathlessly, she replied, "I'll start packing tonight!"

So off we went, visiting Amsterdam's highlights — the Anne Frank House, the Rembrandt and Van Gogh museums — and then to Paris, walking the streets, touring the Louvre, dining outdoors on the Champs Elysee, eating that delicious French food, buying fresh fruit, tomatoes, cheese and baguettes at a local stand and consuming it all while sipping wine from Provence, sitting at a window overlooking the Seine. [See story and photo , "A Picture of Love."]

That was only the first of our trips, journeys that took us to London and Paris again, driving through the Loire Valley, a trip to celebrate Toni's retirement; a month in Puerto Rico, including visiting the Arecibo telescope

"Camping" with our RV in Algonquin Park, Ontario, Canada

239

[see story "Searching Outer space"]; and touring dozens of national parks in the U.S. and Canada which Toni had never experienced: Yosemite, the Redwoods, Olympic, the Cascades, Shenandoah, Algonquin, Acadia, Rocky Mountain, Yellowstone, Mesa Verde, Grand Canyon, the Smokies, Banff and Jasper; you name it, we were there. (This was the second time at all these for me.) Sometimes we were joined by Toni's friends Muriel and Phil and once by Esther's sister Jean and husband Joe, traveling either by rented car or an RV.

In the late 1980s, Toni and Andrea bought a country house in the Catskill Mountains, near Hunter, N.Y. where we spent numerous weekends with family and friends. My job was to mow the huge yards surrounding the house. We went to auctions in East Windham where Zak and Toni bid on a baseball signed by my boyhood hero Joe DiMaggio as a present for me; it still sits in my bedroom baseball display. (Knowing my attachment to DiMaggio, also a hero of Toni's father, she and Zak took me to the Nassau Coliseum when DiMag was signing autographs; we had stuff signed and pictures taken with Joltin' Joe, which are also part of my baseball display.)

Toni, like Esther (and later I was to discover, my long-time partner Vera) were all great dancers. Knowing my inept dancing ability, Toni would twirl me around the living room to the music of Julio Iglesias and was able to drag me out on the floor at weddings and other affairs.

In 1998, the cancer hit the lung area. Chemotherapy caused Toni to lose her appetite and subsequently 50 pounds. A stent was inserted in her hip and I was able to feed her through a tube three times a day. Soon she regained over 20 pounds and we were overjoyed, able to leave the house with her in a wheelchair, to go to the movies and to enjoy the promenade along the East River. I became a 24/7 caregiver. One of her doctors told us it was important to keep her upbeat psychologically, so I would set up a schedule for a friend or family member to visit her some part of each day, seven days a week, which did lift her spirits. Every night and morning we continued our tradition: a kiss the last thing before we went to sleep and a kiss the first thing upon awakening in the morning.

It was during this year that Toni decided she wanted to put me on the building's annual occupancy affidavit, which meant that if she died, I would retain inheritor's right to an apartment in the building. Because of her foresight and love, I have been able to live for the last 20 years in the two-bedroom apartment in which I am now writing these stories of my life.

Gradually the cancer worsened, and at the end of October she entered Sloan-Kettering Hospital. Andrea and I took turns sleeping on a bed in her room for the last ten days of her life. She died peacefully in her sleep in the first week in November.

My love affair with Toni lasted for 14 years, during which she and I were able to live a truly complete life.

A Picture of Love

The time — April 1985.
The place — Paris.

My lovely partner and I are toasting our stay in this glorious city and our feelings towards each other. Through the blinding sunshine streaming through the French windows, we view the Seine River just below and the Louvre Museum on the other bank.

A small table is set between us with wine, a baguette, cheese, grapes and tomatoes, just purchased within the hour from an outdoor market around the corner from our hotel. The fruit and tomatoes look fresh enough to be fairly leaping out of the earth. We thought, "What a lunch this will be!" And so it was.

I felt I was the luckiest guy in the world. It was like a scene we had only read about or seen in a movie. But this was not Ingrid and Humphrey. This was Toni and Wally, gazing into each other's eyes, expressing our love for each other in the city of romance, overlooking the Seine.

It was at that moment that I knew we would spend the rest of our lives together, "until death do us part."

Searching Outer Space

I had never thought much about the search for extraterrestrial civilizations until a trip that my wife Toni and I took to Puerto Rico in January, 1997. We visited the Arecibo Observatory, leading us to a drive beneath what was then the largest radio telescope in the world — a pretty exclusive "tour" as you will see.

The telescope was used to search for radio signals of extraterrestrial intelligence in space. It measures not quite 1,600 feet across and weighs about ten thousand pounds, situated in a hollowed-out basin in the earth. It has enabled astronomers to detect, for the first time, planets outside our solar system and, among other feats, to determine the planet Mercury's rotation period and to detect mountains on the surface of Venus. The damage to the telescope caused by the September 2017 hurricane Irma brought back memories of our visit to the Observatory's museum and the unique experience of enabling us to see the telescope from below.

After looking into outer space through a miniature version in the museum, we strolled back to our car and noticed a man waving to us. He turned out to be the chief engineer on the project, working for Cornell University which was supervising the operation. While in conversation with him he asked us if we'd like to take a drive in his jeep underneath the telescope. Of course

244

we jumped at the chance. We donned hard hats and hopped into his jeep. We then wound our way down into the basin and saw how the telescope looked from below as he described the workings of the various instruments. It was then that he told us we were in pretty exclusive company; while more than 100,000 visitors come by each year, the only people he had ever taken down into the basin was the governor of Puerto Rico and the president of the United States!

Donning our hard hats for the trip below.

(As a sidelight, he said a local family that had visited one day invited him to their house for dinner. As it turned out, they had two daughters and he got the feeling they were hoping to match him up with the older one, but he took a fancy to the younger one, and ended up marrying her. Couples meet in unusual ways.)

Grandchildren — The Lights of My Life

July 22, 1983, was a red letter day for me. That was when Anita gave birth to her first child, my first grandchild, Kevin (middle name Linder, after you know who). When I got the call that morning that she was on the way to the hospital, I immediately caught a flight to Chicago, went to the hospital, and that night around 11:00 o'clock, took the first picture of the little one in the nursery. I had arranged to take off two weeks to help the new parents with their first baby. (I had a special talent, honed with my own kids, for rocking Kevin to sleep while in his carriage.)

My joy knew no bounds when Anita told me she wanted to move to Brooklyn; one important reason was so her children would be close to their grandfather. We re-arranged my six-room apartment to house all of us, with enough separation to ensure privacy, but still enabling my grandkids to grow up close to their granddaddy. A year and a half later, on December 13, 1984, my second grandkid, Peter Sam, was born. Two years later, Anita asked me what I thought about their adopting a third child, guaranteeing, as it were, that it would mean having a girl. "Fine with

246

me," I said. But lo and behold, as if by magic, a week later Anita found herself pregnant. And on April 25, 1987, I had a grand-daughter — Elisa Nicole was born.

In preparation for this family expansion, I asked two comrades, carpenter Davey Matsoukas and plumber Russell Phillips, to create a studio apartment in the basement of our house, freeing space on the first floor to house the three children. Anita would bring the 6-month-old little girl

At the Caref family summer cottage near South Haven, Michigan

to lie on the rug in my studio, and she lay there without a peep, while Anita took Eli's two brothers to a neighborhood day-care center.

I shared their young lives, eating dinner with them four nights a week, playing games and attending their shows in their elementary school, P.S. 254. I was always amused when I took them to the Liberty Science Center in New Jersey and young Peter ran immediately to the gift shop looking for a souvenir, while Kevin scolded him, saying, "Peter, you can't expect Grandpa to spend all this money on stuff you want."

We had great times visiting Toni and Andrea's country house, where I schooled them on how to best win at Monopoly (the "orange" property was the key); on our way to the country house, I always pointed out the "Happy House" — a barn whose lights would shine to spell out that greeting. During the winter, we played in the snow, went tobogganing, sliding downhill on a round red disk, and played hide-and-seek in the many hiding places among the loads of rooms in that large house.

When Anita began teaching a night class in ESL to Haitian immigrants, I prepared dinner; they got a big kick out of their cat "Titi" scurrying up on the counter upon hearing the noise of my cutting the meat with the electric knife; he would sit up next to me and tap me on the arm, requesting a morsel.

In 1999, when an older person close to the family died, the three kids were worried, asking me, 69 at that time, "Grandpa, you're not going to die?" "No," I replied, not thinking what might come next, "I'll be around for another 35 years." They immediately figured out that meant I would last until I was 104. I asked Kevin how old he would be then. "Fifty-one," he said. As a teenager, he couldn't conceive of ever being that age. However, now that I'm approaching 90, they're still holding me to that 104.

That was the year that I ran the New York marathon, and the kids were all there to greet me on Fourth Avenue in Brooklyn, taking pictures and handing me water, before sending me on my way.

When my grandchildren attended Murrow High School in Brooklyn, I never missed, and thoroughly enjoyed, their roles in various musicals and plays. Kevin appeared in nine, including as Oliver in "Oliver Twist." Eli operated behind the scenes in production work, and danced in a chorus role.

I've always depended on the kids' computer expertise. Whenever I got stuck on something, they would either walk me though it over the phone or explain it to me in person at my computer. Eli and Kevin rewired my entire set-up, which was so entangled that their stepfather Doyle was worried it might start a fire.

I guess a highlight of the kids' exploits on my behalf was their participation in organizing a surprise party marking my 80th birthday [See "Surprise! Gotcha!"] Not to be the last party, when I reached 88 they burst into my apartment on May 2, 2018, shouting "Surprise!" carrying loads of food and a birthday cake. Shortly before this event, they organized "Monopoly evenings," coming to my apartment to have dinner and playing our favorite board game.

These are only some of the group memories I can recall. They take me back to my first reaction when I learned of my wife Esther's death: that she would not be alive to enjoy her grandchildren, which she had so been looking forward to (Anita was in her fifth month of pregnancy with Kevin at the time). It is with much sadness that I think of all these joyous moments she could have shared with me. But now I want to recapture many of the memories associated individually with each of these great grandkids.

ELI

I am so thankful that many of the moves that granddaughter Eli has made in her life have been partly motivated by her desire to be close to me. For her college Labor History class, focused on oral histories, she interviewed me about my experiences when working on the railroad and wrote a paper on it (got an A in the class). She then presented that paper with her professor on a panel at the 2009 Labor and Working-Class History Association Conference in Chicago.

That interview was filled with a lot of my communist politics and while Eli never joined PLP, based on her family influences and her own sharp thinking, she regards herself as a communist and has imparted those politics to many of her friends.

When applying to colleges for her Masters degree, Eli chose New York University because she would be living in New York and would be able to visit me often. And during those eighteen months she did just that. When I was traveling on vacations, she came to my apartment to water my plants and helped them stay alive. But Eli has outdone me in the traveling department, however, having already been to fifteen countries, and, now, at only 32 (she still looks like 21 to me), will doubtless be adding to that number.

Eli's life has been guided by her devotion to the environment and teaching others how to preserve it. She's a marine biologist. Her first job after getting her Masters was at The River Project on the Hudson River waterfront, as Director of Education. Currently she has a job as Director of Education at the Sarah Lawrence College Center for the Urban River at Beczak where she teaches about the water, animals and the history of the Hudson River. She also takes the kids out on the river with a 30-foot net to help catch animals.

She has had her own plot in a community garden near her apartment building, where she has planted various fruits and vegetables, depending on the season (and I'm brought some periodically). Eli has a keen understanding of the content of food, which she learned about as a health educator working in a health clinic, always pointing out what's healthy and warning about deceptive labels on food packaging.

I had told Eli about the group my late partner Vera belonged to, Genesis Farm, about a mile from her home in Blairstown, N.J. It's somewhat centered on protecting the environment, among other things, using solar panels, along with actually running an organic farm and promoting local farming. It intrigued her, so Vera invited her to spend a weekend there. Vera served a delicious dinner and took Eli out to the farm where she actually slept that night, returning to Brooklyn the next day.

In April, 2018, Eli had her first peer-reviewed paper — in which she was the lead author — printed in the Journal of STEM Outreach, Vol. 1, No. 2, April 2018, entitled, "If You Give a Kid an Oyster: Reflections on Collaborations in Place-Based STEM Education Through Oyster Restoration Science in New York City." It dispels the Dead River Myth that "the Hudson River is so polluted that nothing could possibly live there. In reality, the estuary is thriving, and The River Project, a marine science field station [where Eli worked] in lower Manhattan exists to showcase its vast biodiversity through place-based education...."

The paper proves that "the Hudson River and New York Harbor are experiencing an ecological revival, with a multitude of native species returning to and proliferating in its waters." The goal of the Project is to help middle-school teachers to bring the "locally relevant topic of oyster restoration into their classrooms." Exposing my ignorance, as a lifelong New Yorker, I never even knew there were oysters in the Hudson. All hail to Eli!

Eli played a crucial role in setting me up to be surprised when the family organized my 80th birthday celebration. [See 80th Birthday story: "Surprise! Gotcha!"] I took her and Vera out to brunch that day, thinking it was to be a surprise birthday party for Eli (whose birthday falls a week before mine) when their aim was to keep me away from the house while the celebration room was being set up. Eli and Vera walked behind me towards the building. Then, as we entered the community room, with the crowd screaming "Surprise!," I turned to Eli exclaiming, "Gotcha!" But she turned to me saying, "No, Grandpa, I got you!" That devil!

I should mention that Eli has a very personable boyfriend, Pascal, who just successfully defended his PhD. thesis about the history of South Lebanon and is a mean Monopoly player to boot.

I'll never forget the message Eli once left on my answering machine saying she was so happy I was her grandpa, a message I kept playing over and over again. This granddaughter has made me one happy grandpa.

KEVIN

July 22, 1983, marked one of the more significant changes

in my life — I became a grandfather. That day Kevin, my first grandchild, was born, and so began decades of memories, embracing a brother and sister to follow, that have enriched my life in ways that nothing else could match. From that day onward I have been carried along for 35 years to Kevin having achieved a doctorate in neuroscience and am now seeing him off to Alicante, Spain, under contract with that city's neuroscience institute. Wow!

As I said in my story about Kevin's mother Anita, when I got word she was on her way to the hospital in Chicago to give birth, I immediately hopped a plane to be there for the first two weeks of his life and help usher him into my world. I enjoyed rocking him to sleep in his carriage as he took his periodic naps. The closest ties began when Anita moved into my Brooklyn house, and he and I were in daily contact.

I particularly remember when my family was preparing a surprise anniversary party in our downstairs apartment for my friends Gertie and Gus, who lived upstairs in our shared two-family house. When we were ready, we sent four-year-old Kevin upstairs to ask them to come down. We told Kevin not to reveal that this was a surprise party. Up he went to tell them to "come downstairs to your surprise party."

In Kevin's earliest years, he seemed to be fascinated with being a classy dresser. He gladly inherited a tweed coat from Toni's grandson Anton, who was slightly bigger and had outgrown it. But then Kevin soon outgrew the coat so I went searching citywide for another in his size for his fifth birthday; I found one in Long Island City. At that age, he also insisted on wearing a sport jacket to school.

Soon Kevin was acting in plays in his elementary school, something he later pursued in high school. He became active in sports, and I would take him and his brother Peter to play baseball in the schoolyard.

In Kevin's freshman year at Murrow High School, he tried out for the chorus of "Oliver Twist," but his high-pitched voice (not having changed yet) led to his selection for the lead role of Oliver. I was amazed to hear the sound coming out of his mouth.

THEATER IN FLATBUSH

Fresh, High Energy *Oliver!* Here for 5 Shows

By Hillary Miller

A review of the current Players' Circle production of the Broadway musical *Oliver!* which opened today with shows through Saturday at the Joseph Arrabone Theatre at Edward R. Murrow High School here in Flatbush at Ave L and East 17th Street.

December 17, 1997. *Oliver!*, the fall musical production of the Players' Circle at Edward R. Murrow High School, directed and choreographed by Mr. Scott Martin, is not merely a production, it is an event.

Oliver! — adapted from Charles Dickens' classic, *Oliver Twist* — tells the story of a young orphan boy fending for himself in London, meeting colorful (and often dangerous) characters along the way.

Kevin Caref's wide-eyed Oliver in this production is innocent enough without the cloying naivete. His voice is sweet, high and clear. After Oliver has been sold by the orphan workhouse to Mr. Sowerberry, the Undertaker, Oliver sings "Where is Love?" and it is here that Caref establishes himself as an Oliver worthy of his rags. Oliver's search for a loving home and family has begun and Caref's warmth keeps us concerned the entire way through.

Soon after escaping from the Undertaker's home, Oliver is picked up, tired and hungry, by the Artful Dodger, played with astounding ease by Steven Pindwin. The Dodger's "Consider Yourself" cheers Oliver and, in the process, woos the audience. Pindwin's free-spirited, rousing and kind-hearted Dodger is one of the highlights of the show.

It is the Artful Dodger who brings Oliver to Fagin's kitchen where he meets a new cast of characters and learns the tricks of the pick-pocketing trade. The ever-amiable Roger Urksman thrills and delights as Fagin the ringleader. Urksman charismatically warbles out memorable tunes such as "Be Back Soon" and "You've Got to Pick a Pocket or Two" in his own quirky style. It is also here that we meet Nancy, who introduces us to life in the underworld tavern, played by graceful songbird Christine DiGuilmardo. Upon hearing the first line of the music hall number "Oom Pah-Pah," the strength and beauty of DiGuilmardo's voice reels us in; one finds oneself awaiting her entrance on stage, hoping the next number will be sung by her.

The ensemble does not disappoint, doing their part to carry the show with beautiful harmonies and lilltwine dance numbers. One moment they're a destitute pack of orphans drooling over hot sausage and custard, the next they're brightly-frocked townspeople hopping, skipping and playfully romping across the stage. The costumes for *Oliver!* are a sight to behold: even the worn and dirtied rags that adorn the orphans seem suited to theatrical perfection.

As soon as the curtain opens, the first glance at the set tells us exactly what we're in for. Ms. Allison Oaker's set design captures industrial London's dreariness through simple design and a mix of blues, purples and browns. The set is at once fun and highly functional one, complete with boxes, barrels, benches and arched bridge upon which the electric cast of *Oliver!* jumps, runs, hides and gabs.

The energy of this production of *Oliver!* stays at a constant high as a result of the talented and water-tight cast, the subtle lighting which eases us from scene to scene, and the phenomenal orchestra which provides the backbone for the entire show, breathtakingly powerful at times and welcomingly understated at others.

This Players' Circle production of *Oliver!* has heart, soul and spirit, retelling the tale of good versus evil in an undeniably entertaining way. The production is fresh and energized, all parts culminating into a powerful and masterly created musical event.

"Consider Yourself" says the Artful Dodger (Steven Pindwin), right, to Oliver (Kevin Caref).

Oliver learns "You've Got to Pick a Pocket or Two" from Fagin (Roger Urksman).

Kevin's "wide-eyed Oliver…"

A rave review in a local paper: "Kevin Caref's wide-eyed Oliver…is innocent without the cloying naiveté. His voice is sweet, high and clear…. Oliver sings 'Where is Love?' and… Caref establishes himself as an Oliver worthy of his rags…. Oliver's warmth keeps us concerned the entire way through." Throughout high school he appeared in nine productions — plays and musicals — which led me to ask him if he wanted to pursue an acting career. "Not really," he replied.

Kevin went on to college at the State University in Binghamton, N.Y., studying computer science, which possibly laid the groundwork for his later studies. He spent one term studying in England, enabling him to travel in nearby Western Europe. By his mid-twenties, Kevin had decided to become a neuroscientist and entered a PhD. program at Einstein College of Medicine in the Bronx, which lasted about seven years. As he neared the finish line, I asked him about the subject of his doctorate. He explained: "You know when you sometimes finish a meal and feel satisfied, but then someone puts down a dessert or some other addition in front of you, and even though you're full, you then fill yourself with something more? Well, there's something in your brain that can trigger that readiness to put some more sugar and/or fat into your system. I'm trying to discover what that mechanism is."

I marveled at what that could produce for the general populace. I told him, "You could solve the overweight/obesity problem in one fell swoop!" When he defended his thesis, the entire family attended the public segment, while Peter recorded it all on his smart phone for me to view on my computer.

During this time Kevin would often come to my apartment to help me with my computer problems, which he usually solved in minutes. When I was lying in bed following the procedure that treated my heart attack, Kevin came to my bedside to chat for hours that afternoon. Somewhere along the line, he met Crystal, a young woman who became his girlfriend. They are now formally engaged and are living in Alicante, Spain, where Kevin has taken a position as a neuroscientist. They reside in a three-bedroom apartment overlooking the Mediterranean Sea. Naturally, the whole family is already descending on Alicante.

Besides his neuroscience expertise, Kevin has become an accomplished cook and a talented "fixer" in my apartment. He raised the height of the seat on my electric scooter, enabling me to get up more easily. And recently he performed some magic on my recliner, which I use at least three hours every night. It changed my life. A part containing four connecting wires had come apart. Kevin rewired them until a new part was to be sent (which never happened), but I was able to use the recliner until delivery of a new one. That was a lifesaver.

I could never have imagined when I was rocking that week-old baby to sleep 35 years ago that he would be "rocking" his 88-year-old grandpa in his golden years.

PETER

Peter Sam came into this world on December 13, 1984. I eventually nicknamed him "the personality kid" — his liveliness carried him traveling and working in country after country, making friends wherever he went. It has been difficult for me to keep up with him. Peter's early years were described in the initial segment of this story. While at the State University of New York in Binghamton where he obtained his undergraduate degree, he spent his junior year in Salamanca and Alicante, Spain, taking an intensive five-day-a-week course learning Spanish.

That prepared Peter for the three years he lived in Barcelona, from 2011 to 2014. There he worked in a travel and tourism agency and organized night-life tours for visitors. His sister and brother made stopovers to see him on trips to Europe. In 2013, I joined our whole family to visit him and met many of his friends while also seeing the sights.

Photo by Peter Caref
Peter hosts the family in Barcelona

In 2015, Peter was "on the road" again, traveling to Nicaragua and then to Guatemala, where he stayed with a friend while working in marketing and also as a bartender. The following year, it was back to Chicago where his mother and stepfather live, while he earned a living selling memorabilia outside the Cubs' Wrigley Field for an outfit owned by his cousin Jason. In 2017, Peter finally made it back to the Big Apple, and during this time we've really became close.

Recently, Peter had a back operation. Before that he had been working two jobs, one part-time for a film production company — operating a teleprompter for a documentary on the Museum of Natural History — and another one attached to a real estate firm. Over this past year and a half, Peter has been coming to my place virtually on a weekly basis. We've been eating dinner together and talking about what's going on in our day-to-day lives. Most of the time he solves a problem I'm having with my computer. Whenever I need immediate advice on a computer glitch, he walks me through it over the phone. He's become very knowledgeable about eating the right kinds of food and clues me in on that, too.

Recently Peter came up with the idea of "Monopoly night": arranging with Eli, Pascal and Kevin to come to my apartment to have dinner and play the game. All this helps fill my days and nights with a companionship that otherwise would be lacking, especially since my partner Vera has died.

Peter is very cognizant of my disabilities. Once when he was sleeping here for a couple of nights, I fell and awakened him to help me get up off the floor (which the weakness in my legs prevents me from doing). During another fall, when he was at Kevin's place, I called him in the wee hours of the morning and he came immediately to help me once again. When, at a friend's suggestion, I contacted the Mayo Clinic in Minnesota to inquire whether they could do something about my myositis disease — which, if so, would require a trip to their hospital which I couldn't make alone — he told me, "Don't worry, Grandpa, whenever that might happen, I'll take you there."

Many of Peter's recent visits have occurred while he's been slowly recovering from his back operation but that hasn't stopped him from visiting his grandpa and together enjoying delicious "take-out" dinners.

Over the past year, Peter has made a real difference in my life. He's helped me overcome many of the hurdles that afflict me on a daily basis. He's what one would call a real "*mensch*."

The Joys of An
Extended Family

Little did I realize that my marriage to Toni would enlarge my family with five wonderful additions: her daughter Andrea, son Zak, son-in-law Jerry, and grandchildren Isa and Anton, all of whom helped make my "golden years" a lot more golden.

The first garbage at the country house.

Actually I had known Andrea before I met Toni [see story on "My Love Affair with Toni], Andrea having worked on our PLP newspaper *Challenge*. A year after Esther died, I remembered her having introduced me to her friend Toni several years earlier. This led me now to ask Andrea for Toni's number and get her encouragement to call her mother. So began a path down my extended family.

We spent many delightful years together, especially in the country house Toni and Andrea

258

had bought in the Catskills. There it was that we spent hours playing games — teaching my new grandkids how to win at Monopoly — watching Isa enact plays with her friends, taking care of the gardens, flowers and backyards, eating the fresh fish that Anton and Zak caught in a nearby stream, being hypnotized by the flames of the woodstove fire and enjoying the inevitable holiday celebrations.

It was in recent years that this family — along of course with my own children and grandkids — played such a meaningful role in easing me through various disabilities that began to affect my life. As my myositis was to limit my walking and eliminate my driving and consequent independence, [See story, "How Myositis Has Not Stopped Me from Living My Life] the members of my extended family stepped up to help in innumerable ways. Not just Andrea and Jerry visiting me for dinners in nearby restaurants or ordering "take-outs" but also Jerry driving me to various doctor and dental appointments, Andrea's regular phone calls checking up on my condition, Isa and Anton coming to my apartment joining Eli, Peter and Kevin for "grandchildren dinners" — all this helped make my life complete in the face of my restricted activities.

Probably the most crucial intervention came when I awoke at 4:30 A.M. on New Year's Day, 2018, with a tightening in my chest, perspiring and with a weakening in my body. I left my bed to rest in my living-room recliner but finally at 6:30 called Andrea and Jerry to describe these symptoms. They immediately said it sounded like I was having a heart attack and should go to the ER immediately. I called Med Alert and they had the EMS come to my house to take me to the nearest hospital.

It turned out they were right; a medical team examined me, diagnosed heart failure, and unblocked my arteries. The operating doctor told me that if I had waited another hour or two, it would have been too late. So my stepdaughter and her husband helped save my life, and I am still here to continue writing these tales.

I am proud of the achievements the members of my extended family have made in their lives. Andrea has become the vice-president of her union — the Professional Staff Congress at the City University of New York and is engaged in signing up new dues-paying members. Jerry, a history professor at John Jay College, has co-authored several books with his brother-in-law on the effects of asbestos, lead and other work-place contaminants affecting workers' lives. He continues to give expert testimonies on behalf of workers who have sued their employers for having hidden the diseases contracted at their workplaces. They are writing an exposé of Monsanto's dumping of cancer-causing PCBs into West Coast waterways and will be writing another article proposing that company executives be tried for murder or manslaughter for policies that lead to workers' deaths. Granddaughter Isa is pursuing a PhD. in political science and is mentoring undergraduates who are aiming for graduate studies. And grandson Anton: — who hopped into an ambulance taking me to the ER where he attended to my various needs, and as a tennis player hitting a wicked serve eluding me, unable to return it — has become an accomplished chef at various restaurants.

As you will have read in other stories, my immediate family — Anita, Andrew, Doyle, Eli, Peter and Kevin — was essential in helping me live a normal life in my later years, fulfilling similar roles as my extended family, including accompanying me to doctors' appointments and hospitals, asking vital questions, making suggestions that improved my daily life and ensuring I received appropriate treatments [also see the story of my years with my partner Vera].

All told, I have been extraordinarily blessed with these loved ones surrounding me. *A La Familia!*

26.2 Miles! — Are you kidding?

While I had been jogging regularly since 1983 as a way to occupy my mind shortly after Esther died, I had never thought of running a marathon. It was one thing to run on a nice flat surface in the park across from my apartment five miles a day, maybe five times a week. But to do those 25+ miles all in one afternoon? Not....

In November 1998, Toni's daughter Andrea was about to run her third marathon, and the course took the runners north up First Avenue in Manhattan. At the time, Toni's cancer was closing in on her and she was a patient in Sloan-Kettering Hospital at East 68th Street off First Avenue. Andrea had asked me to wait with some bottled water on that corner when she passed by. I went up to Toni's bedside to tell her and show the poster I had made: "GO ANDREA! —TONI AND WALLY." Although Toni was filled with morphine and barely awake, she read it and smiled.

I went back to the corner of First and 68th and sure enough there came Andrea, sighting my poster and smiling. She then said to me, "Next year you'll do the marathon!" I told her she was nuts.

A few days later, Toni died. The fact that our last contact was one over that poster which she was able to recognize is a memory that has stayed with me. I guess at that point I sort of — only sort of — vowed to myself that I might enter the following years's marathon.

When application time came, I submitted mine to the NY Road Runners Club and actually won a place in the 1999 Marathon. (I then realized I would be 69 but was aware that plenty of runners were in their 70s, 80s and even 90s.) I followed the Club's practice guide and in May of 1999 began running (jogging?) five days a week. The plan called for five to ten miles a day five days a week. It also scheduled 20 miles three times in the next five months. I would do it by breaking it up into four 5-mile sections, resting in between. Then I thought that if I could do 20 miles, I might very well be able to do 26.

Photo by Kevin Caref

My family greeting me.

I had a T-shirt made depicting the faces of Esther and Toni to wear during the run, figuring it would help inspire me to finish. The first Sunday in November came, and I joined a crowd of 32,000 runners on Staten Island; I met up with Andrea and she insisted on posting my name on the front of my T-shirt, but I didn't want to cover up the images of Esther and Toni so she pasted it on my back. We started out together but she ran ahead once we crossed the Verrazano Bridge into Brooklyn.

Soon I was loping along First Avenue and there waiting for me were family members, Eli, Anita, Peter, Kevin and Zak. A little further along the Avenue at 10th Street was friend Harvey. Thousands of spectators were cheering us on. As we ran up Lafayette Avenue, a band was playing, saluting us. I stopped every so often to drink water. Eventually, we moved into Queens and then turned up the Queensboro Bridge, headed for Manhattan and the Bronx. I never realized how steep that bridge was; after awhile I began walking until reaching the downhill side. I looked around and passing me were some paraplegics in wheelchairs! In Manhattan, up First Avenue, Andrea's husband Jerry hailed me, snapping pictures. Then, after reaching the Bronx, we turned and headed south to Manhattan and finally into the last lap through Central Park. There was son Andrew aiming his camera at his pretty exhausted father.

I was still jogging very slowly, but fast enough to pass several thousand runners who had been reduced to walking. Suddenly shouts of "Go Wally!" arose from the spectators. I realized that as I passed them, they saw my name on the back of my shirt where Andrea had pasted it. I kept raising my hand to recognize those who were cheering me on. I finally reached the finish line in the Park where the Club had set up cameras to automatically record each runner's final steps. (I have that picture framed on a wall in my bedroom, along with other mementoes, in my Marathon montage.)

As it turned out, about 30,000 runners finished ahead of me and about 2,000 behind me. My time (as recorded in the following day's NY Times) was 6 hours and 16 minutes. My legs were so tired I could barely walk the 20 blocks north to Andrew's apartment where I plopped down on his couch. But I was too tired to take the subway so I grabbed a cab to go directly to my

Brooklyn apartment. There I just lay awhile in a hot tub, thinking that Esther and Toni would have been proud. When friends would ask me when I was going to do it again, my consistent reply was this was "the first and last time."

Crossing the finish line!

Chapter Seven
Through the Decades

My Green Thumb

Throughout my first 68 years, using the phrase "green thumb" within the context of my daily life would have been unthinkable. During those decades, particularly in my first half century, a plant never appeared in any apartment in which I lived. My parents never brought any plants into the half dozen places in which I was raised, nor did I introduce them into the several apartments I rented for myself. It never occurred to my first wife Esther and me, throughout our married life, to bring plants into our various residences. This was also the case with Esther's parents, Ida and Sam. It seems plants were never a part of any of their lives, for reasons unknown to me — although they and my father were raised in the Ukraine, probably among peasants on farms.

However, greenery began to edge into our lives once we bought a two-family house jointly with our friends Gertie and Gus. Gus had always yearned to be a farmer, somewhat peculiar for someone raised in the tenements of the Bronx (or maybe because of that?). In any event, he was ecstatic when he saw the postage-stamp-size "backyard" behind our house. A garden was in his eyes. [See "My Friend Gus — A Man of All Seasons."] On top of all this, farmer Gus had more than half of his 24-foot front room populated with a variety of plants, which he would invite us to come and enjoy.

I became a part of Gus's farming ventures when one spring day he asked me to drive out to a stable on the Belt Parkway. Forever searching for ways to improve his crops, Gus had bought three 100-pound bags of horse manure to replenish his farm and wanted to load them into my station wagon to bring home. [That hilarious episode is recounted in "My Friend Gus, A Man for All Seasons."]

After Esther died in 1983, daughter Anita — then living in Chicago — decided to move back to Brooklyn (enabling Grandpa Wally to live alongside grandson Kevin), so we re-arranged the first-floor apartment, with me living in the front rooms. Anita hung some plants in the living room, so for the first time in my life I was walking past greenery every day on my way to the kitchen. And sometimes I would even help water the plants.

Soon plants and I drew even closer. In 1991, I moved in with Toni, who was to become my second wife. Toni's apartment had a terrace on which she had all manner of plants and herbs (the latter she used in cooking), plus a huge plant in the living room. Now the green stuff was staring me in the face — and filling my nostrils — 24/7. At one point, the one in the living room got so huge that Toni decided to donate it to the local library branch to place in their front window. But before that, she took some cuttings from it to grow a new plant. As it turned out I inherited the latter, which now occupies a spot near the windows in my living room, (more on that below). Unfortunately, my life-long separation from plants became evident when one week Toni went to visit her sister in Florida. Upon her return, she surveyed some of her drooping plants and angrily asked if I had watered them. Sheepishly I responded that I had never thought of it. "How could you not see they needed water?" she demanded. Obviously plant-watering was not quite yet part of my repertoire.

But slowly things were beginning to change. Toni and her daughter had bought a summer house in the country with a huge lawn that required periodic mowing. This became my job, first with an electric mower and then with a sit-down one. I was also given the task of using a gasoline-powered weed-whacker to clip the edges of the lawn as well as around the garden where Toni and son Zak and the rest of the family were growing a variety of vegetables. And then there was the time of the year when pails were attached to the trees from which maple syrup could be extracted. Gradually but surely the green life was enveloping me.

Against this backdrop, something we feared might happen came to pass. In November 1998, after having survived for thirty years, Toni died of cancer. I was now alone in a three-bedroom apartment with its terrace — alone but surrounded by plants. Andrea and Zak said to honor Toni, I had to keep the plants alive. "How" I asked. "I know nothing about their care."

"Not to worry," they said. They showed me what to do, how often and how much to water them, and what to feed them. So now my "green thumb" erupted. I followed their instructions, religiously watering and feeding and pruning. The following July, I was offered the two-bedroom apartment in which I've been living ever since. Naturally we moved the plants and placed them in the front of the living room near the expansive windows where the sunlight flooded in.

What we call the "big plant" (we still don't know its name) began growing and growing. From its initial four leaves it expanded to as many as 16, and became much larger in size. It was placed on a stool to be high enough to get the light through the windows but it became so heavy that it was in danger of toppling over. I had an idea, however. I then went to the park across the street and found three boulder-like stones which I put in my shopping cart and brought upstairs. I then placed the stones in the pot, propping up the leaves in such a way that the plant was balanced and no longer in danger of falling. I received much advice about turning the plant periodically so the leaves would grow in the opposite direction and balance themselves, but it had become too heavy to be moved. So there it stood, growing and growing. Son Andrew thinks it may eventually take over the living room.

In addition, I had two other unidentified plants not quite as large as the "big plant," but big enough to be admired, and a jade plant that I kept alive, faithfully spraying daily and watering two to three times a week, depending on the season. When vacations came, I arranged with neighbors to "exchange watering" — they would care for my plants when I was away and I would do likewise when they were on vacation. And in between, granddaughter Eli would come over to take on the watering task.

The "big plant" never stops growing.

Another turning point arrived in my plant-nurturing journey in the person of my companion Vera, who just happened to be a horticulturist/botanist/gardener extraordinaire. In addition to planting trees and gardens outside her house, she had 38 plants which were moved outside in the spring and back into her house in the fall. Every weekend that she came to my apartment, she examined my plants with a fine-tooth comb, pruning, watering when needed, repotting and replanting. When I accidentally tipped over the jade plant onto the floor, she pruned four remaining stalks and, through years of care, the plant grew back to its original size.

We went to nurseries to purchase pots, as well as rods. She showed me how to attach stretchable green tape to falling leaves, enabling them to grow upright. She instructed me how to adjust for the dryness in my overheated apartment to allow the plants to thrive. I have shelves on the wall near the plant section on which are pots and trays and spades and other plant tools. She impressed upon me the amazing natural ability of plants to use water and sunlight to reproduce themselves, and the value of having living things in my apartment.

As the weakness in my legs progressed, I was forced to take my hands off my walker to care for my plants. The danger of my falling increased. This problem was solved in February of 2017 when I contracted for two home health aides — Rema and Sondra — to perform all sorts of tasks that minimize my walking and therefore minimize my knee-buckling and falling. One of these tasks is spraying and watering the plants.

While I've tried to achieve many things in my life, I never dreamed I'd be living with a "floral section" and developing a green thumb as part of my daily life.

Thirty Years a Runner and Jogger — With a Trainer's Help

After my wife Esther died in February, 1983, I was searching for something to help me get through my grief. One idea I came up with was running, to occupy my mind — and as a welcome side effect, losing some weight; at age 53, I was tipping the scale way over-the-top at 174 pounds.

Conveniently, there was a quarter-mile cinder track at nearby Lincoln High School, a five-minute drive from my house. So in March of that year, I began setting out on that track before breakfast, five mornings a week. I was following an Air Force training routine and began by walking 20 laps, five miles a day. Within a few weeks I would alternate, walk a quarter-mile lap, then run a lap. After about four weeks, I was running the entire five miles. I would wear a stopwatch to time myself and found I could do five 7½-minute miles. Once, for the hell of it, I ran one mile as fast as I could and made it in 6½ minutes. But I continued doing the five miles, 7½ minutes each.

A humorous incident occurred one morning when I was out

on my run. The high school was having a fire drill, so several thousand students were directed outside to the grandstand bleachers, which faced one side of the track. I guess the students were bored so when they saw this graying oldster running past them, they started to clap in unison as I passed by. I was somewhat embarrassed, so I changed my routine and began stopping before reaching the stands, turned around, retraced my steps and completed my five miles in that fashion to avoid the students. Was I wrong?

After a little more than two months, combined with lowering my daily caloric intake, I discovered I had lost 25 pounds and my weight was down to 149! I was determined to maintain my running schedule no matter where I was. That summer when I visited my nephew Alec in Alpine, Texas, I kept it up. I continued this routine all through my fifties. In 1991, at 61, I moved into Toni's apartment in Brooklyn Heights, at the foot of the Brooklyn Bridge. There was a park with a 1.2 mile running path across from her building on Cadman Plaza, which enabled me to maintain my routine, doing three-to-five mile runs, three to five times a week.

At one point, the Parks Department began laying down a cork surface on that path, so during construction, I would run on the sidewalk surrounding the park, still maintaining my routine. When the cork surface was completed, it made the run much more comfortable.

In 1999, I decided to do the New York marathon. [See Marathon story, "26.2 miles! Are You Kidding?"] That involved a four-month training schedule, running five days a week, anywhere from 5 to 10 miles at a clip. (Had to do 20 miles, three times.) That summer, I spent a week visiting my friends Clare and Val Woodward in Garden City, Utah, a mountainous area in the northeast corner of the state. I was able to keep training, driving down to nearby Bear Lake and running around a surrounding park, one side of which ran along the lake. It was the most pleasing part of my training schedule.

When I took vacation trips with Toni, and later with Vera, throughout the West, I kept it up. I did my five miles, if not every day, at least every other day, around a lake in the Grand Tetons, near the Everglades in Florida and in the red rocks of Sedona, Arizona, among other places. When I went to my son's wedding in New Zealand, I continued jogging, in Auckland and Christchurch, and then on my solo trip into Australia, hit the trails in Sydney's parks and in Cairns near the Great Barrier Reef. As will be seen in my Marathon story, I did complete that torturous run/walk. The training had paid off.

It was then that I was told by my family doctor that I should adopt an exercise routine. When I arrived home from that visit my mailbox contained a card from a personal trainer — serendipity! He came to my apartment three times a week and put me through a variety of exercises. Soon afterwards he opened a studio in my neighborhood with all sorts of machines which really "exercised" me, again three times a week. It was there that I met Dina, one of his assistants, who became my long-time personal trainer.

Dina, my personal trainer –
and great friend

When the studio owner skipped town, Dina — who had a day-time job as a counselor in a middle school — offered to continue the exercises in my apartment every week. Among her several other clients, she said I was her favorite. But over and above the training, we became fast friends. Even today, when

273

my myositis ailment precludes these exercises at home, our friendship continues, and she periodically visits my apartment. Knowing about my Joe DiMaggio obsession, one year she presented me a really elegant DiMaggio All-Star jersey; when her birthday came, I reciprocated with my home-made key lime pies.

I maintained my jogging for most of the next decade through my seventies, but in later years I slowed down, began walking part of the way, and then, by my 79th year, all the way. It was then that my quads and knees began weakening and my present myositis disease, unknown to me at the time, was emerging, but not diagnosed until seven years later. By 82, I had to stop even a walking routine, and then began using a cane, and now a walker, to get around.

I still do ten leg exercises a day, three to four days a week, which hopefully will help slow down any further deterioration. What were the long-range effects of my running "career"? Possibly a positive outcome aerobically, but maybe not for my knees. In any event, I don't regret having spent those enjoyable years of training, running and jogging, in my neighborhoods and worldwide. I have been able to keep my weight down to around the high 150s, an absolutely positive result. And who knows. Maybe all those years of exercising will have helped me reach my 89th birthday this May.

Wally Plays the Numbers...and the Numbers Play Him

Back in the 1950s — when I started working as a freight handler on the B&O R.R. on Manhattan's west side waterfront — I first came in contact with the "numbers game." My family members were not gamblers, although my father did sometimes "play the horses."

For those few who are unfamiliar with this quest for quick cash — and this was long before the lotteries and off-track-betting — the set-up involved bookies offering 600 to 1 odds if you could pick the last three numbers of that day's local racetrack betting handle. That handle invariably would total hundreds of thousands; for instance, say that day's total was $452,879, so that day's number became 879.

At our workplace, a "runner" took your bet and number every day and would relay it to the bookie, who would collect all the money and then pay off the few (very few) winners. If you picked the winning number, a dollar would get you $600 (actually a net of $500 since a $100 "tip" went to the runner who took your number).

At the West 26th Street freight station where I worked,

Carmine Pirone was the runner. He toured the station every morning (maybe the railroad bosses got a cut to allow him to do this on company time) and picked up everyone's number and dollar. Of course, if you bet $5 or $10 and your bet won, your take was in the thousands.

I was intrigued by all this, watching fellow workers spending their hard-earned wages in the hope of "making a kill." They would go through all sorts of rituals to come up with a wining number. Dreams were a favorite; players would link a particular number to something they had dreamt about the night before. Or maybe it was their girlfriend's birthday that day. Or it was somebody's 20th anniversary.

People would go through all sorts of contortions to come up with a "good number." However, it was well-known among all the workers on my platform — for whom I was the shop steward — that I never played the numbers, so Carmine never approached me.

It was February of 1957 and my wife Esther was pregnant with our first child. She was due near the end of the month. Sure enough, our daughter Anita was born at 2:40 PM on the 27th, so I thought, Why not put a dollar on No. 240 that day? What the hell, in the eyes of my fellow workers this fit the ritual on placing a winning number, the time our child was born. I had fallen into the ritual's trap of thinking, We really could use an extra five hundred bucks with a new baby.

When I offered my bet to Carmine, he expressed shock and shouted out for all to hear, "Hey, everyone, guess what? Wally's playing the number!" This led many of them to think, "What could be a better sign than 240 that day?" Of course, 240 failed, along with thousands of other numbers, except one.

Years passed. On a broiling day in the first week of July, 1960, the guys said it was so hot you could fry an egg on the roof of our freight car. I was part of the usual gang of five unloading that car. Four were "stowmen," who did the physical unloading, two at each end of the car, plus a receiving clerk who would check off the various consignments listed on the manifest as they were being unloaded. On this occasion the foreman happened to assign the clerk's job to me.

To pass the time, the gang members were discussing, among other things, what number to play that day. As I checked off the manifest items, I listened to all the twists and turns they were going through to come up with a hoped-for winning number. Finally I couldn't resist joining the conversation, remarking how crazy I thought it was to plunk down their money on trying to pick one number out of thousands. "What kind of odds was that, a lot more than even 600 to 1?"

Then I said, "Look. To demonstrate the randomness of what you're trying to figure, let's look at today's month, July, the seventh month of the year. Now I'll count up the number of pages in the manifest, 12. So voila, that makes today's number 712."

Much to my surprise, and anguish, several of them said, "Great! Let's play it!" They spread the word to everyone within earshot: "Play 712!" And so they did, with the usual result.

One co-worker, Jackie Abair, told me I'd given him the clue. How? "July 12 falls next week. So that's the time to play 712." He played it every day that next week and wouldn't you know it, 712 came out! (Of course, unfortunately, I didn't follow my own "advice" and neglected to play it.) Jackie, now $500 richer, told me, "I'm treating you to dinner!"

My crazy theory had backfired. I had picked the winner. Word spread throughout the station, "Wally has the clue!" All week long guys came running up to me, asking, "Wally, what's today's number?" I was absolutely dumbfounded.

As it turned out, when Esther was pregnant with our second child who was due July 8, 1960, she was late. I announced that Andrew had "appeared" 12 days later, at 10:06 AM on July 20.

Since everyone knew that the only time I had ever played the number was the time of the day when my children were born, I couldn't avoid putting a dollar down on 106. However, my co-workers, wanting to be "sure" of their chances, played what was called "the box." That is, they played all the variations of 106: 601, 160, 061, and so on. Of course, none came in. I wasn't sure what to do, apologize for having given them the wrong pick, or gloat over the fact that my "theory" was correct.

Visits from "clue seekers" plummeted, marked by the fact that I was not at work, having planned my two-week vacation in order to stay home and help take care of the new baby. However, with no births on the horizon, it seemed my "numbering days" were over.

Mugged Three Times and Lived to Tell the Tale

New York City in the 1980s was all the rage with stories about muggings. Not having been mugged, I tended to dismiss the possibility of it happening to me. Was I ever wrong!

My first encounter occurred in broad daylight at four o'clock in the afternoon in Brooklyn on the corner of Church Avenue and East 18th Street. I had entered a phone booth — no cell phones in one's pocket in those days — to call my wife Esther's cousin Morty. Only a minute or so into the conversation a male voice behind me said, "Don't move!" accompanied by an object being stuck in my back. "I've got a gun!" the voice threatened. "Give me all your money."

I wasn't about to challenge this. Not turning around, I told Morty to "hold on a second" and drew my wallet out of my back pocket, handing him all the bills therein, maybe about forty dollars. During all this, I noticed a guy at the corner waving in our direction, seemingly a confederate giving him the "all clear." As he turned and ran off, Morty kept jabbering away with no response from me. Finally I told him what had been going on, which, of course, he couldn't believe. But I had escaped unscathed.

I had now become a New York mugging victim. For a while I became a little more cautious as I walked the streets, but my next encounter occurred in an elevator, not out in public.

I had come from a downtown Brooklyn Western Union office, having collected $800 in cash, a donation sent from Houston by a PLP member, and was taking it to a comrade in a Crown Heights apartment house across from the Brooklyn Museum. I parked my car about a block away and was about to leave with the cash when a thought struck me. I remembered my recent daytime mugging, and now it was nighttime. Not wanting to chance it while walking to the nearby building, fortunately (as it turned out) I shoved the bills and my wallet underneath the driver's seat, locked the car and left. Entering the building's elevator, I pressed the 8th-floor button and the elevator started moving, but suddenly stopped at the second floor: the door opened and a desperate-looking youth, about 18, entered, flashing what seemed like a pocket knife, and demanding "all your money."

I immediately regretted not having taken a $20 bill out of my stash in the car. I told the young robber, "I have no wallet, only loose change." He looked at me in disbelief and felt my back pocket for a wallet, and realized I had told him the truth. He reached in my front pocket and withdrew about 60 cents. Flustered, and seeing the 8th-floor button lit up, he pressed the 10th-floor button, not thinking I would stop at the 8th floor anyway. He fled, the door closed and the elevator stopped at eight. I went to my comrade's apartment where he saw the jittery look on my face. When I told him the story, his wife remarked that something like that had never happened to them in their building.

My comrade accompanied me down to my car, I retrieved the eight hundred bucks — along with my wallet — and gave him the money (which he would deposit in the organization's bank account).

Having preserved the cash, I had escaped mugging Number Two injury-free.

Now comes the one that tops them all.

One November night around 6:00 pm my second wife Toni and I were driving in uptown Manhattan, headed to a friend of hers in the Bronx who had offered me some videos of Mets baseball classics. Toni said she didn't want to go up empty-handed and asked me to stop at the corner of 96th Street and Broadway to pick up some flowers at a florist around the corner.

I parked on Broadway in front of a bus stop and waited in the car while she went to buy a bouquet. We were on the Upper West Side at a very busy time, with crowds of pedestrians on the streets. Suddenly the passenger door opened and I thought it might be one of the many people I knew who lived in that neighborhood and had spotted me in the car. But much to my shock it was a stranger who sat down, closed the door, put a long knife to my throat and demanded all my money. It was dark and no passers-by noticed what was happening.

Again, I was not about to challenge him, with the point of that knife on my throat. I told him I would reach across my body and get my wallet out of my rear left pocket, but he stopped me and said he would get it out himself. (Maybe he thought I'd pull something else out — a weapon?) He then took out the wallet and stole all the bills, about $80. Meanwhile, Toni had returned from the florist and saw this guy getting out of the car. She later told me she thought it might have been a friend of mine from the neighborhood, and figured I would introduce him. Of course, the guy ran off.

I explained the whole incident to Toni. She examined my neck, which was unscathed, and we took off to the Bronx, where I did get my videos. We were both relieved that it had only cost me eighty bucks.

My three decades since then have been free of muggings.

"Parking" Across North America and Down Under

Who might have thought that half a century of visiting more than 50 National and Provincial Parks in Canada and the U.S. would lead to: contact with an astronaut and seeing the "moonscape" where astronauts trained; catching snakes in Texas; watching thousands of bats flying out of caves; enjoying an open-air Mexican folklore ballet; encountering bears and crocodiles; paddling down the Colorado River in a raft; bathing in hot springs; chatting with a Grouch Marx-loving state trooper; border interrogations about drug-trafficking; holding the Stanley Cup in the Hockey Hall of Fame; witnessing a lumberjack tournament; cooking fresh-caught live lobsters at our campsite, and countless other experiences a city boy from Brooklyn could never have imagined.

For the fifty years beginning in 1955, I was privileged to experience nature's wonders in these national parks in Canada and the U.S., along with trips to Puerto Rico's rain forest and a park near Darwin, Australia. These travels stretched countless miles

— driving in our own car and rented ones, in RVs and camping in tents — from Big Bend National Park on the Mexico-Texas border north to Algonquin Provincial Park in Ontario, Canada; from the Cabot Trail in Nova Scotia and Acadia National Park in Maine westward to California's Redwoods; from the Everglades in the southeastern tip of Florida northwest to Vancouver, British Columbia on the Pacific Coast. And so many of the visits had their own distinctive stories.

Initially, Esther and I got a taste of some of these magnificent vistas on our honeymoon in October of 1955, driving west in our '54 Chevy convertible to reach our destination — stone benches in an open-air theater in the Red Rocks of Boulder, Colorado. This trip triggered a desire to savor the natural beauty of what the continent had to offer. I was to make three or even four trips to many of these parks, first with Esther and our two children, sometimes also with our friends Gertie and Gus Kaplowitz and their kids, sometimes with Esther's sister Jean and her husband Joe, later with second wife Toni, then with companion Vera and some just alone.

THE JOURNEYS BEGIN

In the spring of 1958, my in-laws Ida and Sam (who had never been beyond New York's Catskill Mountains), Esther and I, with 15-month Anita in tow, headed for the west coast. After touring the San Francisco Bay area, we drove down to Yosemite, Kings Canyon and the Sequoias where we motored through a "tunnel" in one of the towering redwoods, the oldest living things on the continent. From there it was east, stopping in the Petrified Forest — where Anita began walking for the first time. Then onto the Mesa Verde Native American "apartments" carved out of mountainous rocks, where Grandma Ida (at 68!) scrambled up a stone ladder to enter one of the rooms. From there to Colorado and Rocky Mountain National Park, driving up onto Trail Ridge Road, more than 10,000 feet above sea level.

Two years later, after having borrowed a tent for a trip to Chenango State Park in upstate New York, we got the camping bug. We bought our own equipment and off we went to Acadia National Park in Maine, a place to which we would return four times. Driving back and forth along its rocky coast, we stopped to pick blueberries on what would become an island once high tide came in, after which we gorged ourselves on fresh-caught lobsters.

Our next trip took us to Canada, to New Brunswick and on ferries over to Prince Edward Island and then to Nova Scotia, where we drove up the Cabot Trail to its northern tip.

In 1974, we planned our first cross-country journey to Glacier N.P. in Montana, a three-day, 2,500-mile drive. Daughter Anita, 17, was working in a summer camp, but Andrew agreed to join us on one condition: that we visit the Hockey Hall of Fame in Toronto on the return home. Andrew had been an avid hockey player and NY Rangers fan since he was seven.

Momma, Poppa and son Andrew set out on the road, 14 hours a day, with me behind the wheel and Esther and our boy playing Monopoly to while away the time. We hiked trails in Glacier, which still had snow on its higher levels, with Andrew sliding down the mountain on a garbage-can cover. From there we crossed the border into Canada and Banff Provincial Park where we bathed in hot springs, temperature 105 degrees, a first for all of us. Then it was north through the Canadian Rockies on the Icefield Parkway — one of the most beautiful roadways we would ever experience — to Jasper Park, where elk and moose visited our campsite.

On our return, we kept our promise to Andrew, driving

through Canadian provinces until we reached Toronto and the Hockey Hall of Fame. We took pictures of Andrew and his heroes and one that Esther had never dreamed of: holding the Stanley Cup!

For the next three decades, I was to take in more than four dozen parks with my family, friends, Toni and Vera. Recounted below are only some of the unique experiences we observed on all these trips. The ones not mentioned include visits to Olympic, Mt. Ranier, Crater Lake, Death Valley, Arches, Canyonlands, Canyon de Chilly, Grand Tetons, Gina Cliffs, Guadeloupe, Badlands, Isle Royale, Indiana Dunes, Great Smokies,

Momma and son
with his trophy for Defenseman of the Year award

Shenandoah, Joshua Tree and Cascades National Parks and Dinosaur National Monument. Here I can recount only some of the highlights that were to cross our paths.

PICKING CHERRIES AND ENJOYING A BALLET IN THE MIDDLE OF A FOREST

It was the summer of 1976 when Esther and I left Salt Lake City in our rented auto and headed south for Bryce and Zion Parks with a one-night stop at Capital Reef N.P. On our way to our cabin, we saw a platform that had been laid down in the park upon which a group of dancers in native costumes was assembled. Here in this wilderness it turned out that the Mexican Folklore Ballet had come to entertain us in celebration of the U.S. Bicentennial!

After a most enjoyable concert, we noticed a grove of cherry trees in full bloom behind us. Since this was Esther's favorite fruit, I turned a picnic table on its end, climbed up and started picking dozens of lush cherries and throwing bags of them down to Esther's waiting arms. That night we gorged ourselves — Esther perhaps a little too much. She spent most of the night in the park's bathroom.

THE OTHER SIDE OF THE MOON

Travelling south from Zion, we reached the north rim of the Grand Canyon overlooking the Colorado River winding its way through the canyon's floor. We hiked several trails, most memorably on a night with a full moon, when the ranger guiding us said not to use our flashlights. He took us to a lookout several hundred yards down, our way lit only by the reflected light of the bright moon that flooded the area. The ranger asked if anyone knew what the other side of the moon looked like. Several campers attempted answers, but none came up with anything conclusive. Then a fellow in the back proceeded to give a meticulous description of the moon's side we couldn't see. The ranger asked how he knew such details. "Because I was there," came the reply, which wowed everyone. Turns out he was Frank Borman, one of the astronauts whose spacecraft was the first one to orbit the moon, see the other side and then return safely to Earth.

WE "SEE" THE OTHER SIDE OF THE MOON

As close as one might ever get to such a sight was the trip Vera and I made into the Craters of the Moon Park in southern

Idaho. The name is an apt description of the park's surface, billed as a "moonscape," so similar to the Earth's moon that the astronauts — who were later to land on the moon — trained there to familiarize themselves with what they would later encounter. With my shaky legs I wasn't about to risk walking on the rocky surface, but Vera was ready to brave it, accompanied by the ranger, reaching the end of the trail and coming back.

PARIS ON THE RIVER!

Toni and I had never been on a raft so we decided it was time to try. We signed up with a guide and a half dozen others to take a short trip down the Colorado River. The guide instructed us how to maneuver ourselves to keep the raft balanced. About half way through, the guide moored the raft alongside a huge flat rock at the side of the river and hauled a huge ice chest out of the raft onto the rock. It was lunch time! We soon discovered it was a Parisian gourmet meal! Out came paté, a crisp French baguette and an assortment of fresh cheeses, meats and wine. I asked what had led her to serve such a spread. "I'm from Manhattan's West Side," she replied. How did she get from there to guiding raft trips here? "My boyfriend has been a guide for years and he convinced me to try it. Now it's how I make a living."

THE FLIGHT OF A MILLION BATS

One of the more extraordinary natural sights I've ever seen occurred on a trip that my nephew Alec took me to Carlsbad Caverns in New Mexico. The roof of the Cavern's cave is a sanctuary for one million Mexican freetail bats. They migrate annually from Mexico to raise their young. Here as many as 300 bats crowd together in one square foot on the cave's ceiling.

We were seated at sunset in an open-air amphitheater facing the mouth of the cave when suddenly a gigantic swarm of as many as a million bats emerged from the cave and blackened the sky, an exodus that can last up to two and one-half hours. Every day they leave their young on a flight throughout the night to forage for insects in the Pecos and Black River valleys. They then return at dawn to the cave to gather at the ceiling and feed their young, where they remain until the next sunset to repeat their daily pilgrimage, throughout the year.

Nature certainly produces some remarkable spectacles...

FURNITURE-MAKING AMONG YELLOWSTONE'S BEARS

We were camping in Yellowstone N.P. with our friends Gertie and Gus and their kids, when Gus saw a lot of dead birch-tree branches scattered on the forest floor.

So Gus — having brought a bunch of tools from home — set about sawing and nailing and constructing a set of chairs and a long table out of the branches [See Story "My Friend Gus — A Man for All Seasons"]. While their daughter Rena was hanging up some clothes to dry, a bear appeared on the other side of the line. "Bear!" she shrieked. Gus, ever ready, grabbed a hammer and started banging it on the newly-made table. Soon the bear stalked off, to be captured by the rangers and returned to its forest habitat.

A HELICOPTER RESCUE FROM EL CAPITAN

While driving through Yosemite N.P., Toni and I stopped when we saw a crowd gazing up at the 3,000-foot ascent of the vertical rock formation known as El Capitan, a favorite of rock climbers. There we witnessed a remarkable rescue by park rangers.

Sitting on a tiny ridge half way up El Capitan were two climbers. As it happened one of them had sprained an ankle and couldn't move, up or down. Soon a helicopter containing a rope ladder with a stretcher at the bottom hovered into view and maneuvered alongside them. A ranger climbed down the ladder to the stretcher and signaled to the copter's pilot to move the ladder to within arm's length of the trapped climber. He reached out and managed to swing the injured climber into the "bed." The pilot slowly pulled the two "passengers" up to the door of the copter and safely inside. From there the injured climber was flown to the nearest hospital emergency room. (We later learned that the Park charged him for the cost of the rescue.)

THE SNAKE-CATCHER

When my nephew Alec and I were returning from Texas's Big Bend N.P. late one afternoon, he suddenly stopped the car, exclaiming, "This is it!" "What?" I asked. "The time of the day when the snakes come out on the road, where the surface is warmer than the bordering grass." Ever since he was three years old, Alec had always been fascinated by snakes, often drawing them, and later in college, seeking an all-purpose serum to treat snake bites. So sure enough, there was a snake sunning itself in front of our car. Whipping out his trusty snake bag, Alec wound the reptile around a long pole and deftly stuck it in the bag, sealing it inside. As I kept furtively glancing at the bag on the back seat, the captured snake accompanied us back to Alec's house.

THE TROOPER WHO LOVED GROUCHO MARX

Anita and I were on our way from Gary, Indiana, driving Anita's brother-in-law Shelley's yellow van to meet up with Esther, her sister Jean and Jean's husband Joe, all of whom had flown into Calgary, Alberta from New York to join us on our way to Canada's Banff Provincial Park. Unfortunately Shelley had been in the process of renewing the vehicle's registration and was supposed to mail it back to Esther before she left Brooklyn. So we were driving with the expired one, through several Canadian provinces, and decided to be very careful, respecting the speed limits and avoid being stopped by any cops.

Lo and behold, in Manitoba we saw flashing lights behind us and got pulled over by a Royal Canadian Mounty, even though we were definitely driving within the speed limit. He asked us politely to get into his car, asked our names, where we had come from and where we were headed. He never mentioned why he had stopped us nor even asked for our registration and driver's licenses. He kept poking into his police radio while starting a meandering conversation which began touching on TV shows. He suddenly asked if we ever watched the Groucho Mark quiz show "You Bet Your Life." I said I did, all the time. "Me too," he said, "and I love it," launching into some of Groucho's jokes from the show.

We were bewildered at all of this but maintained our calm. Suddenly a voice came on the police radio and the trooper responded to the message. We finally found out why we had been stopped. It seemed that a family back in Indiana had been hospitalized and was trying to notify relatives driving in Canada in a yellow van with Indiana plates. The trooper apologized to us, saying obviously we were not the people he was looking for. We breathed easy and went on our way, after being entertained by a Groucho-loving trooper.

DRUG TRAFFICKERS?

When our crowd was camping in Banff, Anita and I had to drive down into Montana to pick up Anita's first husband Ben, who was returning from National Guard training in Georgia. He was wearing his service fatigues and sporting a bald head. As we approached the Canadian border, we were stopped by custom agents holding legal-size pads of paper and told to get out of the car. We couldn't figure out the reason, but I told Anita and Ben we should be certain to tell the truth about how we happened to be there, so if they compared our stories there'd be no contradictions.

As we later discovered, they were searching for drug traffickers and our appearance, especially Ben's, seemed to fit the bill. After they searched our van, we were separated and each of us interrogated by a border agent. We were all asked the same questions, and fortunately gave the same answers. The three agents then compared notes and after about an hour, we were sent on our way, escaping the drug war on the border.

RIVER-BOATING AND BIRD-WATCHING AMONG THE CROCODILES

In 2002, after attending my son Andrew's wedding and touring New Zealand, I vacationed in Australia, flying north to Darwin and taking in Kakadu National Park, a World Heritage site. There we fed some kangaroos and koala bears. While on a river cruise, we marveled at upwards of 60 exotic bird species flocking the shorelines — egrets, sea eagles and five varieties of kingfishers, among others. The guide warned us to keep our arms inside the boat's railings to ward off any salt water crocodiles that frequented these waters, and we did see quite a few jumping above the surface. We had read in a local paper that the previous week a tourist had ignored signs cautioning against swimming in the area. The result: she was swallowed whole by giant crocodile! That was enough to heed the guide's warning.

In the middle of the river, the guide docked the boat near a large, flat rocky area. We disembarked and were treated to a delicious lunch (no crocodile meat!), cooked to perfection on an outdoor grill, capping off a unique trip.

A MIRACULOUS ESCAPE SENDS US ON A TOUR OF SEDONA AND HOME

Traveling east from Los Angeles to Phoenix in our rented 26-foot RV, Toni and I were saved by our safety belts. Toni happened to be driving at the time, going about 50 miles an hour when we felt a bump on the RV's rear end. It swerved to the left and then to the right as Toni tried to straighten it out. But it was impossible. We had been hit in the back by an 18-wheeler. The RV turned over and then turned right-side up and slid down an embankment to the right. The windshield was smashed but our safety belts prevented us from crashing into it. I untied my belt and then Toni's and pulled her out from the driver's seat. We felt around and could not believe we had emerged without a scratch!

The trailer driver got out and came over to tell us that he thought we were about to turn onto a ramp on the right, which, of course, was not the case at all. Drivers on both sides of Highway 10 stopped and ran over to us, offering us towels and water, not believing we were uninjured. They called an ambulance, taking us back to a hospital in Phoenix where we were examined and pronounced fit. We rented a car, stayed in a motel overnight and the next day returned to where the RV had been pulled into a lot, retrieving our belongings. The RV was totaled. We looked up a lawyer to discuss a lawsuit. We were about to decide to fly home but called our daughters, both of whom suggested we spend another few days in a mountain region to relax before returning. So we traveled north to Sedona's Red Rock region where we walked through canyons and experienced galleries of southwestern and Native American art. Now we were ready to put the accident behind us and return to Brooklyn.

ENTERTAINED FOR TEN SUMMERS IN UTAH BY TWO DEAR FRIENDS

The year after Toni died, I met up with long-time friends Clare and Val Woodward. Both had been professors at the University of Minnesota, Clare of Chemistry and Val of Genetics. They invited me to spend an enjoyable week at their summer home in Garden City, Utah. We continued this tradition, sometimes with my partner Vera, every summer for the next ten years. Several of these trips included visiting national parks on the way to and from my friends' home. My first visit took place while I was training for the NYC marathon; I jogged daily around picturesque Bear Lake near their home.

Vera joined the Woodward clan at their Garden City retreat.

Vera and I stayed in a beautiful cabin adjoining my friends' main residence, with a deck overlooking Bear Lake. Our days and nights were filled with Clare's delicious cooking, heated Scrabble games, hikes through nearby hills and forests, and, perhaps best of all, stimulating and scintillating conversation about every subject under the sun (including a detailed discussion of the Mormon Church which Val had left as a teenager). Fortuitously Val suggested that PLP members write a history of our movement, an idea I brought back to New York and which our members have pursued ever since. The Woodward homestead was one of the most delightful "parks" in my treks across the West.

Whirling Around the World

After having already traveled across the U.S. and Canada, in December, 1982, Esther and I took off for Mexico City, where we took in the Diego Rivera and Siqueiros murals, the National Museum and the 700-year-old Chapultepec Park. We then went south to Puebla and Acapulco's beaches where soldiers with sub-machine guns were stationed among the tourists (a little disconcerting).

Toni and I took our first trip across the Atlantic to Amsterdam: the Anne Frank House, the Van Gogh and Rembrandt museums, the Edam and Gouda cheesemakers; then to Paris: the Louvre (see "A Picture of Love"), dining along the Champs Elysee, the view atop the Eiffel Tower. Our next trip, celebrating Toni's college graduation, started in London: the theaters (Agatha Christie, Les Miserables), Karl Marx's desk in the London Museum and his tomb in the High Gate cemetery, Stonehenge and the Bard's hangouts in Stratford-on-Avon. From there it was across the English Channel to Paris again, the Sorbonne and the Loire Valley.

In our last trip beyond the U.S., Toni and I spent a month in Puerto Rico in January, 1997, taking in the rain forest, lobsters in Ponce overlooking the Caribbean and the Arecibo Telescope

295

(see "Searching Outer Space"). I ran on the beach a block from our two-room/patio Hostal Costa de Oro in Santurce, all in sunny 82-degree weather.

My son's marriage in 2002 to a bride from New Zealand sent me flying across the Pacific to Auckland for their wedding on Waihekea Island off the coast. I then went on a trip to the South Island, where we flew in a 10-seat propeller plane (with me sitting next to the pilot as he made his way between the peaks) over the Alps to Milford Sound and the Franz Josef glacier.

On the way back to Auckland, I attended a Maori pageant and a 10-course feast, then flew to Sydney to get a flight to Darwin (107 degrees in the shade!) in the tropics on Australia's north coast — the closest I had ever been to the Equator. There I visited Kakadu National Park. Then it was off to Cairns and the Great Barrier Reef on the east coast, which included a ride in a mini-submarine that submerged among the numerous, wondrous sights of sea life. Returning to Sydney, I visited the Opera House, climbed the High Bridge and jogged in Hyde Park before returning to, yes, Brooklyn.

Finally, with Vera — after taking her to the National Parks she had never seen — it was again across the Atlantic to Paris, visiting her cousins and the elementary school where she had gone to kindergarten and first grade; taking the "bullet train" to a villa her friend owned in Provence; and an Elder Hostel trip in Italy touring Florence, Tuscany, and Pisa. We then drove north to the Alps to visit the house Vera's grandfather had built in the 19th century. We saw the grave of her grandmother in a cemetery surrounded by memorials to the Italian partisans who had fought the Nazis. Finally, the trip that topped them all: in 2011, we celebrated our 10th anniversary on the Orient Express from Paris to Venice to Prague and flew back for another week in Paris. [See story "Vera Completes My Life."]

In August, 2013, I was able to visit the beautiful city of

Barcelona in Spain, accompanying my family in my partially disabled state, taking in historical museums which honored the memories of the anti-fascist Spaniards and the international brigades who fought the fascist Franco. In February 2016, Vera and I went on a cruise to the Caribbean, to San Juan, Puerto Rico, and the adjacent islands.

Growing up in Brooklyn's Flatbush neighborhood, it would have been a wild dream to think I could ever eventually cross two oceans to plant my feet in over a dozen cities in nine countries on three continents — returning a little more worldly-wise to the Big Apple.

Chapter 7 - Through the Decades

Chapter Eight
The Twenty-First
Century

A "Radio Rookie" Jump-Starts My Memoir

My participation in a program sponsored by the New York City public radio station WNYC led to providing me with half the content of this memoir, some of which can be heard on WNYC's website (more of this later).

Back in 1999, my granddaughter Isa had a roommate, Kaari Pitkin, who was interning with the WNYC production of the "Radio Rookie" series, which included training for young people in interviewing others about their life experiences. Isa's roommate asked her if she knew a senior citizen who was loaded with stories and could be interviewed by one of their teenage

Recording at WNYC radio

"rookies."

"I've got just the guy for you," replied Isa, "my grandpa." Isa introduced me to Kaari who explained that one of their rookies, Kady Bulnes, was being guided to interview just such a senior. Kady was a high school student who had emigrated with her family from Honduras. So it was that Kady, accompanied by Kaari, spent tons of hours over several years, partly in my living room and partly in a WNYC studio asking me about my "life and loves." Part of this was recorded onto CDs which became very useful years later when I was beginning to write this memoir.

However, this was not a one-way street. Some of the time I interviewed Kady about *her* life, including when some of her experiences mirrored my own. This was especially true when we exchanged our emotions following the

Kady Bulnes in the WNYC radio studio

death of loved ones, in my case Toni (who died soon before these interviews began) and in Kady's case the death of her beloved grandmother.

This particular story can be heard on WNYC's website by googling <WNYC Wally Linder>. It is one of three stories they broadcast, two of which appear in these pages.

Kady's constant prompting triggered many of the memories I had long forgotten, which became so helpful in creating the foundation for this memoir. Kady was fascinated by descriptions of my family life, of my children and grandchildren, as well as of my communist politics and organizing. Kady said she had never met a communist before. "All I ever heard was that they were bad people," she remarked. "You are exactly the opposite!"

I am truly indebted to Kady and Kaari for drawing out of me the stories of my life, many of which comprise the content of this memoir. Kady is now a nurse in a Florida hospital and Kaari is now the senior producer of WNYC's "Radio Rookie" series.

A Jack of All Trades and Master of Many

When my daughter Anita married Doyle O'Connor on October 30, 2004, how could I have known that a combination electrician, plumber, carpenter, personal advisor, labor lawyer and arbitrator (am I forgetting something?) was entering my life? But I found out soon enough.

In the year 2000, Anita led the organization of the 25th anniversary celebration of PLP's Boston Summer Project, an action in 1975 that had challenged the racist attacks on Black workers and youth attempting to integrate the city's public schools. Anita had originally participated in the '75 Project that drove the racist ROAR fascists (Restore Our Alienated Rights) out of existence.

As the person responsible for the Party's work in trade unions, I had gone to East Lansing, Michigan, prior to the Summer Project, to meet with a group in the Student-Worker Union involved in campus union organizing. Some people in the group were PLP members, and one was Doyle. I suggested that the group participate in the Summer Project, which is how Doyle wound up in Boston, where he and Anita had first met. It took them 25 years to meet up again, at the 25th anniversary celebra-

302

tion, after both had divorced their previous spouses.

Anita and Doyle married four years later, which enabled me to benefit from Doyle's many talents. As an arbitrator, he got a position on a panel to settle disputes, mostly about firings, be-tween the New York City Board of Education and the city's Teachers' Union. This meant that Doyle had to leave his Chicago home and appear at hearings in New York twice a month. Instead of staying at paid-for hotels, we agreed he should stay at my apartment for the two or three days of trials. After a day's hearing, Doyle would come to my place, where we ate dinner together, and then spend the evening chatting, usually about what went on at the trial, and the stupidity of the city's lawyers' efforts in trying to fire teachers.

"I do" in Doyle's Detroit back yard

Often Doyle and I would regu-larly watch one of our favorite TV detective programs, *Murdoch's Mysteries*. And whenever he came across a DVD he thought would interest me, he would send me a copy.

Sometimes I would tell Doyle about a household problem I was having, which led him, for example, to install a sensor in one of my light switches, or affix some 2 X 4s to my bedspring that would raise the height of my bed to make it easier for me to rise from a sitting position. (I have a disease called myositis, a weakness in my quads and knees, which limits my ability to get up from the bed or chairs.) Doyle ordered a new chair whose height would meet my needs. Or he attached a new toaster oven to my kitchen cabinet. Or bought hardware or lumber in the neighborhood to fix stuff in the apartment — all tasks which my condition prevented me from doing myself. I guess you could call Doyle my "home health aide."

Whenever the occupant of the apartment below mine appeared at my door falsely claiming that I was making non-existent noise, Doyle used his lawyer's expertise to shut her down. When one hospital billed me thousands of dollars in spurious charges, his sharp letter forced them to abandon their claims.

Doyle's two-year position at the NYC Education Department hearings ended when the city's lawyers could no longer tolerate his rejection of their claims; they refused to agree to his continuation on the arbitration panel. His pro-working-class stands were highlighted in a case he arbitrated concerning the City of Detroit's attempt to junk the retired city workers' health insurance. His ruling against Detroit and for the workers prompted a tirade in the local media calling for his dismissal as an arbitrator for not being impartial.

And I can't forget Doyle's filing for, and securing, the FBI's 600-page file on my political activities through the Freedom of Information Act.

I have been eternally grateful that Doyle has been — and will continue to be — part of my life.

SURPRISE! "Gotcha!"

Have you ever been unaware you were organizing your own surprise birthday party? That's what happened to me on the occasion of my 80th birthday.

In February 2010, my family members called to say they wanted to have a surprise birthday party for my granddaughter Eli, set for April 25th. Having been characterized as a master at organizing such parties for family and friends, I was delighted at the opportunity to participate. Little did I realize that a cabal — Code Name: "Operation Papa Bear" — of Anita, Andrew, Doyle and Andrea, and later friend Gracie and my companion Vera, were plotting to turn it into a surprise party for me when I hit 80.

As I thought about it, I realized Eli's birthday was a week before mine, May 2. I told Vera I suspected that maybe this had something to do with a party for me. But Vera assured me that I was overly suspicious: "Forget about it," she admonished.

Anita called Vera but felt hesitant about cluing her in on the plot because it might involve some lying, but decided to tell her anyway, stressing that she might have to lie at times to keep it a secret from me. Vera assured Anita that she was "an expert liar."

Now the plotters had to figure out how to "outwit the master," given the fact that they were aware of the many surprise parties I had planned in the past. So Doyle came up with the idea to involve me in the actual planning of my own party, on the pretext that it was a party for Eli. I was asked to rent the building's 2nd floor community room for April 25. Then Kevin printed up invitations (plural) but actually printed only one and gave it to me, which I posted on my kitchen bulletin board. When Kevin reported seeing it there, he informed the plotters and they figured they had me taken in.

Thus the plan proceeded. Assuming this was a surprise party for Eli, it was imperative to keep her away from the party location, so Vera and I treated her to brunch in Manhattan. When we finished, we took the subway to Boro Hall in my neighborhood, but before walking to my building, Eli said she had to get something in the drug store. While Vera and I waited outside, Eli went inside and unbeknownst to me, of course, phoned the plotters to say we were on our way and would be arriving in about ten minutes.

Completely deceived into thinking I was taking Eli to her surprise party, I now had to figure out how to get her into the community room. I told her I had a birthday present for her but it was such a big box that I needed help in carrying it upstairs and therefore had left it with the doorman (who was also in on the plot). When we arrived in the lobby, the doorman told us he had taken the box up to the 2nd floor. So up we went to the community room. As we exited the elevator, Vera hung back to allow me to escort Eli to the room.

The plotters had arranged for Eli's young friends (a number of whom I recognized) to stand in the front, facing the entrance. Seeing them, further led me to assume this was a party for Eli. As we reached the door, a shout arose from the crowd, "Surprise! Happy Birthday!" I turned to Eli and said excitedly, "Gotcha, Eli!" To which she responded, "No, Grandpa, I got you!"

As I noticed the banner that said, "HAPPY BIRTHDAY WALLY!" I smacked my forehead, realizing I had been hoodwinked. That gesture convinced the plotters, and the guests, that I had really been taken in.

The plotters then enacted a skit they had written, which dramatized various highlights of my life. Friends and comrades congratulated me, we enjoyed some delicious food

The plotters outfox me.

and a good time was had by all. They had outwitted the master.

I Am Ordained

Probably the last role anyone might imagine for me would be as an ordained minister, enabling me to legally marry people. But that is exactly what I became in 2008.

In the summer of that year, my friend and comrade Freddie came to me and asked me to marry his fiancée Joan and him. My first reaction was, "Are you crazy, Freddie? That wouldn't be a legal marriage."

"Wrong," said Freddie. "I can show you how you can become a legally ordained minister!"

That floored me but Freddie proceeded to tell me there was something called the Universal Life Church Monastery in Seattle, Washington, that, for a slight charge, legally ordains anyone with the correct credentials to become a minister, and all by mail! At that time, they had already ordained over a million ministers.

And so it was that after filling out the appropriate forms and sending checks for $35.00 and $31.78 (including postage), on July 25, 2008, I received an official Wedding Officiant certificate from the Universal Life Church Monastery. Then on October 3, 2008, I registered at the City Hall Clerk's Office in Manhattan and was given an official number, good for my lifetime. Soon afterwards, I married Joan and Freddie.

I became an ordained minister and was "open for business," ready to administer the sacred vows to any couple who so wished. Over the next several years I married four other couples, some of them friends and some the children of comrades, all "in the name of the powers vested in me by the State of New York" and at least one also "in the name of the international working class."

So now anyone wanting to marry — or those of you who are already hitched and would like to renew your vows — can contact me, the Red Reverend, and I will perform the service, free of charge.

Solidarity Forever

Let me backtrack a few years to November, 1995, when I was proud to go to the city of Nantes in France to represent PLP's support for the millions of workers who had launched nationwide general strikes to protest government cuts in pensions and unemployment benefits, hikes in healthcare premiums and a wage freeze on public workers. I was invited by a French education worker who had become the *Challenge* correspondent in that country, and had been sending us a stream of reports on developments there. (Gene had originally joined PLP in the seventies in Minneapolis and afterwards immigrated to France.)

A total of six million strike days had accumulated over the course of two months and workers had paralyzed the railways, air and bus transport, and utilities (the government had to buy gas and electricity from Britain and Spain); closed the postal system, banks and insurance companies; dockers and truck drivers blockaded the ports; miners and rail workers fought pitched battles with riot police; schools and universities were closed as teachers and students walked out in support. The majority of the population consistently backed the strikers. Striking workers filled the streets of every French city and town.

Our comrade correspondent took me to join a picket line of

striking sanitation workers who greeted me with open arms and fed me sausages grilled on a portable stove they had set up. (See worker on the left in photo, carrying cups of wine — it's France!) On December 15, the government scrapped the pension "reform."

Photo by Gene Zbikowski
An international picket line

On the picket line I answered strikers' questions on our struggles in the U.S. and other countries in which PLP had branches, as well as on what our Party's goals were. They agreed that international working-class unity was crucial to workers winning our battles against the ruling-class's attacks and that it was their experience that the government was not neutral; it was invariably on the side of the bosses.

I left inspired by the militancy and solidarity expressed by these valiant workers. Solidarity forever!

Zak Ades: Creativity Was His Middle Name

My memories of my stepson Zak go back 34 years when I was introduced to him by his mother Toni, who later became my wife. In every room of my apartment there is a memento that ties me to Zak.

There's his gift of pottery from his extensive collection that sits on top of my living room bookcase. And there are the innumerable pieces of his baseball memorabilia that fill the shelves and walls of my bedroom — a plaque depicting a Mets' playoff victory from 1986; a huge framed montage of Lou Gehrig, Babe Ruth and Jimmy Foxx; another one of Roy Campanella, Duke Snider and Gil Hodges; baseball cards recounting the exploits of Jackie Robinson, Campanella and, of course, my boyhood hero Joe DiMaggio.

That involves a story in itself. One summer when we were at the country house near Prattsville, Zak wanted Toni and me to go to a Saturday night auction of sports memorabilia in East Windham. One of the items being auctioned was a baseball autographed by Joltin' Joe. Zak joined the bidding and he was not to be outdone. His and Toni's bid won out and then they presented the ball to me. It sits on a shelf in my bedroom near my bed.

The high point in the DiMaggio saga came when Zak, Toni and I drove to the Coliseum on Long Island where Joe D. was signing autographs and he allowed us to take photos with him. Pictures of DiMaggio with the three of us are hanging on my apartment corridor wall and an autographed, framed picture of DiMag hitting a homerun hangs on my bedroom wall.

Baseball history was a perennial subject in periodic phone calls between Zak and myself. He would call to jog my memory about someone who played for the Yankees or Dodgers 40 years earlier whose card he wanted to purchase, or about some record that had been set by an old-time player. These calls would always bring back

Zak and Joltin' Joe DiMaggio

memories of my attachment to baseball in my youth.

In recent years, these calls from Zak would include his checking on my physical condition as I began to develop various ailments. He would offer advice on how to alleviate some.

Zak's talents were many. At times he would go into the woods near the country house and collect sticks and branches that had fallen off trees or bushes. He'd bring them inside and proceed to construct chairs and tables from them — literally, stick furniture.

He used to take Anton fishing in the river near the family country house and inevitably brought back some fresh fish to cook for a delicious supper that night.

He filled his apartment with the product of his hobby: collecting early 19th century pottery. His collection became notable enough to warrant an exhibition in the Prattsville Museum. He then created a huge diorama of how this pottery had been shaped in the early days, even getting the grandchildren to participate in its construction. Eventually, it was displayed in the New York State Museum in Albany.

Of course, Zak's outstanding talent involved jewelry. He had worked in jewelry shops for many years until the industry went into decline. He would make various rings and other ornaments for family members. After an extended period of Zak's unemployment, I introduced him to a friend and comrade, Derek Pearl, who — also a victim of the industry's decline — taught jewelry courses in Westinghouse High School in downtown Brooklyn. We all encouraged him to apply for a teaching job. Although Zak was initially reluctant (for a reason, see below), a job opened up at Westinghouse when a jewelry teacher was retiring. Derek took Zak for an interview with the principal and he was hired, leading to a 20-year tenure as a teacher.

Zak hated the Board of Education's bureaucracy, but he loved teaching the students. He came up with all sorts of ideas to motivate their jewelry making. One outstanding project was the re-creation of Madison Square Garden's basketball court. He had each student make an action statue of a player on the Knicks and the Chicago Bulls, which were then placed in a "game" on the court. This project was so impressive that it was put on public display in the AT&T building in downtown Brooklyn. After this, I called the NY Knicks community relations director about possibly inviting the students with their display to a half-time ceremony during a Knicks' game. Unfortunately their half-time programs were filled for the season, but he did send free tickets for the students to attend a Knicks' game.

Zak would always regale us with stories about his students' lives, some happy and many sad, but always filled with love for them and feeling for the hard times that many were experiencing.

For me, the topper was the one related to his initial reluctance to take a teaching job. It was at the height of the AIDS crisis and Zak said he feared the students would make fun of him, given his last name being Ades. He was sure they would call him "Mr. AIDS." We argued with him that this was no reason to give up on the opportunity to teach a subject — jewelry-making — that was right up his alley. Having been unemployed for quite some time, he gave in and took the job.

A few months later I asked him, "Zak, what do the kids call you? Mr. AIDS?"

"No," he replied.

"Mr. Ades?"

"No," again.

"So what *do* they call you?"

"Yo, teach, Yo," said these street-smart teenagers. He smiled as we all had a big laugh.

After Zak retired from his teaching career, he began to find it difficult to attend to some of his everyday needs, so his sister Andrea and her husband Jerry began searching for a more suitable living arrangement. They found one on the border of Riverdale and Yonkers, a building for the elderly in which one resided in one's own apartment, could go out independently and could cook for themselves but could also take their meals in a communal dining room — a perfect set-up. They moved all his collectibles to those three rooms. He actually was probably the youngest resident there.

When I was taken to visit Zak, I saw how popular he was as he introduced us to a bunch of his cronies. He looked happier than he had been in a long time. But it was there a short time later that he appeared to have a fatal heart attack and died at the too-young-age of 65.

Zak's creativity, his stories about his every-day life and his wonderful sense of humor will forever be missed.

They Are Still My Kids, at 62 and 58

When I look back to when my kids were born some six decades ago, who could have predicted what they would

Photo by June Linder

Daughter and son at six and three

achieve in their amazing lives? They appear in many of the stories in this book, and inspire a myriad of memories that have filled my life. Both ran toward me screaming "Daddy! Daddy!" upon my return from a two-week jaunt to meet with the Chinese. Both battled it out on the occasion of Anita's Sweet Sixteen party. [For more information about the battle, see "Sweet (?) Sixteen (1973, Before Cell Phones"]. Both urged me on as I ran the 1969 New York marathon. Both were central to the conspiracy that created my surprise 80th birthday celebration, and helped devise the skit that chronicled my life. Both maintain regular and close contact to see me through various ailments that fill my latest years and help make them cheerful ones.

But beyond those collective memories are the many individual ones, as well as achievements that have made me proud.

ANITA, THE DAUGHTER WHO'S A MODEL FOR THE THOUSANDS SHE'S TAUGHT

My daughter's life encompasses both a sharp understanding of the world around her, as well as compassion for both those close to her and for those suffering from, and fighting against, the ravages of racism and capitalism. She certainly fulfilled any expectations her grandparents Ida and Sam might have had in celebrating her birth. [See story: "The Chanzis Clan Celebrates Anita's Arrival]

Anita's sharpness showed early in life when, at eight years old, sitting in our living room, she recognized the Red Squad cops who came to our door to arrest me for defying a grand jury inquisition about the Harlem Rebellion after their initial interrogation a year earlier. [See story "Arrested for Supporting the 1964 Harlem Rebellion"]

Then there was her protest at being put to bed at the same time as her brother, three years younger. When her classmates in the fourth grade asked her if she had seen some nightly TV program, she realized that we were sending her to bed before the airing of that show. She told us there was no way she should put up with such unfairness. Of course, we relented, and gone was her parents' longer evening.

Anita was a voracious reader and never failed to bring along books to devour on our family's numerous camping trips in the late 1960s through the 1970s.

In her early years, she seemed to get along well with younger children, toddlers and those of kindergarten age. Not surprisingly, when she was eight years old, she suddenly announced she wanted to become a teacher of young kids. As a teenager, she worked as a camp counselor, and all that stuck with her after graduating college.

When she went to high school wearing a button I'd brought home stating "Smash Racist Unemployment," and she was taunted by some ignorant classmates, she explained what it meant and put them in their place. She even had to explain international events to her teacher, who had no inkling of the changes in U.S.-Soviet Union relations, saying to her, "If you read the New York Times you'd know that the U.S. is engaged in a friendly *détente* with the Russians."

During Anita's high school years, she joined a protest over budget cuts we had organized at City Hall, and then mounted a

ladder to make a speech through a bullhorn denouncing the politicians cutting funds for schools. This came full circle decades later when she headed the adult literacy

Protesting budget cuts at City Hall.

program at Brooklyn College and there she was again, organizing a demonstration of her students at City Hall, protesting the latest round of budget cuts affecting their ESL programs.

During that period Anita became a member of the Progressive Labor Party, in which she was active for a quarter century, and fine-tuned her understanding of communism as the ultimate solution to the ravages of racism and capitalism. In the fall of 2005, when Anita took her students to a lecture by Jonathan Kozol, who was exposing racist aspects of the school systems, the event was being picketed by a group of Young Republicans espousing racist ideas. Anita began cursing them out. Her students were shocked, never having seen her like that, saying she "had fire in her eyes." The next day they spread the story around the school, and she was congratulated by a number of teachers.

Anita launched her career in teaching ESL when, in her early years while a young mother, she got a part-time job at night teaching English to Haitian immigrants. (She had already been an elementary school teacher in Chicago — 5th and 6th grades — before her kids were born.) Her immigrant students loved her so much that in appreciation, they brought her presents during the holidays.

This led to a full-time job for Anita as an ESL teacher at Brooklyn College, where eventually she became the Adult Literacy Program Manager. During that period, in 2000, Anita helped organize a celebration of the 25th anniversary of the Boston Summer Project, which had fought the racism in Boston's school system and routed its fascist supporters. [See story on Doyle, "Jack of All Trades, Master of Many"]

In the late 1990s, her marriage of more than twenty years fell apart because of her husband's affairs, but she held everything together as a single parent raising three growing children. Seeing Doyle again in 2000, after having initially met him in the 1975 Project, led to their marriage four years later. She moved to Doyle's home in Detroit and eventually to their present residence in Chicago (while teaching in both cities).

Anita still manages to visit me from Chicago and never

misses a week without calling to check up on how I'm handling my life.

I think perhaps the most meaningful hallmark of Anita's life was her ability to draw on her parent's communist principles to become a communist herself. And one might add that her most significant "job" has been bringing three children into the world and raising them to be my three wonderful grandchildren. I am eternally indebted to her for this. [See story, "Is There A Job Harder Than This?"] The four of them have as close a relationship as one could imagine, and are in touch virtually on a daily basis despite living 900 miles apart. (And now, in Kevin's case, 4,000 miles — he's living and working in Spain.) Anita says she attributes her ability to handle family life, with all its problems, to growing up influenced by the relationship between Esther and me. I think, however, having survived her first marriage and now happily established in her current one, she has gone beyond that. She has taught her kids how to handle their problems and also maintains loving relations with a score of nieces, nephews and their parents.

I've been forever grateful to Anita for her decision to move to my house in Brooklyn some months after Esther died, enabling her kids to grow up closely attached to Grandpa Wally, initiating relationships that have made my "golden years" truly golden.

ANDREW, NO FINER SON COULD I WISH FOR

Our son came into this world taking his time, twelve days after his due date — due to a "Stork Strike," see birth announcement — at a hefty 8½ pounds [See story "A Son Who Ushered in A Bright New World."] His early years were marked by a seemingly boundless interest in sports, his favorite being hockey, the roller kind, given the absence of ice rinks. Philip, the son of our close friends Gertie and Gus, influenced him in this direction. They both joined a local hockey league and one year Andrew was named defenseman of the year.

When Andrew was 12, he said he and his hockey mates had found an ice rink on West 33rd Street in Manhattan where they could rent an hour's time to ice skate. Which hour? Turns out to be the only one available: 3:00 A.M.! "What!" I exclaimed. "You're going tramping out in Manhattan at that hour?" "No problem," he replied. "No one will set upon a dozen guys wielding hockey sticks." With much trepidation, Esther and I agreed.

Champion hockey player

I woke up at five in the morning and looked in his room — no Andrew. Before I could do too much about it, around seven A.M. he trooped in with a broad smile. "Where the hell were you?" I roared. "It's okay, Pop. We all went out to a nearby diner for breakfast." Tough to be a parent of a child entering his teenage years.

Andrew's love of hockey is what forced us into that deal we had made with him when he was 14 and refused to accompany us on a planned trip to Glacier National Park and the Canadian Rockies. "Too boring," he said. Anita had a full-time day job as a camp counselor, but we were not about to leave Andrew all by himself all day at that age. He said he would go with us on one condition: on our return home we would have to stop at the Hockey Hall of Fame in Toronto. What choice did we have? So we returned through the western Canadian provinces and stopped in Toronto at that Hall of Fame. Even Esther got into it, having us take a picture of her holding the Stanley Cup (the award to

321

the winner of the annual hockey playoffs). [See "Parking Across North America."]

Around that time, Andrew said he was tired of what he said were the bland meals that we cooked for dinner. As it happened, our friend and neighbor Gus, whose family lived upstairs in our shared two-family house in Sheepshead Bay, had been taking night classes learning to prepare Chinese dishes. Andrew would watch him and soon announced he would be doing the cooking every weekday night. "Great," we said. "You cook, and we'll do the dishes." We bought a wok and all the necessary utensils and for the next four years Andrew prepared all the dinners (both Chinese and others). (He also taught me how to cook those dishes.)

(Interestingly, when Andrew went away to college, he took all the Chinese cooking utensils with him. "Hold it," I said. "How am *I* going to cook those dishes?" "Buy another set," he said, "and I'll print up the recipes." And so he did, entitling the copy, "What is to be eaten: Wally's Guide to Not Dieting.")

When our boy was 15, I asked him if he had thought about what he might do when he graduated high school. I mentioned various choices: college? Learning a trade? Getting a job? "A civil engineer," he replied. Where'd that come from? Not from any family influences. "I like to construct things," he said. While we thought he might not hold to that goal, it turned out he had set himself on a lifelong path, went to the engineering school at the State University in Buffalo and has been an expert in airport design for the past 36 years. (When he received his first paycheck in 1982, half went to a used car and the other half to a season pass to the New York Rangers' hockey games at Madison Square Garden.)

Andrew's affinity for cooking has never left him. While working as an engineer, he took a night class in French cooking, broadening his culinary talents, and at one time even considered changing professions from engineering to becoming a chef. While he didn't pursue the latter, he remains quite proficient in the kitchen, as we all can attest to.

While our family was immersed in a profusion of politics, we didn't push Andrew to become attached to PLP, which may have been a mistake on my part. He did develop an understanding of — and agreed with — what we stood for, and did join a PLP club for a short while. He attended many May Day celebrations and subscribed to *Challenge.*

As Andrew was advancing as an engineer, he vacationed throughout Europe and even went on a safari in Africa. All told he has visited 40 countries. In 1999, two friends told him of this young woman living in London who was coming to New York for an interview, seeking a job in design, and suggested he show her around. Well, as can happen in such situations, one thing led to another and Andrew and Louise were married in 2002. She is from New Zealand, and has a small family, so they

The "bikers" in New Zealand: (from left) the groom, the groom's father, the best man, the bride

decided to have the ceremony in Auckland. This was great for me; I took a four-week vacation and, after the wedding, traveled throughout New Zealand and then over to Australia for ten days.

Andrew and Louise seemed happily married for about ten years, but then Louise — for whatever reason it was difficult to figure out — decided she wanted to leave the marriage and live on her own, which at that time meant living in China, where her job had sent her. Andrew was crushed in the beginning but appears to have come through it, maintaining ties with his family and loads of friends, as well as developing close relations especially with his two nephews, Kevin and Peter, and niece Eli. We'll see what the future holds for him.

Andrew's engineering work has really moved forward. In 2012, his firm won a bid among four proposing firms to almost double the size of Hong Kong's International Airport, based on a proposal that Andrew helped prepare. The contract had to include Andrew working there for what turned out to be 22 months, so he moved, although the contract did pay for three visits back to New York. He was also able to bring Kevin and Eli to Hong Kong during his stay there.

Recently, a similar situation arose, with Andrew's firm winning the bid to expand Singapore Changi International Airport, which also involves his working there, this time for at least two years, with periodic visits back to New York, so that is where he is now.

Andrew has been a bulwark in assisting me through my current ailments. When in New York, he visits me virtually every week and when I suffered a heart attack in the first week of January in 2018, he was there in the hospital, rounding up all the reports that would be needed by my doctors once I returned home. He has guaranteed that in his present job in Singapore, he will always be ready to make an emergency visit to Brooklyn if something happens to me.

The greatest thing that has happened to me is the loving relationship I've had these many decades with my two great "kids."

How Myositis Has Not Stopped Me from Living My Life

In my early eighties, my life was completely disrupted by a disease I had never heard of. I began having trouble getting up from a seated position. I had to press down on the seat with both arms to stand up. Soon I had to place cushions on the seats to raise their height in order to get up. I began finding my knees buckling, leading to falls. My neurologist administered all sorts of tests, including a biopsy of my thigh, but could not figure out the cause. She said, "Walter, I don't know everything. Maybe you should get a second opinion." She directed me to another neurologist, the chief of the clinic at Downstate Hospital. In 2017, he gave me a special blood test which produced a diagnosis: Myositis.

There are five types of this disease. Mine is called sporadic Inclusion Body Mysositis (sIBM). It signifies an overactive immune system, a muscle inflammation of the nervous system which attacks certain muscles and explains why my quad muscles are weak and won't support me when my knees buckle. Thus far it is untreatable by any known medicine. There is currently no cure, although trials, which I have tried to enter, are taking place. There are about 50,000 cases of sIBM in the U.S. My neurologist tests me every six months to determine if it's spreading to any other muscles, but so far it hasn't. However, to prevent falls, I must concentrate on keeping my legs and knees straight. If I allow the least little bend in my knees, I will fall and my legs are too weak to be able to get up myself. It has obviously radically changed my life and my independence.

Probably the most debilitating effect of myositis was it forced me to stop driving. Not only did that mean I had to stop visiting my partner Vera in New Jersey, but in order to keep doctors' appointments I had to depend on family and friends to drive me. I must use a walker to get around my apartment. My family moved furniture to clear space for me to walk. I was forced to give up weekly visits from Dina, my personal trainer, since I could no longer perform exercises involving retaining my balance or lifting my legs, although I am still able to do ten leg exercises a day, three or four days a week. Hopefully, this is maintaining a certain degree of leg strength. (I spent five years in a training studio — where I met Dina. There I worked out on treadmills, Stairmasters and other equipment. Many of the exercises were especially helpful in strengthening my arms and upper body, enabling me to use them to get up from a seated position.)

Fortunately, in 2001 an insurance broker suggested I take out long-term health insurance. Since February 2017, this plan has paid for the hiring of two home health aides to minimize my walking in the apartment. They perform a whole host of tasks: preparing and serving meals and cleaning up afterwards, opening and closing windows, getting my mail, putting away food deliveries, making my bed, doing laundry, helping me shower using a special tub bench, accompanying me to my five doctors and a dentist (ushering me into their offices) — virtually every fundamental chore which I used to do myself.

Minimizing my walking helps to minimize the chances of my knees buckling. I use a food delivery service — instacart.com. On my computer, I order a whole range of foods from the Fairway Market, which are then delivered to my door. In addition, a neighbor who shops at Trader Joe's and Whole Foods takes a list from me weekly to shop for whatever I choose.

All of this, of course, does not eliminate my walking, since I am alone before and after the eight hours the aides are with me. I do plenty of walking around the apartment, even when they're present, trying to concentrate on keeping my knees straight every step I take, while using the walker. If and when I do fall, I manage to call one of three different neighbors who are every ready to enter my apartment to lift me up. Several times when I fell I hit my head, opened a gash in my scalp and ended up in the ER. In the first half of 2017, I fell every few weeks. However, since June, 2017, my knee-buckling and falling has occurred only once every six months or longer. As I write this (March 13, 2019), it has been nine months since my last fall, a record for me. One unrelated setback occurred on New Year's Day in 2018 when I suffered a heart attack and had three stents inserted in two arteries. There have been no after effects since.

None of these problems has stopped me from living my life. An occupational therapist (a friend of my granddaughter's) analyzed my apartment and all my moves in order to make suggestions on how to perform many tasks. She ordered various kinds of equipment to ease my daily living. I now drive an electric scooter to a local farmers' market, to go to the bank, to the library, to spend a pleasant afternoon on the promenade facing the East River, and, most important, to visit most of my doctors who are now in the neighborhood. I switched from the doctors to whom I had to travel by car, and therefore no longer have to spend hours arranging for family and/or friends to drive me. The electric scooter has become my vehicle of choice.

I have a recliner on which I can rest comfortably, read, and watch TV and DVDs. I have complete access to my computer, communicate with family and friends, and have spent the better part of the past year writing these stories and sending them to a copy editor and picture/layout editor for reviewing. I receive frequent visits from my family members as well as from friends, often spending several nights a week eating dinner together and chatting about what's happening in our lives and in the world. Every so often, I use my scooter to join them in a local restaurant. Up until my partner Vera's death in April, 2018, her daughter Lisa would drive her to my apartment once a month enabling Vera and I to spend several days together.

So between the recliner, the scooter, the aides' assistance, the food delivery service, the help of neighbors, continuing my leg exercises, visits from family and friends, and concentrating on keeping my legs straight while using the walker around my apartment, I have managed to maintain a certain degree of independence. Facing up to my ailments has not stopped me from living the life I love.

Fighting Racism in
A Racist Society:
An Unceasing Battle

The struggle against racism is a theme interwoven throughout the stories of my life. Yet, in my first eighteen years, I maintained a virtually exclusive white existence. I had only white classmates and friends in my first seven grades in Monticello's elementary school. My teenage years were spent in Brooklyn's Midwood High, then a virtually all-white school. But thanks to my parents' and sister's guidance, I was able to not only work through capitalism's virulent racism but become an active fighter against it. I came to understand its roots in a society derived from slavery on which U.S. capitalism's economy is based, from super-profits extracted from discrimination against black (and later Latin) workers — all this being used by the exploiting class to depress the working conditions of white workers.

In my case, this transition from growing up in a predominantly white existence didn't just happen. It began with the influence of my Communist parents who led me on an anti-racist path; this is recounted in many of the previous stories you hopefully will have read in this memoir.

In 1962, I participated in the founding of the Progressive Labor Movement, a multiracial, pro-communist organization, bearing an anti-racist stamp. It was the only group supporting the Harlem Rebellion, as the protesters marched through the streets holding PLM's *Challenge-Desafio* English-Spanish newspaper as its flag. The following year we organized the Progressive Labor Party whose anti-racist core principle was fighting racism, exposing it as fundamental to the existence of capitalism. We engaged in mass demonstrations and on-the-job battles on behalf of this principle [See "Launching A New Communist Party"].

My first big struggle occurred at City College in 1949 in the fight to oust two racist professors. The following year, we cheered for CCNY's multiracial team as it won a basketball championship against racist Kentucky's coach Adolph Rupp who had refused to recruit black players.

Later I entered the work-a-day world as a member of Local 65 whose bedrock principle was uniting workers of all backgrounds — black, white, Latin and Asian. This was reflected in its fight against Metropolitan Life's ban on non-white tenants in its Stuyvesant Town housing complex; I marched among 3,000 Local 65 members surrounding the complex to help break this ban.

Soon I was involved in the struggle to merge the 600-member all-black local with the 400-member all-white local into one freight-handler union on the B&O railroad. For the first time, we had black and white committeemen together defending black and white members in both locals and also published our union paper as one representative of both locals — all building toward that goal of a merger.

At the freight handlers' international convention, our New York caucus backed the 150 all-black locals' fight against the failure of the international to end discrimination in job postings in the South.

After being laid off on the B&O, we established the Railroad Workers Unemployment Council, with a multiracial membership and leadership, to sue the railroad for severance pay — organizing protests from City Hall to the White House. We succeeded in our "merger."

My personal life was interwoven with the fight against racism, influenced by my wife Esther and her friendships with interracial couples; by Toni through her establishment of relationships with our black neighbors in an apartment building more than sixty percent black and Latin and whose two grandchildren had a Latino father; and by Vera who was an avowed anti-racist and whose first husband was bi-racial. These anti-racist convictions and relationships were passed through to the next generations of children and grandchildren.

Growing up white in a racist society, it is difficult to completely free one's self from racist attitudes. However, developing multi-racial friendships with black, Latin and Asian working-class people and participating in class struggles united with them, listening to their criticisms, will put one on the path towards a revolution that will smash this racist evil, a goal that cannot be achieved without the international unity of black, white, Latin and Asian workers.

Vera Completes My Life

One's life is composed of thousands of memories and moments. Such was the life my dear Vera and I spent together. We met at an Elder Hostel course entitled "Turning Memories into Memoirs" in Maine, in the second week of October, 2001. Everyone was asked to compose a story which the group would later critique. As luck would have it, the two of us sat at a table across from each other while writing our first assignment. When Vera read her beautiful description of how she had met her late husband Bob, I felt I must get to know her. Never could I have envisaged the 17 wonderful years I would spend with her.

At the conclusion of the course, the instructor Denis Ledoux told us to exchange e-mail addresses and phone numbers so we could later contact each other to compare and criticize our future stories. When we were heading for our cars after leaving the Hostel, I spotted Vera (wearing some pretty sharp sunglasses) and walked over to ask her if I could contact her once we returned home. She said "certainly." (She later told me she thought my request was to compare stories.)

Later that month I called her to say I'd like to take her out to dinner. "You mean a date?" she remarked. "Yes," I replied, so we agreed to meet on Saturday, October 7, at Penn Station in

Manhattan after her trip in from South Orange, NJ, where she was living at the time.

When she arrived, I realized I didn't know much about the restaurants in the area so I suggested we take a 15-minute subway ride to my Brooklyn Heights neighborhood where we could go to a place I frequented. She agreed. When we arrived at my stop, I asked her if she'd like to see my apartment. I had told her about the magnificent view I had of the Manhattan skyline and the glorious sunsets. She said, "Fine" and up we went to the 11th floor of my high-rise. I took her on a tour of my apartment, where she admired the views and the 100 pictures of my life mounted on the walls.

As she strolled down the hallway, she suddenly exclaimed, "Oh, *The Worker*!" She was pointing to a framed front-page picture from the Communist Party newspaper of me pushing my two-year-old daughter Anita in a stroller on a picket line of strikers outside Brooklyn Jewish Hospital.(which is on this memoir's front cover). "How did she know about the *The Worker*?" I wondered, and stored away that thought for future reference.

(When Vera later recounted this visit to her daughter Lisa, she received a sharp rebuke. "Mom, how *could* you?" she exclaimed. "You don't even know this guy and you're going up to his apartment on a first date!" Vera replied nonchalantly, "Oh, please, he assured me he wasn't intending to show me his etchings." And so we went out to the first of many hundreds of dinners.)

As we later parted at Penn Station, I asked her out for the following Saturday to see one of my five favorite movies, "Burn," playing at the Film Forum in Manhattan. Although she said she was very busy preparing some paper, she said "Fine."

We met again at Penn Station and since it was a lovely October evening, I suggested we walk the 40 blocks to the movie theater. "Great," she said (she was an avid walker), so we began the trek from 34th Street to West Houston Street. I had been thinking that I'd better not wait much longer to tell her about my politics, so I asked her how she knew about *The Worker,* which she had mentioned the previous Saturday.

She then related a fascinating tale about a cousin of her mother's, who had appeared at her family's apartment door on Manhattan's East Side in 1946, a year after the end of the Second World War, when Vera was a teenager. The cousin had just arrived from France and asked to see her mother to inquire about possibly staying with them for a short time until he got settled.

Her mother welcomed her cousin with open arms and showed him to a guest room. Vera followed him there and watched as he unloaded his worldly belongings from a large duffle bag. Out rolled dozens of rolls of toilet paper. "What was that about?" thought Vera. It seems he had been active in the Communist-led underground fighting the Nazi occupation of Paris during the war. He was eventually captured and spent the rest of the war in a prison camp. He said he wanted to record a daily diary and the only paper he could get his hands on was toilet paper!

"Wow!" I said. "What a book that would make." But Vera said he never wrote one.

Meanwhile, he had joined the Communist Party in New York and would go out to sell the *Daily Worker* on the subways. He asked Vera if she wanted to join him. "Why not?" she replied and out she went selling this communist paper. So I now opened up about my membership in the CP and why I had quit, explaining all the reasons why I subsequently helped to organize the Progressive Labor Movement and Progressive Labor Party.

She took all this in and while she said she couldn't join, she understood why I had. She herself was very anti-racist and told me about her experience with her first husband, Tom, who came from a bi-racial background. She said when she accompanied him on a trip to visit his black mother's family in Virginia — this in the late 1940s — Tom told Vera she would have to stay in nearby Washington because it would be dangerous (if not unlawful!) for them to openly walk down the streets in the Virginia city as an inter-racial couple.

(As it turned out, Tom had been severely affected by his service in World War II — what we would now call PTSD. Several years into the marriage he suddenly disappeared. Neither Vera nor his family could trace him. She was broken-hearted for a year afterwards, but finally decided she would have to get a divorce, move on and live her life without him. Some time afterwards, she met her second husband, Bob.)

After the movie, Vera and I went to dinner at a nearby restaurant where she opened up a little more. When Bob died in 1988, she had been left with a lot of debts, and went to work at a foundation to try to recover. She said she became very independent and liked that feeling. She said she recognized that although I might be looking for a relationship similar to the ones I had with Esther and Toni, at this time in her life it was not for her. I said, "Fair enough," while thinking to myself, "patience and fortitude" (as the former Mayor LaGuardia used to say). I was amazed about the chances that I would accidentally meet someone like her who was accepting of a Communist, even if she herself wasn't about to become one.

At that time, Vera lived in a large house in South Orange, N.J, with her lovely family, son Mark, his wife Kim and grandsons Jackson and Alexander, about whose abilities she would rave on and on. She was so proud of them. So I pursued a friendship with Vera and visited her periodically at her home in South Orange.

My being tenacious, one thing led to another. By January, she proposed we spend a weekend together at the Jersey shore. My "patience and fortitude" had paid off. In 2002, Vera bought a house in Blairstown, N.J. where I began spending weekends three times a month. Every so often she would come to my place in Brooklyn, looking forward to spending a weekend in the City, which she liked, having grown up in New York and marveling at the diversity of its people.

Vera had an intense interest in my family, especially about how my grandchildren were getting along. She was always asking about their latest exploits. She seemed about as proud of Eli, Peter and Kevin, as well as of Isa and Anton, as I was. When she learned about Eli's attachment to the environment, she suggested I bring her out to Blairstown with the intention of showing her Genesis Farm and its focus on organic farming and supporting local farmers. When I drove Eli out for a weekend, Vera showed her the features of Genesis Farm and Eli actually slept there overnight.

I soon discovered how tied Vera was to the world of plants and animals, heightening my appreciation of that natural environment. She cared for four cats. Her house was filled with nearly 40 plants — which I, and later her daughter Lisa, would help transfer indoors in the fall, and outdoors in the spring. She planted flowers and trees in her expansive yards. Whenever she spent weekends in my Brooklyn apartment, she would nurture my plants, meticulously pruning and repotting them, showing me what I must do to make sure they continued to grow. She always told me, "Wally, you must surround yourself with living things." [See "My Green Thumb."]

Vera had a great passion for feeding birds, especially in the wintertime when the back yard would be frozen over and the birds could not reach their usual supply on the ground. She would go outside in freezing weather to spread bird feed on the snow and ice, to "keep them alive," is how she put it. Even when she came to my place in Brooklyn, she would make sure she brought along bird feed so we could go out to the park across the street to spread the feed on the grass.

When a sparrow flew into my living room and seemingly dropped dead on the floor, Vera instructed me how to save its life: put it in a box with some water, cover it, put it into a dark closet overnight, and in the morning carry it to the park across the street, open the box, and *voila*! out flew the sparrow.

Vera could never stop talking about her love for Genesis Farm, an organization devoted, among other things, to protecting and preserving the environment. She took me to various events there, introducing me to something I had never experienced, a Poetry Slam.

Vera was a talented woman, a writer, a gardener, a botanist, a horticulturist, fluent in French and somewhat in Italian, and was a fund-raiser for her favorite organizations, especially those tied to the natural world. One example of her love of animals: during Hurricane Irene we were about to enter a local restaurant when I suddenly spotted a forlorn-looking cat, moaning and sitting in the pouring rain. I pointed it out to her. When we went inside and were viewing the menu, I looked at Vera and knew what she was thinking. She *had* to save that kitten. We told the waitress we'd be back. We then drove to her house, picked up a cat carrier, returned to put the little thing in it and then drove back to her house where she dried and fed it. Only then could she return to the restaurant to eat dinner in peace. Yes, we named the cat Hurricane, to join the other three she was caring for.

Vera volunteered much time to Genesis Farm and raised hundreds of thousands of dollars, which helped to put the FoodShed Alliance — a group that helps local farmers and wards off greedy developers — on its feet.

Vera was very skeptical of the medical profession, limiting her contact with doctors to as little as possible. This was in contrast with me, who was always getting friends or family to drive me to the five or so doctors I had on tap at any one time. She then joked, "Why don't you just arrange a conference call with all of them so they can discuss your various conditions simultaneously while you sit in your apartment and avoid all those trips." Her curiosity was boundless. Every time I would relate a doctor's new diagnosis of my many ailments, she would tell me to "Ask the doctor for the cause." She was constantly searching for the "why" of things.

Soon Vera and I began our journeys beyond our immediate environment. First, I took her to dozens of National Parks throughout the West. For me, most of these were my second and third visits, but it was Vera's first time and the vistas were thrilling to her. Yosemite, Yellowstone, the Grand Canyon, Bryce, Zion, Mesa Verde, Rocky Mountains and on and on.

In Paris, in front of the Louvre museum
(Vera's favorite photo)

Then we started traveling beyond these borders, off to Europe, to Elder Hostels and on independent trips. Vera had a special affinity for France, especially since Paris was where she had spent her toddler years. She showed me the building where she attended kindergarten and the first grade, introduced me to her cousins, all the time translating for me from her fluent French. We spent hours walking through the streets of Paris, eating delicious food. We toured Provence, staying at a friend's villa near Avignon.

An Elder Hostel trip took us to Italy, the country of her parents. Vera understood enough Italian to help us interact with the local people. We saw the sights and museums in Florence, Pisa and the cities of Tuscany. We then drove North to the Alps, where I took a picture of Vera sitting in front of the house her grandfather had built in a tiny Italian village, and we visited her grandmother's grave.

The trip that topped them all marked our tenth anniversary, in 2011, when we boarded the Orient Express in Paris. We had our own private room, to which a waiter came every morn-

Riding the rails on the Orient Express

ing to serve us breakfast. Fancy stuff — when we had lunch in the dining car I had to wear a tie and jacket. The next morning

Vera's gondola buddies

Prague: At dinner with Jorge, our "private" tour guide

339

we arrived at a three-room apartment in Venice where we spent five days, touring along the Grand Canal, shopping for souvenirs, and taking a trip in a gondola.

From Venice it was overnight on the train for four days in Prague. There we made friends with a young student from Guatemala, Jorge (who spoke Spanish, English and Czech), and who guided us around the city. We went to a wonderful concert in a grand concert hall and took Jorge to dinner afterwards, where we made arrangements to keep in touch in the future. From Prague, we flew back to spend a week in Paris.

In the summer of 2017 when Vera was 89, amazingly she was able to make a trip back to Italy with her son Mark and grandson Alex to visit her parents' region. Early in 2018, she had told me she wanted one more trip to Paris, but soon resigned herself to foregoing that one because of her fading physical condition.

Vera had forgone a doctor-recommended knee replacement some years ago, which she later realized was a mistake. Her knee continued to hamper her walking and then she developed scoliosis, with sharp pain in her left hip. Her doctor said he was surprised that the condition had occurred so late in life, saying that her years of exercising three times a week in a local gym was probably what had delayed it. She was now getting physical therapy which alleviated the pain somewhat, but every time we spoke she would say she felt worse that day than the day before.

In the last week of March of 2018 Vera was able to spend a great weekend with her family in upstate New York, about which she vividly described during our 3-times-a-week phone calls. She was now 90 years old and had finished writing her life's stories, but had never added the accompanying pictures. Her children Lisa and Mark are vowing to finish and publish Vera's memoirs.

On the 5th of April, Lisa called to tell me she had left the house for a short time to walk her dog, while Vera was sitting at her desk. When Lisa returned, she didn't find Vera there, so she went to her bedroom and found her lying in her bed. Lisa realized her mother had taken her last breath. She probably had begun to feel unwell and had gone to lie down. Lisa called the EMS, who came and concluded that Vera had died peacefully in her sleep. Probably her heart had given out.

Vera and I would call each other three nights a week, every Sunday, Wednesday and Friday. As it happened, on that last Wednesday — the night she died — she said it made her very happy that I was writing these stories of my life. Combined with the regular visits I had from family and friends, she felt I seemed very happy. And she said the fact that I was happy made her very happy. Those became her last words to me, or for that matter to anyone, concluding with our usual "French good night": "*Bonne nuit*," she said, to which I responded, "*Bonne nuit*."

When we first met, Vera had said she couldn't become another Esther or Toni, yet Vera was not only my partner for 17 years, she was also my best friend. She filled my life with enormous love and so many new experiences. Vera made my life complete.